BUILDING COSMOPOLITAN
COMMUNITIES

Building Cosmopolitan Communities

A Critical and Multidimensional Approach

Amos Nascimento

BUILDING COSMOPOLITAN COMMUNITIES
Copyright © Amos Nascimento, 2013.

First published in 2013 by
PALGRAVE MACMILLAN®
in the United States—a division of St. Martin's Press LLC,
175 Fifth Avenue, New York, NY 10010.

Where this book is distributed in the UK, Europe and the rest of the world,
this is by Palgrave Macmillan, a division of Macmillan Publishers Limited,
registered in England, company number 785998, of Houndmills,
Basingstoke, Hampshire RG21 6XS.

Palgrave Macmillan is the global academic imprint of the above companies
and has companies and representatives throughout the world.

Palgrave® and Macmillan® are registered trademarks in the United States,
the United Kingdom, Europe and other countries.

ISBN: 978–1–137–26983–6

Library of Congress Cataloging-in-Publication Data

Nascimento, Amós.
    Building cosmopolitan communities : a critical and multidimensional
approach / Amos Nascimento.
       pages cm
    Includes bibliographical references and index.
    ISBN 978–1–137–26983–6 (alk. paper)
       1. Cosmopolitanism. 2. Cosmopolitanism—Philosophy. 3. Human
rights. 4. Globalization. I. Title.

JZ1308.N355 2013
306—dc23   2013004444

A catalogue record of the book is available from the British Library.

Design by Newgen Knowledge Works (P) Ltd., Chennai, India.

First edition: August 2013

10 9 8 7 6 5 4 3 2 1

To Margaret

CONTENTS

Illustrations

Figures

Acknowledgments

This book presents the results of studies and research I have been carrying on for quite some time. I invariably began with seminars and lectures on human rights and cosmopolitanism to my students at the University of Washington in Tacoma and Seattle, then expanded them as papers to be presented at meetings and conferences, and finally reworked the texts based on the feedback I received. I let them rest for a while and then reworked them again for the purposes of this publication. My reflections on the subjects discussed here have benefited from meetings and dialogues with colleagues in the Research Cluster on "Human Interactions and Normative Innovation" at the University of Washington, the Exzellenzcluster "Herausbildung normativer Ordnungen" at the University of Frankfurt in Germany, the Program "Pasado y Presente de los Derechos Humanos" at the Universidad de Salamanca, and "Pensamiento Jurídico Crítico" at the Universidad Complutense de Madrid in Spain as well as the "Programa Interdisciplinar de Direitos Humanos" involving faculty from the Universidade Católica Dom Bosco and Universidade Federal do Mato Grosso do Sul in Brazil. Support from the Simpson Center for the Humanities (University of Washington Seattle) and the Interdisciplinary Arts and Sciences program (University of Washington Tacoma) allowed me to dedicate time to complete this project. Among the many partners in dialogue, I especially thank Matthias Lutz-Bachmann, Bill Talbott, Michael Forman, Johann Reusch, Esther Martínez Quinteiro, Jesús Lima Torrado, José do Nascimento, Margaret Griesse, Andreas Niederberger, Hilário Aguilera Urquiza, and José Paulo Gutiérrez. Eduardo Mendieta, a longtime friend and discussion partner, read parts of the manuscript and provided important criticism and suggestions; so many good ones, that many of them will have to be addressed in a separate volume on which I am already working.

My studies with Jürgen Habermas, Karl-Otto Apel, Matthias Lutz-Bachmann, and Axel Honneth continue to inform my reflections on the subject of this book. I cite the titles of their respective works in

English throughout the text, but make use of their original edition in German. The editorial information provided indicates the year of the original publications or particular editions. For example, references to Immanuel Kant are cited through abbreviations commonly used in the Kantian literature: citations of the *Critique of Pure Reason* [*Kritik der reinen Vernunft*] are identified by *KrV* A 677/B 705, where *KrV* refers to the title, "A" refers to the first edition of 1781, and "B" refers to the second edition of 1787, followed by page numbers. The *Works* [*Werke*], *Collected Writings* [*Gesammelte Schriften*] or *Complete Works* [*Gesamtausgabe*] of Kant and other classic authors are cited in brackets, abbreviated as *W*, *GS*, or *GA*, and followed by the corresponding volume number: for example, *Dialectic of the Enlightenment* was written in 1944 by Theodor Adorno and Max Horkheimer and reprinted in volume 3 of the 1997 edition of Adorno's *Gesammelte Schriften* (Adorno 1997 [*GS* 3]: 1). The translations are mine and some key foreign terms are included in brackets, whenever necessary.

The process of preparing the manuscript involved many other persons. I would like to mention a couple of them. Scarlet Neath was very patient and very helpful with her technical expertise at various phases of the editorial process. I want to express my deepest appreciation to Margaret Griesse, who read the whole manuscript, gave me invaluable suggestions, and offered both important criticism and encouragement throughout the whole writing process. I could not have completed this project without her support and partnership in dialogue. This book is dedicated to her.

INTRODUCTION

1

PLURAL DISCOURSE COMMUNITIES AS POINT OF DEPARTURE

The overall point I want to make can be stated simply: cosmopolitan ideals could be implemented in reality if we relate them directly to global human rights discourses, justify them as universal norms, and apply them differently to various communities. However, the pursuit of this goal requires attention to various complex steps: to select a normative philosophical framework that is robust enough to accommodate this proposal; interpret and define concepts such as community, human rights, and cosmopolitanism; review a growing literature on this subject and search for compelling arguments for the universality of cosmopolitan ideals; and define the compatibility between global norms and the recognition of contextual differences. Obviously, stating the goal is simple, but pursuing it is a daunting task. I could have chosen a simpler undertaking. For instance, to appeal to a vast body of empirical references showing how human rights are being incorporated differently into national constitutions, legal frameworks, and social practices or to refer to the fact that human rights are gaining wide political recognition, legal effectiveness, social acceptance, and concrete application. In fact, the claim that national constitutional frameworks can function as the mediating instance for a possible articulation of human rights norms and effective social institutions at the local level can be taken as uncontroversial. Instead of taking these possible alternatives, I intend to follow the steps above. Despite the many challenges, I want to insist on the idea that plural communities constructed discursively can contribute to the realization of cosmopolitan ideals in different ways by implementing human rights norms in dialogue with their respective social, historical, and institutional conditions. Rather than affirm that cosmopolitan ideals are an end result, I want to take them as norms that help us in the process of evaluating and criticizing cosmopolitan communities under construction.

What makes my main thesis unique is the dual assertion that cosmopolitan ideals are plural and their implementation obeys different and dynamic communicative processes in distinct contexts around the world. I call this the *building of cosmopolitan communities* and argue that this development has an aspirational or heuristic value whose realization requires more attention to multicultural and intercultural interactions. The universality of this process is given by the justification of moral norms that demand the global protection of human rights while the concrete dimension implies acknowledging the different social situations and institutional conditions for the application of such norms. This dual process is a work in progress. To spell out what is involved in such work, it is necessary that I begin with two general remarks.

First, we need to amplify our understanding of *community* beyond the reference to a closed organic structure fixed on a limited and particular locality, group, or national state. Community is a larger and dynamic form of social, cultural, and political relationships that overlap in many ways and are capable of engendering new processes that can transcend established boundaries. The possibility of individuals moving beyond particular conditionings may lead to the constitution of interactive practices at the supranational or regional level, thus generating larger communities of which we have concrete examples today such as the European Union (EU). This more flexible account can be provided by a discursive conception of community.

Second, the addition of *cosmopolitan* as an adjective attached to the term "community" appears as a complicating factor that asks for a few clarifying comments. The use of the term "cosmopolitanism" has a long tradition but we still lack systematic historical research and a detailed mapping of contemporary interpretations of this concept. It has become common to differentiate between moral, legal, political, economic, and cultural forms of cosmopolitanism and each one of them yields a different position. For instance, some recent interpretations insist that *moral cosmopolitanism* is utterly individualistic and incompatible with strict communitarian values while others affirm that *political* or *legal cosmopolitanism* requires global structures that are incompatible with any other institutional arrangement at the local or national level. The challenge here is an *all* or *nothing* approach. Many political cosmopolitans expect an empirically viable institution at the global level, a super state or a global constitution as the condition to implementing cosmopolitan ideals; if attempts to answer these questions fail, they see no other alternative because the only resort would be to fall back into the particularity of local communities and nation-states with their propensity to pursue their self-interest by means of conflict and power relations. However, there are, indeed, other alternatives! Moral cosmopolitans insist on the ideality of universal principles and norms related to individuality, even if they are not yet fully achieved. For instance, they search for a guiding element that motivates us to move forward and uphold ideals such as human dignity, individual autonomy, justice, and solidarity; they insist on social justice and recognition of differences precisely because such ideals have not yet been fully realized. Moving in-between these views, it is possible to refer to multifarious positive individual interactions that occur beyond the limits of particular communities and nation-states but have not yet reached universality because cosmopolitanism is obviously a critical ideal, not an empirical reality. If we take this third possibility into account, cosmopolitanism could be seen as a *process of transgressing borders* according to normative ideals expressed in a consensually valid repertoire of human rights; it is not necessarily the concrete *end result of a perfect borderless* world society, but it is a movement forward.

As an initial reference to support this claim, it is important to be reminded that Immanuel Kant was the first to talk about a community of world citizens involving all peoples on Earth [*weltbürgerliche Gemeinschaft aller Völker auf Erden*]. Note the talk about earth, not heaven! This is a modern idea that, on Kant's own account, was becoming reality. He saw cosmopolitanism as a *point of view* and as a *process*. Notoriously, he also related this process to the growing need for a new legal framework, a law of global citizenship [*Weltbürgerrecht*] that would have to be based on the defense of human rights [*Menschenrechte*]. Although there is a clear ethical and universal dimension to this claim, it is important to differentiate the legal, political, economic, and cultural aspects implicit in Kant's views on cosmopolitanism. In his essay on "Idea of a Universal History in Cosmopolitan Intention," in *Perpetual Peace*, his *Doctrine of Right* [*Rechtslehre*], and other writings, he was consistent enough to apply the cosmopolitan point of view to morality, politics and war, colonialism, and trade as well as cultural history. Today, we can make similar distinctions. From an ethical point of view, one can talk of cosmopolitan ideals in terms of global norms, refer to all human beings, transcend particular conditionings, and define very demanding individual or collective obligations—even if the conditions for their fulfillment are not yet given. A political form of cosmopolitanism would then consider the possibility of implementing peaceful and just structures of power, decision making, procedures, and governance institutions within or beyond the nation-state, a task that would require the creation of new legitimate realms for public expression and participation in political processes, which also demand a juridical approach. Kant saw cosmopolitanism as compatible with some kind of patriotism. From a juridical point of view, we have witnessed the expansion of the design and application of public and private law to the international arena, which is overcoming the boundaries of nationalism and defining the framework of what can be properly considered the legal rights and duties of persons, corporations, and states, but the problem in this case concerns whether a juridification process is subordinated to ethical principles, has primacy over political procedures, or can be independent of economic interests. The possibility of an economic cosmopolitanism has been more controversial, but this idea has both historic antecedents and current prospects due to globalization, such that the need for ethical, legal, and political regulations of economic practices becomes even more urgent. Also here, debates abound concerning the shape of such cosmopolitanism, for it could be based on economic incentives and injunctions that contradict the assumptions that economic interests are seemingly conflictive or conducive to belligerent actions. Culturally, there is much discussion on intercultural communication as an alternative to cultural imperialism and as a way of making the affirmation of diverse particular identities compatible with universal values. Are there guarantees that this cosmopolitan situation could be either fully achieved or assumed as perennial? Unfortunately, I am in no condition to offer such guarantees. Nobody is! Notwithstanding, the cosmopolitan universal ideal remains an aspiration worth pursuing, even if aspects of this ideal and the conditions for its application are found only partially today in regional communitarian contexts that do not yet correspond to a truly global cosmopolitan society.

These initial remarks should be enough to reveal the position I take in order to defend the possibility of *building of cosmopolitan communities*. I now need to make explicit the conceptual basis upon which I stand.

A CRITICAL STANDPOINT AS POINT OF DEPARTURE

This project is inspired by a philosophical tradition that starts with the "Criticism" inaugurated by Immanuel Kant, a tradition that is then expanded by Karl Marx's critique of political economy and taken up by the Critical Theory of the Frankfurt School, before finally reaching the current stage of a "Critical Discourse Philosophy" proposed by Jürgen Habermas, Karl-Otto Apel, and other contemporary authors.

I am focusing on a line of thought that has its roots in the German context and inspires contemporary philosophers who not only rescue the Kantian project and reconstruct or transform his transcendentalism in light of the *linguistic turn*, but also criticize the totalitarianism of Marxism and the subjectivism of critical theorists such as Theodor Adorno and Max Horkheimer. This line updates the original insights of previous positions and translates them into the fresher analytical terms of contemporary philosophy, everyday discourse practices, and current political challenges raised by globalization processes. Through new initiatives within this Critical Discourse Philosophy and two complementary but distinct projects defined as "Discourse Theory" and "Discourse Ethics," Habermas and Apel have influenced new generations of scholars working specifically on cosmopolitan values, the communitarian-liberalism debate, human rights, and normativity. This book is to be placed within this critical tradition.

However, some may not share the premises I just laid out or be persuaded about the explanatory power of Critical Theory and the authors I mentioned. Even those who happen to agree with these introductory remarks may have different interpretations or give a distinct accent to particular aspects of the critical tradition. Therefore, I would like to expand my remarks a little further and present my take on Critical Discourse Philosophy—and its internal differentiation in Discourse Theory and Discourse Ethics—in order to clarify some points regarding my own theoretical position.

First of all, what is "critique" or "criticism"? This term has an original meaning in aesthetics and art, related to the act of carefully appreciating and appraising not only objects that may have aesthetic value, but also the very process of subjectively ascribing such aesthetic value to particular objects. This initial definition evolved to include a series of other uses, such as the evaluation of public affairs in daily newspapers, careful analysis of political arguments, moral judgment of social behavior, revealing and questioning of implicit premises in theoretical works, or the examination of weaknesses and strengths of particular arguments or even research programs. This variety yields a plethora of philosophical practices and programs that are now available, such as critical thinking, critical analysis, and critical theory. Among the various versions of critical theory one can mention linguistic pragmatism, feminism, and postcolonialism, but my focus here will be on Critical Theory, in capital letters. Because various theories aim to be critical, using the very term "critical theory" would appear misleading. Hence, I will follow the common practice of using capital letters and identifying Critical Theory in a narrow sense that refers to a specific school of thought involving several generations of German theorists who affirmed the importance of upholding human rights and emancipation ideals while questioning the oppressive structures of society that contradict these rights and ideals. I probably need to explain why I choose this particular branch of critical theory: this German tradition of Critical Theory with roots in Kant reaches all the way to contemporary Discourse Philosophy and provides one of the most ambitious theoretical programs available. This theory focuses on normative questions concerning human rights discourses that *could* be related to other theories that deal with issues of gender, ethnicity, race, culture, and economy, among others. With the careful use of the expression *could*, I express my agreement with a common criticism that Critical Theory has often failed to address these issues in more detail. Nevertheless, it can be said that this theoretical framework has proven to be broad and flexible enough to serve as a starting point that is open to other contributions and to corrections.

Surely, Critical Theory is not free of problems and there are differences even within this tradition. Many authors side with Adorno and Horkheimer and reject the reconstruction of Critical Theory proposed by Habermas, while others focus on Habermas, but do not take his dialogue with Apel into account. Still others perform a radical division between Habermas's Universal Pragmatics and Apel's transcendental-pragmatic version of Discourse Ethics. Some neglect the contribution of newer generations of critical theorists who discuss issues such as gender, colonialism, globalization, and multiculturalism. I argue that Critical Discourse Philosophy is at the center of all these debates and, therefore, I take this model as a frame of reference. Still, some may question, why would this reference be better than, say, Adorno's emphasis on aesthetics or Michel Foucault's genealogy? A simple answer is that Habermas and Apel were able to update and translate many of the previous claims of Critical Theory in terms of discursive practices that can be revealed and criticized in everyday life and at the same time keep the emphasis on discursive universality.

What is meant by "discourse"? If one takes daily political practices as example, one may be tempted to consider the discourses of political campaigns as an empty form of speech that abuses rhetoric and provides little information because it is geared toward persuading people by means of a strategic use of communication. Indeed, there is a long history of suspicion against the association between rhetoric and politics and the reference to discourses without explaining their meaning. Another possibility is to take discourse as a technical tool that requires expertise in its use. In view of all these options, an initial clarification of this term is, therefore, in order. I will have a chance to discuss this issue in more detail later on. The Latin term *"discursus"* was originally used to denote the course of thought or flow of ideas, but this term was appropriated differently in specific European philosophical traditions and has different interpretations today. Let me refer to those that are inspired in traditional European views.

In the British tradition, one can single out John Locke's *Essay Concerning Human Understanding*, where he defines reason as a discursive faculty and explains that words and arguments are parts—or rather "particles"—of a coherent discourse capable of expressing all kinds of connections in areas such as science, morality, and art. However, he reserves the expression "Philosophical Discourse" to the most precise and coherent form of rational discourse, thus justifying the use of the term "discourse" as the very title of his systematic works. The British empiricism that expands on Locke's philosophy of language yields not only a rich tradition of linguistic semantics, but also influences Charles S. Peirce in the United States and his use of the term "semiotics," which had been originally applied by Locke at the end of his *Essay* in order to define a third branch of science. Contemporary semantic theories follow this line, but are more interested in analyzing the meaning and reference of specific units within a discourse in artificial or natural languages.

In the French tradition, we can go back to René Descartes's *Discourse on Method* as a famous example equating discourse and scientific rationality. But others went beyond his work to find a linguistic definition of discourse that refers not simply to mathematical or scientific statements, but also to different forms of communication, their users, and the contexts in which they are embedded. An example of a complex definition of linguistic discourse can be found in the eighteenth century in the works of Étienne Bonnot the Condillac, which was expanded upon by contemporary authors such as Ferdinand de Saussure and his *semiologie* as well as the poststructuralism of Jacques Derrida and Jean-François Lyotard. It is to Michel Foucault's merit to have studied this French tradition of discourse analysis and revealed the institutional background to discursivity. Through his "archeology of knowledge" [*archeology du savoir*] and "genealogical analysis" he uncovers a history of power, control, domination, and oppression that leads to the imposition of specific values and exclusion of certain peoples by particular institutions—the university, hospital, prison, and others. All this is revealed through a deconstructive analysis of the power implicit in discourse.

In the German tradition, some interpreters go back to Meister Eckhart and Martin Luther to show the beginnings of a linguistic reflection on German language in the sixteenth century, but it is mainly in the anti-Enlightenment reaction to Kant that we find an explicit philosophy of language, best exemplified by the so-called three Hs: Johann G. Hamann, Johann G. Herder, and Wilhelm von Humboldt. In reaction to the publication of Kant's *Critique of Pure Reason* in 1781, his close friend Hamann wrote but never published a *Meta-Critique of the Purism of Reason*. Similarly, Herder wrote his *Meta-Critique of the Critique of Pure Reason* in 1799 while Humboldt published a treatise on *Thinking and Speaking* already in 1795, which was later complemented by a series of empirical studies in comparative linguistics. The point of these critiques is the same: Kant neglected the dimension of communication. Their work on language has been reappraised in the twentieth century in the philosophical hermeneutics of Martin Heidegger and Hans-Georg Gadamer, but it is primarily in Karl-Otto Apel and Jürgen Habermas that we find a systematic attempt to reconsider this tradition in philosophy of language and establish a dialogue with another conception of formal linguistics that had emerged in Germany: a research program on formal language that goes from Gottfried Leibniz to Gottlob Frege and on to Ludwig Wittgenstein and Rudolf Carnap, later merging with Anglo-American analytical philosophy.

In their articulation of elements from both the continental (French and German) and analytical (British and American) heritages of linguistics and philosophy of language, Apel and Habermas were able to come to a bold definition of discourse that is applied in theory and practice. From a theoretical perspective, discourse is a *form of communication through rational arguments* in which specific validity claims are raised in relation to given domains of reference. From a practical perspective, discourse is a self-referential *ethical norm* prescribing what can be agreed to as universally valid and morally acceptable as well as a range of social practices that implicitly rely on such a norm. In both theory and practice, discourses rely on the pragmatic and compelling "power of the best argument" and constitute the fundamental aspects of a *Critical Discourse Philosophy*. This is, in my opinion, the best term to characterize the general philosophical project developed jointly by Habermas and Apel as well as a way to architectonically organize various contemporary contributions to Critical Theory. Of course, there are differences to acknowledge. For instance, Habermas describes his views as "Universal" or "Formal Pragmatics" as well as "Discourse

Theory"—which is applied differently to legal, political, educational, and other institutional settings—while the terms chosen by Apel are "Transcendental Pragmatics" and "Discourse Ethics." In both cases, however, they go back to Kant, inherit the critical tradition, and interpret him in light of new theories of discourse and contemporary challenges. In both cases, there are also limitations that need to be criticized, such as relying on the particularities of their social context while claiming universal validity, lacking a systemic approach to art, aesthetics, and culture while claiming to inherit the tradition of Kant and the Critical Theory of the Frankfurt School, or failing to engage in a discussion of economic issues such as global poverty although they have the potential to update Marx's critique of political economy. Most important for the purpose of this book is that they both have contributed to debates on community, human rights, cosmopolitan ideals, and normativity. I will, therefore, focus on these aspects.

Observing the examples above, it is easy to conclude that while discourse can be closely related to the notion of a logical argument and to specific forms of rationality, it can also refer to formal structures that give them validity, institutions that define their rules, social practices that emerge in relation to these structures, political programs that implement them, and ethical norms that guide such practices. An objection could be raised that according to this view, everything would be defined as discourse. This is not necessarily so, but I do take that discourse is continuously presupposed in our interactions. This also means that discourse cannot be dismissed as simply the strategic use of rhetorical devices in order to persuade or deceive someone. To say this, one would have to make use of discourse to say that discourse should not be taken seriously, and this would be a self-contradiction. Therefore, discourse has to be seen as a *normative criterion*, a principle to orient human interactions and a tool to evaluate real individuals and communities in pursuit of human rights and cosmopolitan ideals. In the terminology of Discourse Philosophy, we can define these instances as discursive communities or *communities of communication*. This discursive approach will, therefore, guide us in analyzing the process of *building cosmopolitan communities*.

I will have the opportunity to provide more details about these concepts later on. For now, I just want to inform the reader that my use of these words are influenced by these philosophical meanings and loaded with their technical implications. In what follows, let me show the steps I will take in order to make the case for a constructive and dynamic view of cosmopolitan communities under construction.

COMMUNITY, HUMAN RIGHTS, AND COSMOPOLITAN IDEALS

This book is divided into two parts preceded by this introduction and complemented by the conclusion. Part I has two chapters. Chapter 2, "The Transformations of the Critical Tradition," is *a genealogical* introductory discussion that situates this project as a contribution to Critical Theory and prepares the argument that human rights and cosmopolitan ideas need to account for both the *ideal* normative aspirations and the *real* communitarian conditions and possibilities to implement them. As mentioned before, Immanuel Kant is the starting point of this tradition and he established basic references that were important to Georg F. Hegel and Karl Marx. While Hegel criticized Kant's abstract views, Marx provided a critique of Hegel's philosophy of law and explicitly discussed questions of humanity, rights, and cosmopolitanism with an emphasis on political-economic aspects. Max Horkheimer, Theodor Adorno, and other representatives of the Critical Theory of the Frankfurt School touch on some of these themes, but add social and cultural dimensions that had been neglected until then. Beyond these authors, this chapter progressively prepares the way to introduce the work of Jürgen Habermas and Karl-Otto Apel, who reassess Critical Theory in terms of an elaborate Discourse Philosophy that connects community, human rights, and cosmopolitanism to normative communicative procedures. This has led to a new research program about the formation of normative frameworks, which is being carried out by new generations of critical theorists who are more open to global issues. This chapter concludes by insisting on the need of a more incisive global approach.

Chapter 3, "Discourse Philosophy as a Critical Framework," adopts a *pragmatic* approach, introduces this theoretical position in more detail, discusses communicative processes in communitarian settings, and highlights the application and internal differentiation of practical discourses within institutional realms. To pursue this general goal, I first provide more details about the philosophical project developed jointly by Karl-Otto Apel and Jürgen Habermas. This chapter then accounts for the internal differences within Discourse Philosophy by showing the importance of the concept of *communication community* in Apel's Discourse Ethics developed in light of his Transcendental Pragmatics and the concept of *rational discourse* proposed by Habermas in light of his Discourse Theory and Formal Pragmatics. I finally argue that despite these internal differences, this joint program provides a useful basis for the critique and updating of Kant's views on cosmopolitanism and human rights. But again, this program needs to be corrected and expanded in certain ways, especially regarding the inclusion of a global approach that should be complemented by a more explicit and systematic commitment to plurality. Therefore, I propose the model of a *multidimensional discourse community* to address this issue.

Part II includes three chapters that expand on the historical and theoretical basis offered in the first two chapters. They interpret *communities, human rights,* and *cosmopolitan ideals* as fundamentally plural concepts that need to be read in counterpoint with the theoretical framework presented earlier. This part deepens the discussion of Critical Discourse Philosophy and introduces new elements that complement my presentation of Apel and Habermas. For instance, they see community as both a norm and an institution. Moreover, they define three historical moments or paradigms in terms of metaphysical, epistemic, and discursive approaches that help us sort out the different kinds of arguments regarding human rights and cosmopolitanism. However, instead of simply affirming or imposing their theories, I actually expose them to the contemporary diversity of positions, thus opening their views to new challenges and adaptations. Also, this part reminds the reader that Kant argued for a new political order based on cosmopolitan law [*Weltbürgerrecht*], the right of humanity [*Recht der Menschheit*], and the condition of hospitality [*Hospitalität*], which need to be upgraded in terms of contemporary global human rights discourses.

Chapter 4, "Individuality and Collectivity in Changing Concepts of Community," adds more complexity to the general picture presented thus far by including and radicalizing the element of diversity and plurality. By means of a *sociopolitical* description, it reveals the contemporary quest for community and shows the variety of perspectives at play in emphasizing community values and norms. These values and norms need to be understood in light of a wider context that factors in the challenges of individual diversity, multicultural societies, and contextual differences. This discussion invariably leads to a consideration of communitarianism, but in this chapter I argue for a reconsideration of the contemporary call for community according to a critical normative principle, so that we can better qualify the kind of community at stake whenever we talk about the possibility of a cosmopolitan community. First, it is important to consider the ways in which individuals can move in and out of specific communities as well as keep in mind the fact that conceptions of community are continuously changing. This realization helps us to grasp the tense relationship between autonomy and belonging, which always emerges in discussions about communities. I conclude this chapter by reiterating the proposal for a *multidimensional community of communication* or *multidimensional discourse community* that accommodates issues of individuality and promotes plurality by going beyond communitarian particularism and recognizing the cultural differences and diversity inherent to modern societies.

Chapter 5, "From Plurality to Global Human Rights Discourses," applies the paradigmatic models offered by Discourse Philosophy to a *legal-critical* consideration of human rights and argues that the discussion concerning rights can be traced back to three moments. These include, first, the ancient metaphysics that reaches the traditional "law of peoples" [*jus gentium*] and natural law in medieval Europe; second, the modern epistemic approaches to rights that were pursued by nations in Europe and the Americas during modernity and led to the establishment of constitutional law; and third, the contemporary discourses on human rights that emerged after the adoption of the *Universal Declaration on Human Rights* in 1948 and are still being debated. In this chapter, I hope to show two things: first, that all these paradigmatic models are still available in different contexts and sometimes interact in either a conflictive or interactive way; second, that we can claim a theoretical superiority of a discursive conception of cosmopolitan ideals and human rights which leads to a new understanding of norms. Guided by this understanding, I question contemporary human rights conceptions that simply rely on a legal reading of existing documents such as the *Universal Declaration on Human Rights* and I also reject assumptions that see positive law as the sole instance for the normativity of human rights. Instead, I highlight alternative "processes" that lead to the pursuit of cosmopolitan ideals and propose a discursive or communicative understanding of global human rights. This chapter highlights the importance of *bottom-up* processes that rely on human rights discourses and motivate positive changes at both the community and global levels. In the course of this discussion, different contexts are observed, the common normative structure of encompassing discourses is revealed, and the possibility of amplifying this process to integrate global issues is proposed.

Chapter 6, "Cosmopolitan Ideals and the Norms of Universality," begins with a *historico-critical* perspective and tries to apply the three paradigms defined in Discourse Philosophy to the concept of cosmopolitan ideals. This concept has been classified in historical terms before, but I think its meanings can be better sorted out at the macrophilosophical level if we interpret it according to the stages defined in the previous chapter: the ancient cosmopolitan metaphysics of Diogenes the Cynic or Cicero is a political position based on a distinction between the real city [*polis*] and the *metaphysical* structure of a *cosmic city* [*cosmopolis*]—while modern cosmopolitan ideals emerged in the European context as an attempt to articulate individual rights, sovereign political units, and an incipient *international* structure aimed at avoiding wars among peoples and nations. Contemporary cosmopolitan approaches, however, not only require a *postmetaphysical* perspective and a transition to a *postconventional* level of normative reflection, but also need to recognize a *postnational constellation*.

After the second part, I offer a conclusion by providing a brief systematic synopsis of the issues discussed before. Building on the previous discussions, chapter 7, "Cosmopolitan Communities under Construction," summarizes my proposal to relate cosmopolitan ideals to concrete global human rights discourses and differentiate their application processes according to the paradigmatic references and communitarian frameworks discussed previously. I therefore reiterate my point that the model of a *multidimensional discourse community* provides a robust normative framework that helps us to avoid the problems of ancient metaphysics, supersede the limits of modern *politics* centered on the Westphalian State, and consider the contemporary *postnational constellation* that emerges with the globalization process. While recognizing the importance of strong technical definitions of norms in logic, law, and politics, attention is given to understandings of norms in the anthropological, sociological, legal, and ethical sense. Relying on these considerations, I conclude that it is reasonable to aspire to ethically or morally defined universal norms if we relate them to plural communication processes, apply them to the justification of cosmopolitan ideals, and connect them to the process of implementing global human rights discourses in reality. This is certainly a difficult task, but the theoretical elements presented in previous chapters provide us with a general framework for the process of building cosmopolitan communities. This is done by differentiating the justification and application of norms at various levels while including the possibility of constructing communities beyond state-centric approaches, which promote human rights at all levels. Global human rights discourses is what we have now, which help us to pursue the aspirational dimension of universality expressed in a cosmopolitan ideal that is capable of passing the test of *being multidimensional enough* to account for individuality, collectivity, multicultural and intercultural plurality, and global universality.

This assessment leads then to my supposition that it is possible to redefine cosmopolitan ideals in terms of contemporary human rights discourses without forgetting the deep historical, cultural, and contextual dimensions of their implementation. At the same time, these discussions constitute the normative framework that allows us to evaluate and criticize contextual applications at each level. This explains why it is crucial to rescue and articulate disconnected aspects of the discussion on cosmopolitan ideals and also design new tools to better define the kind of normativity required to make sense of the global role that human rights discourses could play in the twenty-first century. Global human rights discourses can be more specifically related to the dynamics of communitarian belonging, but we also need to provide more specific references regarding the types of norms individuals and groups may appeal to when moving in and out of specific communities. If, on the one hand, it is possible to *justify* human rights as an aspirational process or a form of cosmopolitan transgression of communitarian boundaries, it is also necessary, on the other hand, to *apply* these rights by taking into account the conditions and situation of particular contexts at a global level. The normative guidance in this case is given by the process of building cosmopolitan communities from below, in plural, as opposed to imposing cosmopolitanism from the top down.

Based on these views I think it is possible to consider different ways to pursue cosmopolitan ideals and implement human rights according to their specificity and context. The process of building cosmopolitan communities would serve as an important mediation link that needs to be included more prominently in reflections about cosmopolitanism. Another issue that emerges is the tendency to affirm globalization and universal values without recognizing the interaction of communities and networks that include different voices, cultural experiences, specific challenges, and geopolitical issues. I attempt to rescue and articulate neglected and disconnected aspects in abstract conceptions of cosmopolitanism, normativity, and human rights in order to provide a more immanent and scalable approach to reach the goal I proposed at the beginning.

Motivations, Limitations, and Projections

In the remainder of this introduction, I would like to make more explicit some of the motivations that guide my initiative by answering three main questions.

The first is, what do I hope to accomplish with this book? The main goal is to propose a critical framework to articulate community, human rights, and cosmopolitan ideals in a way that expresses the intrinsic plurality of individual perspectives, community settings, contemporary societies, and cultural worldviews. In formulating my views for a constructive conception of cosmopolitan community, I try to pay attention to contextual differences without losing the universal perspective. Thus, I situate myself in the middle of current, decentralized sociopolitical issues particular to contexts in which I have lived and worked, such as Latin America (Brazil), Europe (Germany), and North America (the United States). At the same time, however, I am always reminded of the experience of transcending cultural, linguistic, and political boundaries by the possibility of establishing communicative interactions and concrete relationships beyond borders.

Human relations and claims for human rights are occurring at a faster pace due to an ongoing *globalization from below*, which has been enabled by social movements, education, tourism, communication networks, business practices, immigration, and other bottom-up processes. Moreover, many other forms of interactions are influencing the shape of societies in both the global North and the global South—including the challenges of financial instability, poverty, and violence. Conceptual discussions need to consider these interactions and refer to them not merely as interesting empirical cases, appendices, or footnotes, but rather as important conditions that affect the way we think about cosmopolitan ideals. I attempt, therefore, to see historical and current events involving social actors and contexts as concrete factors that need to inform both theoretical and practical models. By insisting on the recognition of these contextual references as necessary to making sense of community, human rights, and cosmopolitan ideals, I hope to contribute to the further transformation of the critical tradition.

The second question is, what does this book leave out? I am aware that this book does not address many specific issues related to the general topics of community, human rights, and cosmopolitan ideal, which are the subject of a growing literature. Although I do provide a general perspective on ethical or moral cosmopolitanism in terms of Discourse Philosophy, I do not deal with specific questions that emerge in recent analytical literature on theories of justice and democracy. Neither do I get into details about questions that emerge regarding minorities, gender relations, racial and ethnic identities, and religious groups that question the limits and power of the nation-state. Issues of governance, representation, and economic relations are also left out. However, what I regret the most is that the limits of this book did not allow me to delve deeper into other "traditions of critique," especially the liberation thinking that evolves in the Latin American context. I hope to pursue this goal in another volume.

The third and final question to be answered would be, what are possible ways of expanding on the work I present here? In defining my theoretical standpoint, I engage in a conversation with both historical and contemporary authors in the perspective that I call the "tradition of critique." I hope to have contributed to the task of demarcating this area. I have focused on the German tradition. By doing so, I also "situate" and "contextualize" the theoretical perspective I am following, instead of affirming its universality as a given or simply imposing my views. As I do so, it is important to indicate that many others within this tradition are in direct and indirect communication with their antecessors and contemporaries, so the mapping of these dialogues is very important. Moreover, although I simply indicate other traditions in other contexts, they deserve more attention. I have also attempted to argue for a concept of *cosmopolitan communities* as a way of speaking in the plural. While acknowledging a variety of existing approaches, I had to focus on specific examples and cultural experiences related to Europe. Also, here is much room to expand, especially in considering other regional frameworks in different parts of the world.

I believe that an expansion of our frame of reference and consideration of specific cases in our justification and application of cosmopolitanism, community, and human rights is an urgent necessity. Hopefully, this book will help us to articulate these different aspects in a dynamic way that highlights the process of transgressing boundaries and enlarging perspectives. This leads to my final point: instead of simply focusing on particular documents and merely formal frameworks for human rights, we need to explore how interactions among humans from many contexts and the process of coming in and out of different communities transcend specific borders and generate new flexible communities of communication in which new values, processes, and norms emerge. These communities can be defined as cosmopolitan, not necessarily based on predefined static structures but rather on the community record of continuously implementing dynamic communicative processes compatible with the norms that contribute to the increasing realization of cosmopolitan ideals.

I

A CRITICAL AND MULTIDIMENSIONAL APPROACH

2

THE TRANSFORMATIONS OF THE CRITICAL TRADITION

Before considering how community, human rights, and cosmopolitan ideals can be articulated within a normative philosophical framework, we need to go back to the eighteenth century, take Immanuel Kant's views on *Criticism* as point of departure, and show how the tradition he inaugurated has been changed and updated. The focus here is not necessarily on the epistemology of Kant's three *Critiques*, but rather on the critical method he initiated and the practical applications of this method in history, ethics, politics, law, and aesthetics. The focus is not solely on Kant either. He is the starting point of a series of definitions of cosmopolitanism, community, human rights, and normativity that still inform Critical Theory. These definitions were important for Georg Friedrich Hegel and his critique of Kantian formalism, but because Hegel remained bound to idealism and to the German status quo, his views had to be superseded. Therefore, it is in the materialism of Karl Marx and Friedrich Engels that we see a radical rejection of Hegel's views, which represented an abstract "critique of heavens" that never came down to a "critique of earth." This subtle but radical change in the meaning of critique becomes explicit when Marx upgrades the critical tradition by proposing a "critique of ideology" and a "critique of philosophy" as conditions for a *Critique of Political Economy*. This is not simply a new term, but a new program affirming the materiality of life, priority of human needs, rejection of workers' alienation, and promotion of social transformation. We cannot, however, stop at Marx. There were new developments in Marxism, strong opposition to it, and also a particular alternative approach to "critique" represented by Max Horkheimer, Theodor Adorno, and other members of the so-called Frankfurt School.

The Frankfurt School revised the conceptions of "critique" in Kant, Hegel, and Marx in order to define a new approach, *Critical Theory*, designed to include important social and cultural issues that had emerged in the first half of the twentieth century but were neglected by political parties in Europe. This program is not static, but rather dynamic, and renews itself to include a "critique of instrumental reason" or "critique of positivism" as well as a "critique of society" and a "critique of culture" that led to Adorno's transformation of Critical Theory into an "Aesthetic Theory." My point so far should be obvious. There are many dimensions of "critique" and Critical Theory itself is a project "under construction." Hence, the Frankfurt School cannot be our endpoint either. Authors such as Adorno and Horkheimer remained prey to a certain pessimism that was superseded by a more hopeful approach based on a turn to a pragmatic "critique of meaning" provided by Jürgen Habermas and Karl-Otto Apel. By transforming both Kant's Criticism and Critical Theory in light of the *linguistic turn*, Apel and Habermas initiated a new program: "Critical Discourse Theory." Yet, this program remains in flux, as evidenced by Habermas's changes in his own position, his differences with Apel, and the emergence of new generations of philosophers who build on the strengths of Discourse Theory while recognizing its shortcomings.

This summary indicates already some key shifts within a critical tradition in Germany. While Kant, Hegel, and Marx clearly emphasize the importance of science, the members of the Frankfurt School question scientificism and turn to social and cultural issues. But here also there are differences, not only among the members of this group but among also what has been called the different "generations" of the Frankfurt School. While Adorno and Horkheimer represent a first generation of the old Frankfurt School [*alte Frankfurter Schule*], which remained limited by the subjectivism and pessimism of the period between World War I and World War II, a second generation identified with a new school [*die neue Frankfurter Schule*] linked to Habermas, Apel, Albrecht Wellmer, and others, stressed intersubjectivity and expanded the scope of the critical tradition once more while collaborating with partners in the United States, such as Thomas McCarthy and Richard Bernstein, to propose a new program that defines critique as the pragmatic analysis of validity claims and their meaning. A third generation of philosophers directly or indirectly related to the Frankfurt School, such as Axel Honneth, Matthias Lutz-Bachmann, Martin Seel, and Christoph Mencke, was extended to include the collaboration of philosophers in the United States, such as Seyla Benhabib, Nancy Fraser, and James Bohman. With this, they widened the scope of the critical tradition by including themes such as community, gender, democracy, and cosmopolitanism. A more recent group of authors such as Cristina Lafont, Rainer Forst, Max Pensky, Eduardo Mendieta, Andreas Niederberger, and many others constitute a fourth generation that takes multiculturalism, race, cosmopolitanism, and globalization into account while paying attention to specific contexts and contemporary challenges to normative theories. This generation not only expands the repertoire of themes and initiates a fruitful dialogue with contemporary positions, but also reestablishes the link with the original sources and intentions of the critical tradition.

In providing an overview of these developments and links, this chapter introduces and exposes in more detail the key concepts I presented in the introduction. I make explicit my commitment to Critical Theory and at the same time identify the kinds of "critique" available today. As it will become clear later on, by providing this overview, I rely on a key methodological contribution of Discourse Theory, which Apel calls the "transformation of philosophy" and Habermas defines as "historical reconstruction." Based on this reconstruction, we will see that the scope of "critique" has definitely expanded and included many of the elements needed to discuss community, human rights, and cosmopolitan ideals.

THE CRITICISM OF IMMANUEL KANT

The conceptual history of the term "critique" can lead us all the way back to ancient Greek times (Koselleck 1977), but I will start with some key modern references that point directly to Kant. The term "*critica*" was used in eighteenth-century Italy by Giambattista Vico (1725) to characterize a method based on imagination [*fantasia*], which aimed to study the creativity and authenticity of human artifacts (Verene 1981; Pompa 1990), while "criticism" was applied in Britain by the Earl of Shaftesbury and Joseph Addison to characterize the process of informing the general public about the need to examine concrete artworks, appreciate their impact on spectators, and express this appreciation through informed judgment. In his three-volume collection of essays, *Characteristics of Men, Manners, Opinions, Times* (Cooper 1711), Lord Shaftesbury defends the role of the art critic as an interpreter of artworks. At the same time, in a series of 11 essays published in *The Spectator* under the title "The Pleasures of Imagination" (1711), Addison considered questions such as why pleasure is produced by external objects, how people experience the external world, how one can describe and judge artistic objects based on the theories of John Locke and Thomas Hobbes, and how Descartes explained the functioning of the mind. Addison answered these questions to provide a model of the "true Critick" who should be able to analyze literary works and understand the role of imagination as a faculty related to both morality and aesthetics (Addison 1711, "The Spectator" 412). The Common Sense Philosophy of the Scottish Enlightenment followed a similar line of thought: Francis Hutcheson published his *An Inquiry into the Origin of Our Ideas of Beauty and Virtue* in 1725, Edmund Burke's *Philosophical Inquiry into the Origin of Our Ideas on the Sublime and the Beautiful* appeared in 1757, and, shortly thereafter, in 1762, Henry Home (Lord Kames) published his *Elements of Criticism* in three volumes. He defended the advantages of studying criticism not as a mere exercise of the imagination but rather as a rational endeavor to guide reflection and judgment (Home 1762:7–10).

Why do we need to know all this? These references are relevant insofar as they influenced the beginning of a tradition of critical philosophy initiated by Immanuel Kant. Most of the works mentioned above were translated into German between 1762 and 1773 and Kant had access to them. He was deeply influenced by the Scottish Enlightenment (Kuehn 1987). Also, among these philosophers, Home—Lord Kames—was the one to exert a central influence that led to Kant's adoption of the term "criticism." Home had shown that, differently from metaphysics and mathematics, criticism had "the tendency to improve social intercourse" (1762:11). Another important point he made is that "the science of criticism appears to be an intermediate link, finally qualified to connect the different parts of education" (1762:10). Kant quoted Home in scattered notes written at this time—later collected as *Reflexionen*, numbered from 1 to 6455, and published in volumes 15–18 of the *Akademieausgabe* of his *Gesammelte Schriften* [hereafter, *AA*] (1902). One of them confirms this influence, even if only elliptically: "Fine art allows only critique. Home. Therefore no science of the beautiful" (*Reflexionen* 1588). This is an interesting statement because it presents "critique" as an instance between natural science and arts while showing us where Kant got the idea of an intermediate method capable of articulating different but complementary forms of cognition. Kant's statement in his *Reflexionen* 1588 provides us with an important point, stressed later in further developments of Critical Theory: criticism is related not only to science and society, but also to aesthetics and culture.

Next, I focus on his own conception of critique, which will later help us define community, human rights, and cosmopolitan ideals in terms of individual autonomy and membership in an extensive social unit within and beyond the limits of the nation-state.

A disclaimer is necessary before I proceed. Although Kant synthesizes previous trends on cosmopolitanism and anticipates many themes later introduced in the *Charter of the United Nations* in 1945 and the *Universal Declaration on Human Rights* in 1948, it is possible to identify and criticize many anachronisms in his work. This includes errors in his views on history, geography and anthropology (Mendieta and Elden 2011), traces of pietistic religious metaphysics in his teleological thinking (Apel 1997; Kuehn 2002), the bias of German political chauvinism, lack of consideration for women and gender issues (Kleingeld 1993; Shell 1996), and the affirmation of racist assumptions (Bernasconi 2001, 2003, 2006; see exchange between Kleingeld 2007 and Bernasconi 2011). As we recognize these shortcomings in an author that was bound to eighteenth-century Europe, it is still possible to find many important elements in Kant's thinking (Habermas 1996). First, however, we must step back and exegetically consider the meaning of "criticism" and "critique" as well as the contemporary influence of these concepts. Kant provided us with a tool to criticize his own work and our own shortcomings, so this explains why the tradition of critique is in constant transformation.

Critique or *Criticism* was the very denomination chosen by Kant to characterize his philosophical program. So much so that his philosophy is now classified into two moments: the *precritical* period between 1755 and 1769 and the mature *critical* stage inaugurated with the publication of his *Critique of Pure of Reason* [*KrV, AA* 4] in 1781, which was prepared by reflections and discussions in the 12 years between 1769 and 1781 (Kreimendahl 1990). The precritical period shows the influence of ancient metaphysics while the "critical turn" in his philosophy represents a shift toward modern science in order to reject untenable metaphysical assumptions and define the limits of reason. This shift can be identified in the very titles of his books. While his precritical work on aesthetics carries the Burkean title *Observations on the Feeling of the Beautiful and Sublime* (1764 [*AA* 2]) and is influenced by empirical anthropology, the work published on this same topic in 1790, thus after the "critical turn," is titled *Critique of the Faculty of Judgment* [*KdU, AA* 5]. The difference in these titles is reason enough to ask a few questions.

If Kant's mature thinking was based on science, why does he use the aesthetic concept of "criticism" to identify his mature thinking? A partial answer is given by recalling the methodological twist given to this term by Home when he saw criticism as a procedure to guide judgment. Mirroring Home's proposal, Kant proposes a tripartite division of knowledge according to the methods of science, historical discipline, and critique (*Reflexionen* 622, 623, 624, 626). Moreover, he introduces new layers of meaning that add complexity to his use of the term. In the announcement of his lectures for 1765, he practically presents the plan for his future career and provides the architectonic design of his intellectual program: first, he divides philosophy into metaphysics, logic, ethics, and physical geography, and then he relates criticism to logic. Accordingly, his *Lectures on Logic*, offered annually since 1765 but published in 1800 by Gottlob Benjamin Jäsche (*Logik* [*Jäsche*] in *AA* 9), defines logic as a canon that serves the goal of criticism. Although Kant concedes that the axiomatic statements of mathematics could be defined as dogmas, as Christian Wolff had suggested, he rejects the extrapolation of this mathematical "dogmatism" because it claims absolute certainty in areas to which mathematical proofs could not be applied. Second, Kant recognizes the possibility of using David Hume's skeptical method to question particular statements, but avoided the generalization he identified negatively as "skepticism." In his view, "both methods are faulty, if applied too generally" [*beide Methoden sind, wenn sie allgemein werden, fehlerhaft*] (*Logik* 84; also *KrV* A 424/B 451). This explains why he avoided both extremes and followed Home in proposing an "intermediate link," an alternative between these two, which he called criticism.

Third, in his *Announcement of the Program of His Lectures for the Winter Semester 1765–1766* Kant adds that critique as a whole had the double task of projecting the edifice of reason [*Gebäude der Vernunft*] in theoretical terms and relating it to practical life (1765/1766:10–13 [*AA* 2] and *Logik* 8). Therefore, criticism can be interpreted as the architectonic plan upon which different forms of cognition could be organized as complementary, with a look at both logical and abstract issues on the one hand and an eye on their possible application on the other. He did not stop there. Shortly thereafter, in a letter to Marcus Hertz on February 27, 1772, this project evolved into a general method based upon which he characterized his whole philosophical endeavor, dividing it into a critique of reason [*Kritik der Vernunft*] and a critique of taste [*Kritik des Geschmacks*], later to be defined as aesthetics. There is at least one other perspective relevant to the understanding of Kant's criticism at this time, found in the *Critique of Pure Reason* (*KrV* B 741–742) and in three versions of a manuscript entitled *On the Progress of Metaphysics since Leibniz and Wolff* (prepared in 1790 but published only posthumously in 1804 [*AA* 20]): criticism is to be identified as the last of three historical stages in the evolution of philosophy. Dogmatism corresponds to an old attitude that is questioned by skepticism, which is then superseded by criticism (*AA* 20:281–282). We will later see how this evolutionary idea remains throughout the transformations of the tradition of criticism. All these aspects show that criticism is more than an aesthetic method as it has logical, architectonic, methodical, and historical connotations.

A second question is unavoidable: How does Kant apply the concept of criticism to these various areas? The three *Critiques* constitute the pillars of his Critical or Transcendental Idealism and provide a summary answer: the *Critique of Pure Reason* [*KrV*], originally published in 1781 and revised in 1787, dealt with matters of metaphysics and epistemology; the *Critique of Practical Reason*, published in 1788 [*KpV*], is related to norms for social behavior; and the *Critique of the Faculty of Judgment*, of 1790 [*KdU*] (see Kant 1960), connected aesthetic and teleological judgments in an attempt to complete the systematic project Kant had delineated in 1765. Let me simply highlight some important aspects of these three important works, which will be relevant for us later on.

The first *Critique* deals with the tension between metaphysics and natural science. Its main goal is to expound the "human standpoint" that conditions knowledge and to demarcate the bounds of reason. Nevertheless, Kant establishes connections between epistemology and juridical, logical, political, moral, and cultural issues (Henrich 1973; Kaulbach 1982; Lyotard 1986:34–46; O'Neill 1989:3–27; Korsgaard 1996:114–122; Wood 1999:111–155; Longuenesse 2005:236–241). For instance, he identifies dogmatism not merely as a procedure in the field of mathematics alone, but also as the method of both speculative metaphysics and political despotism, which are not transparent about their procedures and, therefore, bring about injustice [*Ungerechtigkeit*]. In the same way, skepticism's strong focus on causality is characterized by its hopelessness that leads to indifference (*KrV* A viii/B xiii, xx–xxii). Keeping an eye on these two extremes, Kant engages in a critical search for a middle term. Leaving aside the complex discussions on perception, logic, and dialectics, I limit myself to the juridical images in central passages of the first *Critique*.

In the preface of the first edition of 1781, he says that the instance to answer all possible philosophical questions is the "tribunal" [*Gerichtshof*] of reason (*KrV* A viii–ix, A 443/B 491). This expression reappears in several passages (*KrV* B 529, 697, 768, 779, 815) and is considered by many as the main structural metaphor of the first *Critique* (Vaihinger 1892; Henrich 1963, 1973; O'Neill 1989). Indeed, his discussion of sensibility as well as of the antinomies was permeated by juridical language (*KrV* A 43/B 66, 331).

Moreover, when he prepares the transcendental deduction, Kant not only uses the word "deduction" in its juridical acceptation but also proposes a distinction between facts and values by using two terms taken from jurisprudence—"*quid facti*" and "*quid juris*"—(*KrV* A 68, 84/B 99, 116). Toward the end of the *Critique*, he is more explicit about the legal, political, and cultural implications of the critical method. After showing that the pure unity of reason is the final instance for the answer of theoretical questions (*KrV* A 475/B 503; see A 680/B 708), he concludes that practical questions about freedom, immortality, and God cannot be answered by theoretical reason. Consequently, the second part of the *Critique* (the Transcendental Doctrine of Method) reiterates the need for an architectonic project (*KrV* A 832/B 860) and uses legal and political terminology once again in order to define the task of philosophy: philosophers should not follow a "dictatorial authority" (*KrV* A 739/B 767), but rather pursue "the peace of a state of law" (*KrV* A 751/B 779) and require "the agreement of free citizens" (*KrV* A 739/B 767) who submit social and political structures to the scrutiny of reason. Kant obviously returns to the point of departure spelled out in his preface and, moreover, anticipates themes that will be central to his cosmopolitan project. This project also implies a "method of institution" (*KrV* A 478, 751/B 506, 779), based on a human "love for system, i.e. for a whole according to laws" [*Liebe zum System, d.i. einem Ganzen nach Gesetzen*] (*Reflexionen* 1434) and the need for social "order and connection" (*Reflexionen* 626). Many of these ideas reappear in Kant's political writings such as "Idea to a General History in a Cosmopolitan Perspective" and *Toward Perpetual Peace*.

There is much opposition to and misunderstanding of Kant's architectonics because it seems like an archaic "Baroque" structure imposed upon the whole only for the sake of symmetry (Strawson 1966). It also gives the impression that he insists on given institutions and espouses a certain functionalism that accepts the status quo and, therefore, contradicts the goals of criticism. Nevertheless, it is possible to argue that the legal and political metaphors he uses are compatible with his original intention (O'Neill 1989:3–27; 1992; Saner 1983). These metaphors provide us with a glimpse of how practical questions related to morality, social life, and legal norms emerge at crucial points in the *Critique of Pure Reason* when Kant attempts to define the limits of reason. Also there are complicated questions here that I cannot address within the limits of this section. For example, his attempt to reintroduce the question about God and "make room for faith" would be a fall back into the metaphysics he tries to criticize. I will not address this issue, but rather indicate that this very question allows us to see the role of critique: all questions need to be brought before the tribunal of reason, the instance to decide about the *validity* of competing claims. While summarizing this difficult book in a couple of paragraphs does not do it justice, I hope to have presented at least some key points relevant to the discussion about the meaning of criticism.

The *Critique of Practical Reason* [*KpV*] must be seen as a necessary complement to the first *Critique*. Because the "human standpoint" defended by Kant in the first *Critique* implicitly touched questions regarding morality, social behavior, politics, and law, he was prompted to move to the realm of practical reason. This turn was prepared by the *Groundwork to a Metaphysics of Morals* (1785 [*AA* 4]), where Kant denounced the "*philosophia moralis* of the old times" for grounding the duties of the person in God's will and saw this as incompatible with the Enlightenment and its ideal of freedom (*KpV* v, 18). He thus proposed a *philosophia practica universalis* centered on individual autonomy, capable of addressing the tension between particular and universal conceptions of freedom, and robust enough to make freedom compatible with a universal law (1785:29–31, 34; *KpV* 87–115). This tension between freedom and determinism, anticipated in the third antinomy of the *Critique of Pure Reason*, becomes a new methodological crucis that demanded a different kind of approach. What is this approach? The *Critique of Practical Reason*—which includes a discussion of moral feelings, virtues, and duties—attempts to solve the antinomy of practical reason by affirming the primacy of practice as the "keystone of the whole architecture of the system"—a point already indicated in the first edition of the *Critique of Pure Reason* (*KrV* A ix–xii) and discussed in detail in the second *Critique* (*KpV* 48–51, see § 4, 7). Following the model of the first *Critique*, Kant now attempts to mediate between rationalism and empiricism in ethics and to provide a foundation for morality by means of another deduction (Allison 1990:11–29). The images of the tribunal reappear: he affirms that each person has the right to be his own lord [*sui juris*] and the duty to uphold the universal moral law, but then he realizes that he could not deduct a moral law in the same way he had arrived to the "I think" in the *Critique of Pure Reason*. Therefore, instead of focusing on the *quaestio juris* of the first *Critique* he turned to the *quaestio facti* and proposed a solution to this problem in postulating a "fact of reason" justifying a "law within" ourselves as a tacit presupposition to any moral behavior (*KpV* 3, 9, 56, 72, 74, 81, 96, 163, 187; See Beck 1960, 1961; Henrich 1973, 1975; Willaschek

1991; Proops 2003). This sudden and controversial move has puzzled many interpreters, but it is possible to interpret it constructively as a concrete fact or deed that makes *evident* the rational presupposition to any moral action (Rawls 1980; Allison 1990; Lukow 1993; Kleingeld 2010). This solution has been criticized for committing a "naturalistic fallacy" in trying to derive a moral norm from empirical facts (Ilting 1972) Also, this postulate appears to search for the foundation of morality *in abstracto* and beyond real human interactions (Allison 1990:191–192; Herman 1993:1–44). Following some recent interpretations, these tensions can be reconciled if we see the practical application of reason not as logical deduction but as a capacity to judge that enables us to relate our particular actions to universal laws without contradicting our free will. Kant's controversial solution can be interpreted as a formula that allows a complex interplay between positive and negative freedom (Allison 1990). However, even if this is granted, there are other problems: Kant maintains the dualistic structure of his methodical criticism, still sees the foundation of morals *in foro interno*, and deducts this "fact of reason" in subjectivity instead of explicitly relating it to intersubjective interactions. He maintains his traditional dualism by separating and drawing a series of parallels between law, morals, and politics, while insisting on a subjectivistic definition of human agency at different levels represented by individual freedom of will [*Willkür*], social reciprocity [*commercium*], political general will [*gemeinschaftlicher Willkür*], and communitarian universality [*communio*]—although he does not clearly articulate these dimensions at this point. He was much criticized by Hegel and other authors for this dualism.

Finally, the *Critique of the Faculty of Judgment* [*KdU*] claimed to systematically bring together the two dimensions of theoretical and practical reason. It is fair to expect that the unresolved problems reappear in the third *Critique*, but I want to focus on the meaning of criticism in relation to judgment. Also here the juridical metaphor sheds light on the concept of "judgment." In one of his previous *Reflexionen* he had written the following: "The judge should 1. proceed analytically as inquirer and...2. as judge he must proceed synthetically" (*Reflexionen* 3357). Furthermore, in the first *Critique* there was a chapter on schematism in which Kant explained the general structure and function of judgments, while in the second *Critique* he considered moral judgments according to Common Sense philosophy. In this third *Critique,* he attempts to devise bridges to connect both theoretical and practical thinking and close the gap between subjective freedom and natural causality (*KdU* § 15). The problem of dualism reappears because he proposes two complementary forms of critique related to the specific forms of judgment applied to the domains of arts and sciences (i.e., in relation to freedom and nature): the "critique of aesthetic judgment" and the "critique of teleological judgment" (*KdU* 192–198). He provides a bridge between these two extremes by defining a transcendental principle of formal purposiveness [*Zweckmässigkeit*] (*KdU* [*Erste Einleitung*] 217–221). For many interpreters, this solution simply appears to force a synthesis between two elements that do not seem to stick together. In any case, the relevant point for us is that Kant recognizes a gap between theoretical and practical reason and, consequently, proposes a middle term between these extremes: the "*sensus communis*" in case of aesthetics and "*biological organism*" in the case of life sciences (Zuckert 2007). Whether we agree or not with this outcome, his solution consistently applies what he had defined previously as "criticism" and comes full circle, retrieving the original connotation proposed by Home.

All this should suffice to show the methodical importance of Kant's criticism and realize how he applies this method to different aspects of his philosophy. It is also important to see the juridical and political aspects involved in this project, which emerge later in his cosmopolitan project. Some problems of his method became evident, and they were assessed by other critics who attempted to update the critical tradition. Let me turn my attention to some of them.

DIALECTICS AND CRITIQUE OF POLITICAL ECONOMY IN HEGEL AND MARX

In the transition from the eighteenth to the nineteenth century, we observe an important political tension between the old regimes and a new democratic model inspired on the ideals of the Enlightenment. The attempt to put these ideals into practice could be witnessed in the American Revolution of 1776 and the French Revolution of 1789 as both emphasized democratic values and the "rights of men"—since women were not considered citizens. Kant reacted very positively to the French Revolution in several of his writings (Burg 1974), seeing it as an important event for politics and law. But on moral grounds he opposed the execution of Louis XIV, the state of terror, and the war between Prussia and France. This differentiation between legal and moral standards was a point of contention for many who question Kant's formal dualism and equate the critical attitude with the dynamic use of the dialectical method. Why did Kant make strict use of dialectics and stop at an arbitrary synthesis instead of exploring all the possibilities of this dynamic method? This is the question asked by Georg Wilhelm Friedrich Hegel.

Since Hegel has been appropriated by many conservative authors it is fair to ask what is critical about his philosophy. He criticized Kant's views as too abstract, formal, impracticable, and disconnected from social and political reality. Against Kantian formalism, he proposed the concrete universality that is expressed in different moments of a dialectical progression of the "Spirit" [*Geist*]. Beyond mere dualism, his *The Phenomenology of the Spirit*, published in 1807, exposed the affirmation, negation, and sublation of the opposites contained within the Spirit (1970 [*W* 3]: 141–142). Thus, Hegel conceived of dialectics as an alternative to Kantian bifurcations and as a way of radicalizing "the negation of negativity" (Benhabib 1986). Dialectics becomes, in Hegel's hands, a dynamic tool to show thinking, acting, and history making as a process of "becoming" autonomous. For Hegel and many Hegelians, Kant was not critical enough because he refused to open reason to historical experience and submit it to natural evolution (Smith 1987:99–126; Pippin 1989; Buchwalter 1991; Westphal 1998; Sedwick 2012).

Another dimension of Hegel's thought is his insistence on concrete social practices. Taking this dimension as reference, he reveals dialectical moments in which tensions between abstract and concrete dimensions are resolved. For example, he shows the constitution of a family based on individuals who form a certain unity based on love, which is negated when civil society supersedes individuality and family to forge a community based on law and rights, then to be sublated by a more general conscience of a national Spirit [*Volksgeist*] expressed in a Constitution—or, more precisely, in a law-giving system based on a particular ethos (Hegel *Enziklopädie* [*W* 8] § 517; *Rechtsphilosophie* [*W* 8] § 33, §§ 261–269). For Hegel, the French Revolution was the political realization of an absolute free will that, at least initially, expressed something even larger, the Spirit of the world [*Weltgeist*] (Ritter 1965; Ilting 1971). However, as he was concluding the writing of his *Phenomenology of the Spirit* and witnessed the invasion of Jena by Napoleon Bonaparte, he also experienced firsthand the negative impact of historical events on the dialectical movement. He concludes that the *Weltgeist* should not be equated with a despotic state, but rather with the advent of civil society [*bürgerliche Gesellschaft*] as an association of self-sufficient individuals and legal institutions. This is a central point of his *Philosophy of Right* (*Rechtsphilosophie* [*W* 8] § 187), which indicates his alignment with the liberal bourgeoisie. This was later appropriated by conservative interpretations of history (Riedel 1975; Henrich 1983). Nevertheless, Hegel's dialectical method remains an important contribution to the critical tradition (Marcuse 1955; Honneth 1992, 2001; Salter and Shaw 1994; Salter 2003).

Not so for Karl Marx. According to him, the bourgeois perspective stressed by Hegel was not enough to motivate the revolutionary impetus. Marx witnessed and participated in the attempts to promote revolutionary change in Germany during the nineteenth century and was inspired by Hegel's philosophy and the "Left Hegelians." He became influenced by the ideas of French socialism and pursued the possibility of using these ideas to spark a political revolution in Europe. The first political opportunity for the implementation of this plan was during 1848, when different groups took arms in order to promote regime change. Although these attempts failed, Marx and Friedrich Engels persisted in their goals, by rescuing the tradition of criticism and stressing the need to bring the theoretical and practical dimensions of politics together in a new political program. In this process, they added a radical twist to the meanings of "critique" and "dialectics." While Marx turned to a "critique of Hegel's philosophy," Engels studied the history of revolutionary movements—including the peasant movement led by Thomas Muenzer in sixteenth-century Germany. They both came to the conclusion that the revolutionary theories and practices involving the bourgeoisie and peasant movements were too utopian and, therefore, disconnected from social reality. A new historical agent for change needed to be found. This implied a new understanding of critique as a "critique of Hegel's philosophy of politics and right" and questioning of his emphasis on the bourgeoisie.

This critical intention is easily identifiable in the very titles of many of Marx's writings. In his "Contribution to the Critique of Hegel's Philosophy of Right," published in the *Deutsch-Französische Jahrbücher* in 1844, he begins with a bold statement, "For Germany, the *criticism of religion* has been essentially completed, and the criticism of religion is the prerequisite of all criticism" (Marx and Engels 1958 [*MEW* 1]:30). He then adds, "Thus, the criticism of Heaven turns into the criticism of Earth, the *criticism of religion* into the *criticism of law*, and the *criticism of theology* into the *criticism of politics*" (*MEW* 1 :32 [emphasis in the original, here and in the following passages]). He is obviously talking about Kant and Hegel while recognizing that a *practical* and effective politics in Germany still demanded the negation of abstract philosophy. In affirming this point, he has harsh words against Hegel: "The criticism of the *German philosophy of state and right,* which attained its most consistent, richest, and last formulation through *Hegel,* is both a critical analysis of the modern state and of the reality connected with it, and the resolute negation of the whole manner of the *German consciousness in politics and right* as *practiced* hereto, the most distinguished, most universal expression of which, raised to the level of *science,* is the *speculative philosophy* of right itself" (*MEW* 1:97). However, he concludes that in politics, "the Germans *thought* what other nations *did*" (*MEW* 1:97). A new mission required a consideration of *real humans* in real historical conditions to promote real change.

This point was expanded in Marx's discussion of the "Jewish Question" (*MEW* 1:147]). For him, the Jewish community was aspiring to the emancipation ideals of the French Revolution without asking the fundamental question, what kind of emancipation? By asking this question, Marx reveals hidden religious assumptions of politics and economics and affirms that people should be free and emancipated from religion because religion was the "opiate of the people," just another form of illusion as those denounced by Kant. Beyond Kant and Hegel, however, a new form of human emancipation was necessary, which would be not merely political or legal but rather economic because it would question the individualism that lies at the core of capitalist, liberal, and bourgeois society. To show the subtle differences in the kinds of emancipation, Marx compared the several bills and declarations of rights available at the time and showed that the problem was the individualistic interpretation of natural rights. Accordingly, he adds, "This *man,* the member of civil [*bürgerliche*] society, is the basis, the precondition, of the *political* state" (*MEW* 1:363). The problem, for Marx, was that *man* was reduced to an egoistic, independent individual moved by economic self-interest. The goal, therefore, was to criticize this individualistic premise in the conception of rights and citizenship by means of a new form of critique: the "critique of ideology."

What is the role of this new form of critique and how does this differ from previous critiques? For Marx and Engels, the goal was to reveal the influence of capitalism on people's own consciousness. As a result, in *The German Ideology,* a book considered to be jointly written by Marx and Engels and published posthumously (*MEW* 3), Neo-Hegelians are criticized for their failure to realize how their ideas and representations were still framed by the social and historic conditions of the bourgeoisie. As a result, bourgeois society had to be dialectically superseded by the needs and conditions of the proletarian class. As Marx—then inspired by Feuerbach—insists, one of the essential aspects of life is the concrete relation to nature and the work performed by humans. Still, the question concerning the positive possibility of a German emancipation remained open, so his answer points to a class that had a universal character because it experienced universal suffering as a result of universal wrongs: the proletarian class of workers who were treated as objects, so that the bourgeoisie could accumulate capital at the expense of natural and human exploitation (*MEW* 3:70–77).

The next step in Marx's renewal of the critical tradition was a "critique of philosophy" for its failure to see the poverty of the world as well as its own intellectual poverty. In his famous thesis against Feuerbach, Marx had famously stated, "The philosophers have only interpreted the world, [but] the point is to transform it" (Thesis 11, *Ad Feuerbach* in MEW 3:7). This insistence on transformation is indebted to Kant and Hegel and a fundamental aspect of critical philosophy (Negt 2003:44). Such realization helps us to understand the status of Marx's concept of critique (Rancière 1967; Schmidt 1962). Critique is still a rejection of illusions by means of the dialectical method, but the difference now is the emphasis on revolutionary practice as the answer to profound class differences and "class conflict." This program was clearly expressed by Marx and Engels in the *Communist Manifesto* from 1848 (*MEW* 4:571–590), which marks the transition to a "critique of political economy," a program that became central to Marx's philosophy.

This is Marx's most important contribution to the tradition of critique. The "critique of political economy" is not only the title or subtitle of several manuscripts he writes during his exile in London—especially *A Contribution to the Critique of Political Economy* of 1859—but also the main topic of his *magnus opus, Das Kapital,* whose first volume appeared in 1867 (Rancière 1967:125). In drafts for a critique of political economy which were completed in 1858 [*Grundrisse: Einleitung zur Kritik der politischen Ökonomie—Rohentwurf*] (*MEW* 13), the Kantian language is evident, especially when Marx discusses the method of political economy as a process that starts in a concrete intuition and abstracts from them to create representations and concepts (*MEW* 13:632; *MEW* 42]:15, see 99–115). But in the preface to *A Contribution to the Critique of Political Economy,* written in 1859, this project is summarized in Hegelian terms:

The first work which I undertook to dispel the doubts assailing me was a critical re-examination of the Hegelian philosophy of law; the introduction to this work being published in the *Deutsch-Französische*

Jahrbücher issued in Paris in 1844. My inquiry led me to the conclusion that neither legal relations nor political forms could be comprehended whether by themselves or on the basis of a so-called general development of the human mind, but that on the contrary they originate in the material conditions of life, the totality of which Hegel, following the example of English and French thinkers of the eighteenth century, embraces within the term "bourgeois society" [*bürgerliche Gesellschaft*]; that the anatomy of this civil society, however, has to be sought in political economy. (*MEW* 13:7)

These fragments eventually made it into *Das Kapital*, which is a critical, dialectical, and political enterprise that summarizes Marx's development (Hoff, Petriolo, Stueltzer, and Wolf 2006:27–28). Marx states clearly at the beginning of the book that "dialectics is essentially critical and revolutionary" (*MEW* 23:28). This is nothing but a radicalization of Hegel's "negation of the negation" (*MEW* 23:791), for the critique of bourgeois political economy requires the negation of the capital (Haug 1973). What was the impact of this whole endeavor? Undoubtedly, Marx and Engels motivated initiatives that were later labeled "Marxism" and influenced the Bolshevik Revolution in Russia in 1917. Although this revolution fascinated many at the beginning, it was later questioned for its violence, totalitarianism, and conceptual problems. For instance, the term "dictatorship of the proletarian class" was taken to justify all kinds of atrocities by the regime of Josef Stalin and the expansion of the Soviet Union, a project that was then criticized by many, including Marxists. However, we cannot forget the German context and the several groups that presented alternative understandings of "critique" and "revolution." They advocated different strategies to attain the goal of a classless society (Sassoon 1996). I will refer to some of these positions, so as to prepare a transition to the Critical Theory of the Frankfurt School.

   One of the many groups to inherit this tradition was the "orthodox Marxism" of Klaus Kautsky and Eduard Bernstein, who followed the writings of Marx and Engels literally. "Reformism" held that the transformation of society would have to occur by means of improving already existing conditions of a given democratic society, since it would be impossible to have a new start in history. Among the advocates of this position were those who followed Lenin's ideas in Western Europe. "Revisionism," in turn, suggested that the original revolutionary tactics proposed by Marx and Engels had to be changed because capitalism had reached stages not previously envisaged by them (Kolakowski 1978, vol. 2; Sassoon 1996). "Anarchism" had its origins as an alternative to communism and was based on the libertarian socialist ideas of Mikhail Bakunnin, but it often merged with Marxism in the context of the first congress of the International Working Men's Association (IWMA). Gustav Landauer was one of its main strategists and advocated the organization of strikes. In the context of the Second International at the beginning of the twentieth century, Rosa Luxemburg defended a more radical revolutionary approach against the revisionists while "syndicalism" insisted that Marxism should be based on the organization of unions in order to better prepare workers for the class struggle at the national and international levels (Forman 1998). "Austro-Marxism" was a doctrine influenced by Neo-Kantianism and developed in Vienna under the leadership of Max Adler and Otto Bauer around 1904, who adopted the positivism in vogue at the time and argued that Marxism needed to be backed by rigorous science, concrete evidences, and bold ideals (Bottomore and Goode 1978). A wing of the women's movement had its inspiration in Marxism, included Marx's daughter, Jenny Marx, and continued with the participation of Clara Zetkin and others in the Second International (Lopes and Gary 1993).

Despite all these competing and conflicting views, Marxism eventually became the most important doctrine for the German and European Left, but several problems became evident: the Marxist doctrine had insisted on the revolutionary practice with the sole goal of conquering power, but had not prepared the proletarian class to steer political institutions. Also, Marxism disregarded other institutions in society and contradicted democratic principles. This can be seen not only in internal tensions after the Russian Revolution of 1917, but also in the German social-democratic experiments during the Weimar Republic in 1919. According to many analysts, the failure of these experiments motivated the reaction and popularity of the German National-Socialist Party (NSPD) headed by Adolph Hitler, which eventually led to the National-Socialist dictatorship. It is in this context that we can better understand the so-called Neo-Marxism of the Frankfurt School: it emerged during the times of deep economic difficulties, experienced the social turmoil during the Weimar Republic, witnessed a period of cultural effervescence, and observed the rise of a new dictatorial regime that provoked World War II and perpetrated the Holocaust of European Jews and other minority groups. Under these circumstances, the German tradition of critique was indeed in need of updating.

THE FRANKFURT SCHOOL: FROM CRITICAL THEORY OF SOCIETY TO AN AESTHETIC THEORY

Many studies have provided detailed accounts of the emergence of the Frankfurt School, its members, its impact beyond Frankfurt, and the problems in identifying and classifying its members (Jay 1973; Tar 1977; Dubiel 1985; Wiggershaus 1989). Based on these studies, all we need to do is briefly show how its members continue the tradition of Kant, Hegel, and Marx. At the same time we can expand our understanding of the concept of critique.

Before anything, I need to stress that the expression "Frankfurt School" is a result of the affiliation of many intellectuals with the University of Frankfurt. The university was founded in 1914 with the support of private donors, politicians, and citizens, and became one of the first institutions in Germany to grant professorships to intellectuals of Jewish ancestry. Between 1919 and 1933, the university sponsored the creation of a new Lectureship on Jewish Religious Studies and Jewish Ethics as well as the first Chair of Jewish Studies in Germany involving Franz Rosenzweig and Martin Buber (Schottroff 1987, 1990:69–131, 2000:112–119; Zank 2006:11–28). The newly founded university was also the stage for many philosophers such as Hans Cornelius, Max Scheler, and Paul Tillich, who were inspired by a new interest in Kant and neo-Kantianism as well as a combination of humanism and socialism (Jay 1973:24–25; Wiggershaus 1989:91–116; Gabus 1998). In 1923, the university sponsored the creation of the Institute for Social Research [*Institut für Sozialforschung*] initially involving Kurt Albert Gerlach, Karl Korsch, and Carl Grünberg (Wheatland 2009). These and other initiatives explain how the university was able to attract a constellation of young academics, many of them of Jewish descent, who later became known as members of *the Frankfurt School*. They were directly or indirectly related to the institute, and contributed to the formulation of a "Critical Theory of Society" (Kellner 1989).

In what follows, I will focus on key representatives of what came to be characterized as the old Frankfurt School [*Alte-Frankfurt Schule*] or its first generation, which included scholars such as Max Horkheimer, Theodor Wiesengrund Adorno, Walter Benjamin, Siegfried Kracauer, Leo Löwenthal, Erich Fromm, Herbert Marcuse, Otto Kirchheimer, Karl Wittfogel, Franz Neumann, and others. Although different authors stressed different aspects of the issue, common *Leitmotive* can be traced in their work. Moreover, the persecution of Jews, socialists, intellectuals, homosexuals, and minorities by the Nazi dictatorship in Germany provoked a diaspora of those working for the Institute for Social Research. First to Paris, then London, and eventually New York, where many became involved with Columbia University and the New School for Social Research (Wheatland 2009:43–50). Although Walter Benjamin did not survive the war, his works were published and he is now recognized as a leading representative of the Frankfurt School (Tiedemann 1973, 1983; Benjamin 1989 [GS 1]:605–653), especially for his study of the concept of "art critique" [Kunstkritik] in Romanticism (1989 [GS 1]:62–86) and his groundbreaking essay on the technical reproductibility of art in modernity (Benjamin 1989 [GS 1]:431–469). I want to highlight the indebtedness of Critical Theory to Kant, Hegel, and Marx as well as the internal transformations in the critical tradition. From Kant they took the idea of a critique of reason and expanded it in terms of an ethical critique of the positivist conception of rationality, science, and technology. From Hegel, they radicalized the negativity of the dialectical method. From Marx, they took the emphasis on human "alienation" that resulted from economics and technology, and based on this concern they established a connection between the economic "alienation of labor" and the "collective alienation" of society by a "cultural industry," as denounced by Adorno and Horkheimer in their joint book of 1944, *Dialectics of the Enlightenment* (reprinted in Adorno 1997 [GS 3]). In this process, the critical tradition was updated in terms of a "critique of instrumental reason," a "critique of society," a new "critique of ideology" in a neo-Marxist sense, a "critique of culture" that focused on the manipulation of mass media, and a "critique of art and aesthetics."

First, there is the very definition of "Critical Theory" in Horkheimer's now famous article "Traditional and Critical Theory," which is inspired by his work on Kant and a radical critique of positivist scientific theory (Horkheimer 1989 [GS 1]). Horkheimer revealed how the concept of science had turned into an ideological and reified category, hypostatized in the mathematical ideal of the natural sciences (1989 [GS 4]:12–56). Rejecting its Cartesian matrix and the fact that knowledge was reduced to highly specialized ends such as war and the manipulation of society, he observed that reason and science had lost their critical and existential dimension. Opposed to the traditional scientific theory based on logical positivism and the pretension of a "unity of science," Horkheimer concluded,

> The critical theory of society…has for its object men as producers of their own historical way of life in its totality. The existing relations

which are the starting point of science are not regarded simply as givens to be verified and to be predicted according to the laws of probability. Every given depends not on nature alone but also on the power man has over it...Critical theory is not just a research hypothesis which shows its value in the ongoing business of men; it is an essential element in the historical effort and powers of men...Its goal is man's goal is man's emancipation from relationships that enslave him. (*Zeitschrift für Sozialforschung* 1937: 625–626, 244–246) (cited in Benhabib 1986:3)

Second, this conception of critical theory had many interdisciplinary applications in the social sciences. I will focus on the case of psychoanalysis. Erich Fromm was involved in the School of Jewish Studies initiated by Rosenzweig, was affiliated to the Institute led by Horkheimer, and worked in the Frankfurt Institute for Psychoanalysis. His most important contribution to the Frankfurt School was both the combination of Karl Marx with Sigmund Freud and the scrutiny to which he submitted these two theories. Against orthodox Marxism, Fromm rescued Marx's early manuscripts from 1844 and highlighted their "humanist" dimension, which inspired his proposal for a "humanist socialism" based on the "critique of alienation" [*Entfremdungskritik*]. Against Freud, he downplayed the role of sexuality—already in "The Social Conditionality of Psychoanalytical Therapy" [*Die gesellschaftliche Bedingtheit der psychoanalytischen Therapie*], originally published in 1935 (Fromm 1999 [*GA* 1]:115–138) and again in later texts. Although he used these theories in an important collective research on the rise of authoritarianism in Germany, *Studies on Authority and Family*, published in 1936 (1999 [*GA* 1]:139–187), by 1956 he had moved beyond them in order to emphasize the "art of loving" the role of family, and the formation of individual and social character (1999 [*GA* 9]). As a matter of fact, Fromm was one of the first to criticize Freud for his patriarchalism and repressiveness. After his move to the United States during World War II, he published books on themes such as *Escape from Freedom* in 1941 (1999 [*GA* 1]) and *The Revolution of Hope* in 1968 (1999 [*GA* 4]). Due to this heterodox combination he was considered a "revisionist," who seemed closer to Hegel than to Marx (Noerr 2000).

A similar combination can be seen in Herbert Marcuse. He was originally involved with a circle around Martin Heidegger and later approached the group in Frankfurt, for which he had written a series of articles for their journal *Zeitschrift für Sozialforschung*. Like Fromm, he also combined Marx and Freud. The very titles of popular books he published later on, *Eros and Civilization* (1962) and

One-Dimensional Man (1964), make evident the connection between his approach and the "critique of ideology" inspired by Marx. His most specific contribution to the demarcation of Critical Theory can be read in "Philosophy and Critical Theory" published in 1937, where he considered that reason, as a formal and fundamental concept of philosophical activity, had been open to any form of ideology. Marcuse then reappraises the critical dimension of Hegel's political dialectics in *Reason and Revolution: Hegel and the Rise of Social Theory* (Kettler 1975). Through his reflection, the traditional epistemological dimension of idealism became more directly related to social and political movements of liberation (Farr 2009:1–5), but the important point for me is his reassessment and reinterpretation of Hegel's philosophy in his proposal for a "critique of society" [*Gesellschaftskritik*]:

> The dialectical conception of change was first elaborated in Hegel's philosophy…Hegel himself used the dialectical conception in the field of social philosophy by analyzing Civil Society as developing through the antagonism between self and common interest, accumulating wealth and increasing poverty, growing productivity and expansionist war. (Marcuse 1998:131, cited in Rockwell 2004:143)

Third, there is a dialectical critique of the Enlightenment. While Kant had asked about the meaning of Enlightenment and answered that it should be seen as the audacity to know, Horkheimer and Adorno restated the same Kantian question in their book *Dialectic of Enlightenment*, but arrived to radically different answers (Adorno 1997 [*GS* 3]). They showed that the idea of autonomy had lost its actuality and the early promise of happiness had turned into a nightmare under the lead of scientific reason. Even more radically, they concluded that the state of society in the 1940s was in total contradiction with the picture elaborated in the Enlightenment as the fields of art, religion, and culture were now administered by instrumental reason. Their conclusion, stated right at the beginning of the book, is that the rationality of the Enlightenment reverted to mythology and was responsible for a series of oppressive events.

Fourth, this diagnosis motivated the upgrade of critique to a "critique of positivism" and its application to social engineering and a "critique of instrumental reason." As Horkheimer stated in *Eclipse of Reason* in 1947, the "subjective reason" of Kant's *Critiques* had morphed into a mere "instrumental reason" that supported a technological manipulation that needed to be critically scrutinized. In the 1950s, however, Horkheimer and Adorno returned to Frankfurt to reassume their positions, reestablish the Institute for Social Research, contribute to a reassessment of the Nazi past, and pick up their intellectual discussions where they had left off before World War II. The critique of positivism can be traced back to as early as 1934 in Horkheimer's article, "The Debate on Rationalism in Contemporary Philosophy" [*Zum Rationalismusstreit in der gegenwärtigen Philosophie*] (Horkheimer 1989 [*GS* 6]:163–220), but it was radicalized in the controversy between Adorno and Karl Popper, made famous as the "debate on positivism" held during the German Congress of Sociology in 1961 (Adorno, Popper et al. 1976). Popper had claimed the Kantian heritage and defined his program as "critical rationalism," a position based on the principle that "everything" needed to be considered fallible. He had prepared 27 theses proposing a logic for the social sciences related to the ideas he espoused in *The Open Society and Its Enemies*. This attempt, backed by Ernst Topitsch, Hans Albert, Niklas Luhmann, and others, was refuted by Adorno in a long reply in which he opposed the formal exigencies of fallibilism and equated this position to logical positivism. Although Popper was not directly aligned with positivists, he did think that his method should orient not only the verification of conjectures of scientific research, but also the work of the social sciences. Moreover, he considered ethical issues as a matter of personal choice based on a "situational logic" that would not be open to rational criticism or verification—what was then defended as an individualistic "decisionism." Adorno concluded that "the irrationality of the current structure of society does not allow rational developments at the theoretical level" (Adorno 1997 [*GS* 8]:359). For him, instead of being so abstractive a "theory had to be critical" and based on an analysis of social relations (1997 [*GS* 8]:196–197).

Fifth, a "critique of culture" and art was the other dimension in Adorno, Benjamin, Marcuse, and others. Expanding on the cultural critique expressed in *Dialectics of the Enlightenment* and many papers on literature, music, psychoanalysis, and culture, Adorno provides a theoretical definition of his critical procedure in *Negative Dialectics*, originally published in 1966 (Adorno 1997 [*GS* 6]:7–9). Here, he relies more on Hegel's dialectics and his conception of negativity, but he does have something to say about Marx (Honneth and Mencke 2006). Right at the beginning of *Negative Dialectics*, he contradicts Marx's early verdict of philosophy by saying that "philosophy, which once seemed outmoded, remains alive because the moment of its realization was missed. The summary judgment that it had merely interpreted the world is itself crippled by resignation before reality, and becomes a defeatism of reason after the transformation of the world failed" (Adorno 1997 [*GS* 6]:10). In the conclusion, however, Adorno radicalizes Marx's call for a critique of "what is" by stressing "what is not" (1997 [*GS* 6]:345–346). This is the theme of the not-identical [*das Nicht-Identische*] ontological search for what is hidden or occluded by means of a formal principle that rejects identity, promotes difference, destructs formalism, questions authoritarian totality, and opposes the reification of the subject. As his method is applied to empirical studies and analysis on several cultural themes, Adorno reveals the rational administration of all spheres of life, including art and culture, but at the same time finds an alternative for the preservation of the human being from the administered world in the sphere of aesthetics and art, as seen in his collection of essays, *Cultural Critique and Society* (1997 [*GS* 11]). His critique of culture evolved into art criticism and, more specifically, a critique of modern music (1997 [*GS* 10, 11, and 14]).

Finally, with Adorno, Critical Theory becomes an "aesthetic theory." *Aesthetic Theory* is the title of his last book, published posthumously in 1970 (1997 [*GS* 7]), which brings us back to the original ambiguity of the term "criticism" before Kant. Based on his view that "critique is not external to the aesthetic experience but immanent to it," Adorno brings social and artistic dimensions together in a complex and negative way (1997 [*GS* 7]:515). His writing is notoriously difficult, precisely because he packs all these dimensions into a single phrase. For instance, he says that art is conditioned by social issues (1997 [*GS* 3]), so that the analysis of music can reveal class tensions, technological developments, industrial manipulation, and political imposition. At the same time, he adds that music escapes societal conditionings in order to express something new and liberating, which points toward something utopian. This is what Adorno states in an opening paradoxical passage of the *Aesthetic Theory*: "It is self-evident that nothing concerning art is self-evident anymore" (1997 [*GS* 7]:9). This refers to the ambiguous fate of modernist works of art: they are concrete artifacts (Bürger 1974) but abstract and autonomous enough to be irreducible to instrumental rationality (Adorno 1997 [*GS* 7]:26–30, 287–296). With these views, Adorno surely opened new venues for a critique of music and art, but he has been criticized in many respects as well: he did not value popular music because he considered it fetishized, his views are extremely pessimistic, he assumes that there is something authentic in art even in the age of cultural industry, he holds a very subjectivist view of art and aesthetics, and his dialectical critique of the Enlightenment leads to a dead-end. As a result, a new generation of scholars undertook the task of researching a rational element not

yet fetishized or instrumentalized, which presented a positive inheritance of the Enlightenment. They also questioned Adorno on many
other fronts: he focused only on certain aspects of the Enlightenment,
his critique of the Enlightenment relied on the tradition of critique
inaugurated by Kant but he did not acknowledge this inheritance, his
views on culture and music were elitist and Eurocentric, and his writing style was too dense and cryptic (Pensky 2005:10).

Despite all the problems we find in this first generation of Critical
Theory, there are some aspects that remain valid. What have we
learned so far? We started with a definition of critical theory, observed
applications of this theory as a psychoanalytical critique of alienation, observed a critique of positivism and instrumental reason, and
observed the expansion of critical theory to culture, art, and aesthetics. By the 1960s, the combination of all these forms of critique and
the proliferation of liberation movements in several continents turned
the philosophical program of a Critical Theory into a very influential
form of social activism. A case in point is the Student Movement in
Germany (von Friedeburg, Habermas, Oehler, and Weltz 1961), and
the United States (Marcuse 1972). Eventually, students came to question not only the patriarchal, archaic, and dictatorial structures still
present in German society, but also the extreme pessimism, skepticism, and Eurocentrism shown by Adorno and Horkheimer. Echoing
Marx, a new generation saw the possibility of putting Critical Theory
into practice through their engagement in liberation movements that
were emerging during the 1960s (Farr 2009). From a theoretical
point of view, intellectuals in Frankfurt were also attempting to provide a more positive evaluation of reason, contrary to the sole focus
on "instrumental rationality."

By this time, however, the first generation of the Frankfurt School
was fading—Adorno died in 1969, Horkheimer in 1973, and Marcuse
in 1976. Nevertheless, the field of Critical Theory was well demar-
cated, despite the difficulties in circumscribing the several themes
touched upon. Each one of the forms of critique and their applications
evolved into specific areas of study—literary criticism, film criticism,
social criticism, and other fields. I hope to have shown that Critical
Theory is an interdisciplinary project originally informed by the particularities of the German context, inspired by the critical tradition
of Kant, Hegel, and Marx, and motivated by new challenges that
emerged as a result of two World Wars in the twentieth century, the
political upheavals in Europe during the 1920s and 1930s as well as
the persecution, emigration, and adaptation of Jewish scholars to new
contexts and cultures (Honneth and Wellmer 1986; Stirk 2000; Rush

2004). As they tried to come to terms with these experiences, they were prompted to renew the tradition of "critique" by specifying its epistemic, social, ideological, and cultural or aesthetic applications. The "linguistic turn," that is, a new philosophical emphasis on language analysis, communication, and discourse will lead to yet another contribution to the tradition of critique and help us answer the question regarding the need for a new transformation of Critical Theory.

THE LINGUISTIC TURN AND CRITICAL THEORY: DISCOURSE THEORY AND DISCOURSE ETHICS

The path I have revisited up to now is well trodden, but I hope to have shed light on the nuanced conceptions of critique at play in the authors reviewed. My main point is that the definition of Critical Theory is fluid enough to include many persons and themes loosely related to an interdisciplinary program, with its self-corrections and different applications. Now it is important to mention that this dynamic program inspired a new generation of scholars who gave a new turn to the tradition of critique (Rasmussen 1996). Qualifying the members of the Frankfurt School or those associated with Critical Theory is not always easy or useful because these terms were not necessarily used to self-describe a position or to identify membership. Moreover, many authors reacted against this label being applied to them. As Jürgen Habermas once affirmed regarding the time he was working with Adorno, "for me there was never a consistent theory. Adorno wrote essays on critique of culture and also gave seminars on Hegel. He presented a certain Marxist background—and that was it" (Wiggershaus 1989:2). Despite this statement, it is possible to trace many elements that connect different aspects of the critical tradition I am reviewing here. The question is, what counts as continuity or rupture in this process? The answer is that a reassessment and transformation of Kant's philosophy definitely remains fundamental to Critical Theory; the turn to Hegel and Marx is certainly a commonality; and these affinities are evident in the work of philosophers who studied or taught at the University of Frankfurt or worked at the Institute for Social Research under the guidance of Adorno and Horkheimer and ended up continuing the critical enterprise.

By the 1960s, a new group of philosophers was emerging, who came to be defined as a "second generation" of Critical Theory, later labeled the *Neo-Frankfurt School*. This group included Jürgen Habermas, Albrecht Wellmer, Ludwig von Friedburg, Oskar Negt, and later joined by H. Schnädelbach and Karl-Otto Apel (Honneth and Wellmer 1986:10; Honneth 2007). This new generation took up the question about rationality not from the exclusive point of view of the consciousness privileged by German Idealism—which strongly influenced the earlier group of researchers—but rather in light of the paradigmatic concept of communication and discourse that emerged after the "linguistic turn" in twentieth-century philosophy. This is what leads to yet another transformation: a radical turn in Critical Theory as it is morphed into a "Critical Discourse Theory."

Undoubtedly, the main role in this transformation is due to Jürgen Habermas, who developed a new project for Critical Theory in partnership with Karl-Otto Apel. As one of the main heirs of the Frankfurt School, Habermas studied with Adorno, wrote a groundbreaking study on the "public sphere" and the importance of participatory democracy (1962), and became interested in Marxism, but later criticized Marxism for not paying attention to the interactive dimension of working relations (1963) and questioned the subjectivism and pessimism in the critique of society of Adorno and Horkheimer (1971a). In dialogue with Apel, he focused on a *reconstruction* of Critical Theory in terms of discursive analysis, as seen in his book *Knowledge and Human Interests* (1968a) and in debates with Niklas Luhmann (1968b and 1971b/1982), in which Habermas insisted on a normative definition of "rational discourse" (1971b/1982:418). In a series of papers and books during the 1970s, he not only expanded the application of Critical Theory to address the demands of political legitimacy through participatory political processes (1973, 1976) but also developed his Discourse Theory by proposing a division between theoretical and practical discourses, as registered in the two volumes of his *Theory of Communicative Action* (1981a). While the first volume establishes the "idea of discursive redemption of validity claims" in relation to the natural, social, and expressive worlds as the basis for a new communicative theory based on intersubjectivity and the "unforced force of the best argument" (1981a:28; 1984:144, 177; see also 1991a), in the second volume as well as in *Moral Consciousness and Communicative Action* (1983) and *Justification and Application: Remarks on Discourse Ethics* (1991b), he advances the Discourse Principle [*Diskursprinzip* or (*D*)] and the Principle of Universalization [*Universalisierungsgrundsatz* or (*U*)] as the core normative elements of a discursive ethics (1983:92). Bringing these elements together in a series of texts before and after the publication of his book *Between Facts and Norms* (1992), he amplified this conception of discourse in terms of law and politics, defining new applications of discourse in the form of a Principle of Universalization in morality, a Principle of

Adequacy or Appropriateness [*Angemessenheit*] for juridical discourses, and a political Principle of Democracy [*Demokratieprinzip*] mediated by the use of "communicative power" [*kommunikative Macht*] in deliberative processes (Ingram 2010:163–165; Baxter 2011:65; Forst 2007:16–163 and 2011:125–127). Finally, similar applications were developed for international politics—defined in terms of a transformation of Kant's cosmopolitan project (1996, 1998, and 2005)—and an assessment of religion in a postsecular society (2001b, 2005, and 2012)—in which he affirms that different cultures and religions need to be able to bring their claims and concerns in the terms of the public discourse accepted by liberal democratic societies.

This proposal for a Critical Discourse Theory was built in constant dialogue with Apel, but key differences emerged between them. Apel's central concern was the role of language as foundational to philosophy. He not only analyzed this issue in different historical periods (1963) and focused on the study of hermeneutics, pragmatics, and semiotics (1967), but also discovered a complementary relation between the "linguistic turn" within analytic philosophy and the hermeneutic tradition and their corresponding methods of analytical explanation [*Erklären*] and hermeneutic understanding [*Verstehen*] (1967, 1979). In this process, he did not give up the transcendental dimension, but rather stressed the need to uphold the Kantian a priori and "transform" it, as proposed in a series of articles gathered in the two volumes of his book *Transformation of Philosophy* (1973). Holding on to the idea of language as a priori, Apel transformed Kant's philosophy by questioning its subjectivism and interpreting it according to the pragmatist concepts of an indefinite community of investigation or inquiry (Peirce), a community of interpretation (Royce), and the universal community of discourse (Mead), which allowed him to define an "ideal unlimited community of communication" [*unbegrenzte Kommunikationsgemeinschaft*] (1973 2:376–377; 1994:231–253) as the fundamental presupposition to philosophy— very similar to Habermas's early definition of an "ideal speech situation." Moreover, he expanded this concept of a community of communication to practical philosophy in *Discourse and Responsibility* (1988:38–39). Although he maintained his dialogue with Habermas and shared many of his positions, Apel came to emphasize the primacy of an ethical conception of discourse as responsibility and question Habermas's consideration of morality simply as a form of practical discourse among others—such as politics and law (1998). It is also important to say that, initially, Habermas and Apel were in agreement about the need for a "reconstruction" or "transformation" of

Critical Theory. However, as Apel furthered his critique of positivism in a metacritique of critical rationalism and argued that this universal or transcendental pragmatics would have an "ultimate foundation" [*Letztbegründung*], differences emerged between these two authors (Habermas 2005).

Despite this difference, it can be assumed that Habermas and Apel share the basic assumptions of Discourse Philosophy and develop complementary perspectives. They also share a basic problem of Discourse Philosophy, namely the lack of a systematic consideration of aesthetics, art, and culture, which was fundamental to Adorno, Benjamin, and Marcuse. Nevertheless, there is a division of labor within a newer generation of critical theorists, so that other authors provide an interdisciplinary complement to this philosophy in areas such as aesthetics, politics, culture, communication, social theory, and politics. Adorno's aesthetics was reconsidered by Peter Bürger in terms of a theory of avant-garde art (1974) and in relation to postmodernism (2000). Herbert Schnädelbach dedicated himself explicitly to the relation between Hegel's philosophy, the question about rationality (1987), and the challenges of Aristotelian and neo-Aristotelian versions of virtue ethics to Discourse Ethics (1992). Helmut Dubiel reappraised the history of Critical Theory (1985), directed the Institute for Social Research, and studied the impact of neoconservative politics in Germany and the United States. Alfred Schmidt continued Horkheimer's research and showed the inner relation between the concept of nature and the materialist critique in Marx (1974), while Ludwig von Friedeburg led the Institute in Frankfurt and continued his involvement with questions concerning education and cultural formation in Germany (1989). Rolf Tiedemann was responsible for the edition of Adorno and Benjamin's works and a series of monographs on their philosophies (Tiedemann 1973, 1983, 2007). Albrecht Wellmer deserves a special reference for his contributions to aesthetics. Although viewed as hesitant in espousing a specific position (Honneth 2007), he can be characterized as providing a constant reassessment of Adorno's aesthetics and critique of positivism (1969), based upon which he also questioned some aspects of the project defended by Apel and Habermas, such as the lack of an analysis of art and culture (1985), its strong claim to truth (1986), and its need to reconsider rationality as open-ended (1991). This provides an important argument for the consideration of Discourse Philosophy as a "school" because many philosophers related to this second generation claim the inheritance of Critical Theory, affirm their allegiance to the Frankfurt School, accept the "linguistic turn," and provide corrections and complement to what is missing in Habermas and Apel.

Thus far I have indicated differences and transformations while also indicating continuity within the critical tradition. Still, one may ask, what is new in this second generation? The "critique of instrumental reason" remained a constant as well as the "critique of ideology," but these tasks are now achieved through a "critique of meaning." Next, I will have an opportunity to discuss these issues in more detail. To conclude this chapter, let me briefly refer to more recent developments in the tradition of critique that point toward a necessary "critique of globalization" capable of addressing current global challenges.

GLOBAL CHALLENGES AND NEW DEVELOPMENTS IN CRITICAL THEORY

What happened during the 1960s with the first generation of Critical Theory in Frankfurt could be observed in the 1990s, when Habermas and Apel retired while a third generation of scholars emerged and attempted to continue the critical tradition. Also here, classifications are difficult and the targets are constantly moving because this generation is still at work. A good overview of this group is provided by Joel Anderson (2000), who offers a frame to identify this "third generation" as including Axel Honneth, Matthias Lutz-Bachmann, Hans Joas, Wolfgang Kuhlmann, Hauke Brunkhorst, Dietrich Böhler, Matthias Kettner, Martin Seel, and Christoph Mencke. That women are not mentioned in this list already indicates a serious deficit in Critical Theory. I can neither do justice to the work of these authors nor correct this problem in the limited space I have in this chapter, but a few points can be mentioned regarding the expansion of Critical Theory and the inclusion of newer agents who bring their contexts and differences to the debate on community, human rights, and cosmopolitan ideals.

The issue I would like to highlight is that beginning with this third generation it was possible to observe an initial opening and outreach of Critical Theory and Discourse Philosophy toward other perspectives, including the cultural and gender differences that were somewhat neglected by previous generations. Also, this led to a more global perspective that prompted a dialogue with other traditions. One way of mapping the internal change and the external influence of this third generation is to observe the new themes, issues, and intercultural references that emerge in their work. Another way of documenting this process is evidenced by the growing openness to emerging studies, themes, and researchers from different countries. There is a lack of research about the global impact of Critical Theory (Pensky 2005; Mendieta 2007) and this cannot be addressed in detail here. Nevertheless, despite the risk of omitting names, I will attempt to briefly mention the diversity of contexts and highlight the plethora of themes and authors beyond the German context. In doing so, my point is to show that new developments in this critical tradition point toward a more global perspective.

The dialogue with the Frankfurt School could be observed early on in many European contexts. In England, John Thompson, David Held, and Andrew Linklater focused more on the sociological and political aspects of Habermas's theory (Held 1980, 1995a, 1995b; Archibugi, Held, and Köhler 1998; Linklater 2007). In France, Rainer Rochlitz and Gérad Raulet were the early translators of Critical Theory, including the works of Adorno and Benjamin (Höhn and Raulet 1978), while Jacques Poulain collaborated with Apel and Jean-Marc Ferry worked with both Habermas and Apel translating their work (1987, 1994). In Spain, Manuel Jimenez Redondo, Javier Muguerza, Adela Cortina, José Rodriguez Ibáñez, Victoria Camps, Carlos Thiebaud, José Maria Mardones, and Jesús Conil form a group of important mediators of ideas by Habermas and Apel (Mardones 1990; Gómez 1996). Through their reception of Discourse Philosophy, a new generation of students was formed in this tradition. In Hungary, Agnes Heller and Ferenc Féher provided the link between the critical tradition inaugurated by Lukàcs and the more recent work of István Féher while in former Yugoslavia there was the *Praxis* group, which was later dissolved in view of the conflicts in the area and the involvement of Mihailo Markovic with the regime of Slobodan Milosevic—charged with crimes against humanity in connection to wars in Bosnia, Croatia, and Kosovo (Crocker 1983; Doder 1993). Their journal was later published in the United States as *Praxis International* and eventually renamed *Constellations.* Undoubtedly, the United States was the most visible of the spheres of influence of Critical Theory (Wheatland 2009). Although Thomas McCarthy and Richard Bernstein were more contemporaries of Habermas and Apel and helped to translate and publicize their works in the 1970s, the names of authors such as Seyla Benhabib, Nancy Fraser, Kenneth Baynes, James Bohman, and Iris Young emerged in the late 1980s as philosophers contemporary to the third generation of Critical Theory who addressed issues that had been neglected until then such as feminism, postmodernism, communitarianism, and liberalism (Bernstein 1994. See also Benhabib 1986; Benhabib and

Cornell 1987; Fraser 1989; Benhabib and Dallmayr 1990; Young 1990, 2000; Calasanti and Zajicek 1993).

At one point, however, the need to "globalize critical theory" (Pensky 2005) became evident as intellectuals aligned with the Frankfurt School began to form a new generation of students trained in Discourse Philosophy. For instance, the influence of the first two generations of Critical Theory can be traced in Latin America. In Argentina, Dorando Michelini, Ricardo Maliandi, and Julio de Zan focused on discourse ethics (2007) and developed a group that includes Graciela Fernández and Alberto Damiani. In Bolivia, this can be seen early enough in the work of Hugo Mansilla (1970). In Brazil, this trend is represented by José Merquior, Roberto Schwarcz, and José Herrero who started by presenting Adorno and Horkheimer to the Brazilian public in the 1970s and then translated works by Habermas and Apel in the 1980s. Barbara Freitag (1987) and Sérgio Paulo Rouanet (1991), for example, centered their attention on Habermas's appropriation of Kohlberg's postconventional ethics while Oliveira (2003) was more interested in Apel's transcendental pragmatics. In Mexico, Adolfo Sánchez Vásquez and Bolívar Echeverría were one of the first to directly engage the ideas of the Frankfurt School (Gandler 1999) and later Enrique Dussel initiated a dialogue with Apel and Habermas, involving many other Latin American philosophers (2000, 2009). Similar processes could be observed in Japan and Korea as well as in South Africa. This is an area that deserves more research. As younger philosophers had the opportunity to study in Germany and became directly involved in debates concerning a more contextualized Critical Theory, the tradition of Critical Theory began to be confronted more directly with global questions: David Held has championed this issue in an impressive project on global governance (Held and McGrew 2003), Hauke Brunkhorst introduces the theme of global solidarity (2002), James Bohman discusses transnational democracy in relation to pluralism (2007), and Matthias Lutz-Bachmann proposes a philosophy of international relations focusing on cosmopolitanism as the answer to global challenges (Lutz-Bachmann and Bohman 1996, 1997, and 2002; Lutz-Bachmann, Köhler, and Brunkhorst 1999; Lutz-Bachmann, Niederberger, and Schink 2010).

These references may suffice to provide a glimpse of new developments related to a third generation of philosophers. Criticisms become evident as well. It is not surprising, therefore, that a new group emerges, corresponding to a fourth generation based on the critical tradition, which infuses newer elements into Critical Discourse Philosophy, such as discussions on globalization, multiculturalism, climate change, gender issues, poverty, and other recent economic issues (Nascimento 1998b). Among the exponents of this new generation one can mention Rainer Forst (1994, 2007, 2011) and Klaus Günther (1988, 2005), and Cristina Lafont (1999). My critique of the critical tradition is that it has not made a turn to an explicit "critique of globalization" yet, although Pensky (2005), Mendieta (2007), and Niederberger and Schink (2011) advance new perspectives in this direction. I insert myself within this context and see my work as part of a dialogue with these authors (1997a, 1998b, 2003a, 2003b, 2006, 2007a, 2007b).

This genealogical perspective provides the mapping and overview of the critical tradition and its transformations as well as the opportunity for me to articulate my own position because I share much of the intellectual lineage mentioned above and accept many of its theoretical assumptions. Therefore, I recognize the contributions of many of these authors and affirm the importance of "critique" as a methodological procedure that is constantly under scrutiny and revision. As a result, some key elements such as the importance of reason, its upgrading as communicative rationality, and its application to social issues by means of discursive procedures in ethics, politics, and law will reappear later in our discussion. However, in bringing my own hermeneutic conditioning to this discussion, I see the need to refer to other traditions beyond the original German context of Critical Theory and present my own critique. For instance, members of the first generation had notoriously limited Eurocentric views and—despite their sensibility to the plight of Jews in Europe—did not consider other cultures and persons, a point that has been brought up in discussions on multiculturalism in the Americas. Moreover, the second generation represented by Habermas and Apel advanced only partially in this area, making only a minimal formal acknowledgment of the critical claims of feminists and minorities but failing to engage in a more direct consideration of their theories (Fraser 1989:113–143; 1997:69–98). Also, while they contributed greatly to questioning German chauvinism by looking at moral and philosophical resources in the cultural and philosophical history of the United States—such as pragmatism and liberalism—and engaged in a dialogue with Enrique Dussel and the Latin American tradition of liberation philosophy (Mendieta 2007), they remained bound to a North Atlantic bias.

Members of the third generation do not merely repeat what they inherited from the critical tradition but also question their predecessors and advance new ideas. They express reservations to Habermas's ideal speech situation, Apel's proposal of an ultimate foundation, the formalism of Discourse Ethics, the exclusion of gender and cultural issues, the lack of reflections on aesthetics, and the limited reference to economic issues and the social struggles in the global South. Yet, in his dialogue with contemporary French philosophy, Honneth considers Michel Foucault and postmodernism and develops a theory of recognition that relies partly on the tradition of Hegel and Marx, but refers only briefly to Frantz Fanon and his reinterpretation of Hegel (Honneth 1992:256), neither exploring this link nor advancing a more fruitful dialogue with postcolonial and race studies (Nascimento 2012). David Held and Daniele Archibugi have an important contribution to studies on global democracy and cosmopolitanism, especially in their plea for a new structure for world governance that would avoid the current problems facing the United Nations. However, their approach is rather formal, has been accused of being elitist and top-down, relies heavily on an Anglo-German axis without considering the contributions of peripheral movements that are active in the World Social Forum, and refer only *en passant* to the role of social movements on a global scale (Patomäki 2003, 2011; Patomäki and Held 2006). Adela Cortina has advanced Apel's position and developed a new program on global ethics and cosmopolitan ideas, but fails to address an important Spanish tradition that is now being reassessed, namely the work of the Salamanca School and its influence in Latin America. This aspect is somewhat corrected by Matthias Lutz-Bachmann, who rescues a critical theory of religion, connects it to the Salamanca School and liberation movements in the global South, and develops a new approach to cosmopolitanism (Lutz-Bachmann and Bohman 1996; Lutz-Bachmann, Fidora, and Wagner 2010; Lutz-Bachmann, Niederberger, and Schink 2010). Still, his views on globalization and cosmopolitanism have not taken into consideration important aspects related to global environmental challenges that require a critical approach. Nancy Fraser presents important critiques to Habermas's position, faulting his theory for not being critical enough because it fails to consider feminist perspectives. She also criticizes Honneth for limiting his approach to recognition without including disadvantage groups that also raise claims to redistribution as a way to address social injustice (1997, 2003). However, she commits the same fault of projecting a form of feminism that does not account for the differences represented by Latina, womanist, and Third World approaches, even though she raises a universal claim in her proposal for a critical feminism (Aslan and Gambetti 2011).

It is obvious that the critical points mentioned above refer to a lack of a truly participatory and inclusive global approach in theory and in practice, which realizes that—as part of its transformation process—Critical Theory and Critical Discourse Philosophy have to become more global and include more voices. There are limitations, however, on how many of the philosophers above engage in a dialogue with these global voices. In view of these limitations, I want to radicalize the open-ended character of the interactions and movements we have observed in the critical tradition. Especially as we deal with themes such as globalization, the role of civil society organizations beyond state borders, and the different expressions of cosmopolitan hopes, there is the urgent need to recognize the agents of these processes, who come in and out of different contexts and establish a dialogue within multicultural societies and with intercultural structures at the global level. As we consider community, human rights, and cosmopolitan ideals in a critical perspective, it is possible and necessary to update this tradition of critique in light of recent perspectives, making it compatible with recent critical discussions about Eurocentrism, immigration, racism, gender justice, and multicultural identities while finding ways to avoid many of the shortcomings mentioned throughout this chapter. It is also possible to reassess Marx critique of global capitalism as a tool for an understanding of the peripheral situation of many of the agents who are now participating in this wider dialogue. In the same way, Habermas's discussion about the "colonization of the lifeworld" and Apel's dialogue with Latin American intellectual traditions open new venues for a consideration of the limits of Eurocentric, statecentric, and corporatecentric strategies that negate the real situations of global oppression, discrimination, and impoverishment. We need to establish new bridges between the tradition I have presented and several other traditions, so that we can expand the critical approach and address issues neglected until now.

We can conclude that the critical tradition still offers many important insights for the discussion and resolution of novel challenges in times of globalization. Criticism was an idea originally related in Europe not only to science and society, but also to aesthetics and culture, and Kant later defined "critique" as a tool to submit social and political structures to the scrutiny of reason. Kant's critique of reason inaugurated a German tradition that was expanded in many ways. It now needs a progressive opening toward global issues through the work of several generations. These "transformations" reveal that the critical tradition is a "work in progress" and that it is still in need of continual upgrading in order to be relevant at the global level. Based on this realization, I will take up this tradition but also acknowledge that some critical theorists have failed to move beyond their specific contexts when they deal with global and cosmopolitan issues. I will attempt to reread this tradition and find some entry points that allow us to include and make sense of alternative models. So far, however, I have only defined the general interdisciplinary tradition within which I insert my work and indicated that this tradition is dynamic and in continuous transformation. I also highlighted that under this "critical tradition" there are different forms of critique that can be applied as tools to address different issues. Finally, I indicated some of the limits in this tradition, which need to be overcome by turning to a more global perspective. With this reclaimer, I can now focus on Critical Discourse Philosophy as the specific theoretical approach that I will follow in my attempt to apply the tradition of critique to contemporary issues related to community, human rights, and cosmopolitan ideals.

3

DISCOURSE PHILOSOPHY AS A CRITICAL FRAMEWORK

After having provided a general overview of the transformations within the critical tradition, I briefly indicated the need for a more expanded consideration of plurality and globalization. I shall now discuss in more detail the *Discourse Philosophy* developed jointly by Jürgen Habermas and Karl-Otto Apel. They provide a basis upon which I can address this issue. In relying on these two authors, I relate their respective positions on normativity to questions about community, human rights, and cosmopolitan ideals and acknowledge their internal differences: the *Discourse Ethics* developed by Apel according to his *Transcendental Pragmatics* stresses the importance of a *community of communication* while the *Discourse Theory* based on the *Formal* or *Universal Pragmatics* brought forward by Habermas emphasizes the concept of *discourse*. Despite differences between them, they both rescue and update Kant's views, review the shortcomings of Critical Theory, and offer a robust communicative account of normativity. Habermas's defense of the juridification and institutionalization of legal and political norms are widely known, but I establish a counterpoint between his views and Apel's approach to the justification and application of ethical norms. Apel's philosophy has been accused of being highly abstract, but this criticism can be addressed by accepting some of Habermas's suggestions. Their respective views need to be more explicitly integrated as complementary parts of a common framework that will help us understand the purpose for building "cosmopolitan communities."

The general term "Discourse Philosophy" is the best way to characterize the general philosophical project developed jointly by Habermas and Apel and to architectonically organize their various contributions to the critical tradition. *Discourse* is a traditional *terminus technicus* in philosophy, which can be traced back to ancient times, but the new meaning of *discourse* is the achievement of a *linguistic* paradigm that includes recent critical programs in the history and philosophy of science (Kuhn), postmodern philosophy (Lyotard), poststructuralism (Derrida, Foucault), psychological and psychoanalytical theories, and feminist positions as well as the recent emphasis on "discursive constructions" in the social sciences (Habermas 1985a). I focus, however, on a specific technical understanding of this term based on a scheme initially proposed by Charles Morris, for whom the study of language and discourse can be divided into *syntactics, semantics,* and *pragmatics* and included into *semiotics* (Morris 1938).

The emphasis on syntactic, pragmatics, and semiotics is one of the corollaries of the "linguistic turn" in philosophy and it helps us to understand language in its multifarious functions (Rorty 1967:1–39; Dummett 1993:4–14). Which functions? In the traditional logical syntactics and semantics of Gottlob Frege, one takes sentences [*Sätze*] as the central unit of analysis in formalized languages of logics, mathematics, and science. On the one hand, thus, logical empiricism, the Vienna School and the earlier Wittgenstein used various terms to identify such sentences [*"Protokollsätze," "Pseudosätze," "Satzzusammenhang," "unsinnige Sätze"*] and attempted to avoid abstract psychological aspects in order to concentrate on the structure and sense of statements (Dummett 1993). The problem with psychological statements, they said, was their self-referentiality and logical circularity. On the other hand, Martin Heidegger introduced the hermeneutic notion of a historical "context of meaning" [*Sinnzusammenhang*] and "hermeneutic circle" to explore the self-referential aspects that are always implicit in our use of language (1927). This perception was later recognized in analytic philosophy of language by means of a "pragmatic turn" represented primarily by the later Wittgenstein (1953) and the speech acts theory of John Austin (1962) and John Searle (1969), who moved beyond the study of mere formal sentences in order to value the use of ordinary language in everyday life. This included the analysis of assertions, utterances, expressions, and a variety of speech acts that anchor a sentence to a given context and to the performance of a given task. As a matter of fact, what Frege had formulated earlier as the "context principle" in syntactics—"it is only in the context of a sentence that a word means something" (Frege 1884:§ 60, 62; Dummett 1973:83–93)—was then generalized and actualized pragmatically in speech acts theory in much wider terms: we can only understand something if we take into account the contextual background of communicative practices.

These discussions in philosophy of language led to the conclusion that there are unavoidable presuppositions to the empirical act of speaking a language, presuppositions that can be known by reference to both the social context and the conventions that reveal the background of concrete communities—including their cultural, political, and legal practices (Winch 1958; Hart 1962:v, 14). Of course, there are many other elements such as gestures, signs, unconventional or new uses of communication that go beyond this original conception (Grice 1981; Habermas 2012:54–76), but they can be viewed as parts of sign-relations that refer to the concrete object or reality, to the medium of expression or to communication process, which are also subject to the context of a community (Peirce 1931 [*CP* 5]:120–150; Apel 1975). By adopting the linguistic turn in its hermeneutic, pragmatic, and semiotic variations, Apel and Habermas account for the multifarious use of communication and grant new meaning to the concept of *discourse* as a complex form of interaction among humans embedded in concrete communities. However, tensions arise between a theoretical, practical, and subjective application of discourse (Bühler 1934; Habermas 1981a), and a strong appeal to normative aspects implicit in such discourse (Apel 1976a; Habermas 1976b, 1984). For analytical purposes, I will consider Apel and Habermas separately, beginning with a review of Apel's position before I turn to Habermas.

A DIALECTICAL CONCEPTION OF COMMUNITY

Karl-Otto Apel's philosophy can be defined as the pursuit of a transformation of Kant's transcendental philosophy with the tools of linguistic analysis (Nascimento 1996; Mendieta 2003). Already in his doctoral dissertation, *Being-there [Dasein] and Cognition: An Interpretation of Heidegger's Philosophy According to the Theory of Knowledge* (1950), he compares Kant and Heidegger, takes a hermeneutic point of view, criticizes methodical solipsism and individualism, uncovers the "*a priori* commonalty" of Being-with-others [*Miteinandersein*] (1950:59–64), and stresses the role of language in this process. This leads to the lengthy historical study, *The Idea of Language in Humanistic Tradition: From Dante to Vico* (1963), in which he comes closer to Hans-Georg Gadamer's project of a philosophical hermeneutics, but then criticizes Gadamer for forgetting the transcendental dimension of reflection and validity (1963, 1994, 1996a). On this basis, he moves away from the mere concern with Being to a more radical interest in the normativity of language (1973 1:228). In the same way as Heidegger had asked the question on the sense of Being, Wittgenstein searched for the sense of philosophical sentences, and Peirce proposed a *Critical Common Sense*, Apel's project takes these positions to perform a transformation of Kant's critical philosophy into a "critique of meaning" [*Sinnkritik*]. To this end, he adopts the architectonic structure of transcendental philosophy and defends his project in terms of two complementary perspectives:

> On the one hand that of *transcendental semiotics* as the novel, post-linguistic turn paradigm of First Philosophy as theoretical philosophy; and, on the other hand, that of *communicative* or *discourse ethics* as the corresponding paradigm of First Philosophy as practical philosophy. (Apel 1994:viii)

One question is unavoidable here: Why is such a reappraisal of Kant necessary? Apel could simply start with contemporary positions. His answer is that orthodox Kantians remain faithful to Kant but fail to make the linguistic turn while many who make this turn reject the Kantian approach. Another question is, what is critical about this move? Answers to these questions would contribute to our understanding of the reach and limits of Apel's program. I will attempt to answer these questions by uncovering the main lines of his architectonic project, starting with his views of theoretical philosophy before I turn to practical philosophy.

First, the transformation of Kant's theoretical philosophy implies a turn to language and emphasis on a hermeneutical conception of community. In his early writings, Apel delineates a project in which a concrete "corporeal and historical being-in-the-world of a linguistic community" is defined in the obvious terms of Heidegger's philosophy (1973 1:122, 132, 137). Following Heidegger, Apel concludes that in a factual linguistic community, human beings are historically bound to cultural forms, but the language of such communities provides the medium for a reflection on the very conditions of knowledge and culture (1963: 150, 315–317; 1973 2:311–329). This, however, cannot be thought of as a conventional community that projects its particular culture toward others without recognizing general cultural values. For Apel, this would amount to a fall back into G. F. Hegel's definition of "ethical life" [*Sittlichkeit*] (Hegel *Rechtsphilosophie* [*W* 8]:§ 129–130; Apel 1988:81–83), that is, the concrete ethos and objective moral customs of a particular people, represented by the spheres of family, civil society, and the state. To avoid what he sees as Hegel's conventionalism, Apel stresses the need to go back to Kant and retrieve the reflective and transcendental character of language. Yet, he accepts Hegel's point against abstractions. Thus, he concludes that since language is both a concrete medium of reference and a tool that allows us to surpass empirical limits because humans are capable of expressing ideals through linguistic means, it is possible to have a *Transcendental Hermeneutics*, where the "transcendental" is a correction to the traditional historicist and empiricist view (Apel 1963:43–44; 1973 1:35–36; 1973 2:334–335; 1994:35–43; 1996b:200).

Second, the close connection between hermeneutics and Hegel's views on historicity prompts Apel to make a turn to pragmatics, which is a concrete way of going beyond the limits of solipsist views on language. This move starts with Wittgenstein, who shows the impossibility of a private language and stresses the multiplicity of particular "forms of life" [*Lebensformen*] and language games [*Sprachspiele*], but ends up in an anthropological relativism that does not consider reflectively the fact that a universal standpoint is the condition to affirm plurality because to affirm diversity one necessarily needs to transcend one's own community. Apel rejects this solution as particularist, but concomitantly rescues a concept of "transcendental language game" from his interpretation of Wittgenstein (1973 1:365–366; 1973 2:71–72, 161–164, and 255–256; 1994:1–50). As a result, he recognizes that there is a variety of forms of life, but does not draw radical relativist consequences from this as Wittgenstein and Winch did. Instead, he combines Kant with Wittgenstein's pragmatics and the speech acts theory developed by Austin and Searle to propose a *Transcendental Pragmatics* (Apel 1976a), whereas the transcendental standpoint can be made explicit in discursive terms (1979:132–133).

The term "transcendental pragmatics" requires an explanation; although the pragmatic use of language clearly shows a concrete dimension beyond metaphysics, Apel's insistence on the transcendental seems suspicious to many. In the two volumes of *Transformation of Philosophy*, he advances one more step in his definition of the "transcendental" by going back to Peirce in order to define a *Transcendental Semiotics* and adopt the Peircean concept of a "community of inquirers and interpreters" (1973 2:114, 121–137, 157–158, 215–219; 1994:95, 102, 127; as well as 1975/1981:84–85, 134–135). The basic insight taken from Peirce is that even the search for truth in science *presupposes* a community whose members are open to a communicative process that includes peer-review and verification processes informed by both fallibilism and meliorism. Based on fallibilism, community members project their hypotheses almost as a method of trial and error, but with meliorism they have the motivation to pursue truth through a process of presenting arguments that presuppose a wider normative context as reference. This context has been defined by pragmatists in many ways: as an indefinite community of investigation or inquiry (Peirce 1931 [CP] 2:655, 5:356), a community of interpretation (Royce 1913), and a universal community of discourse (Mead 1934:51, 327). By combining these approaches with Kant's universalism and showing how Peirce provided a transformation of Kant's transcendental logic (Apel 1973 2:157–177, 208–209, 223–224; 1975/1981:35–34), Apel arrives to a synthetic concept of transcendental community. He progressively delineates three different programs that highlight the transcendental dimension and connect this dimension to a communitarian context: transcendental hermeneutics, transcendental pragmatics, and transcendental semiotics.

We can now clearly spell out the question asked by many of Apel's readers: What does he mean by "transcendental"? The answer to this question requires that we review a threefold dimension in Apel's philosophy, which resembles Hegel's triadic scheme and at the same time attempts to avoid the problems that Hegel found in Kant. There is a social and historical implication of transcendental that should not be misunderstood, for transcendental should be seen as a way of "transgressing given limits," a way of going beyond solipsism, particularism, and relativism. Simply put, transcendental means the reflective awareness of biases and boundaries represented by particular language games, institutions, or cultures and the process of searching for implicit universal assumptions that allow us to question and overcome such boundaries. For Apel, it is precisely at this point that we have the transformation of Kant's theoretical philosophy, that is, the substitution of the highest point of the *Critique of Pure Reason*, the "I think"—which, for Kant, was implicitly attached to all representations—by the idea of a linguistic community that serves as the a priori structure which constitutes the condition of the possibility of interactions among real human beings. This means that before the "I think" there must be a community as the very condition for sharing a language and expressing one's thinking. Moreover, Apel adds that by the very act of speaking, members of this real community implicitly project a normative ideal of mutual understanding to be fulfilled in the long run, in an "ideal unlimited community of communication" [*unbegrenzte Kommunikationsgemeinschaft*] (1973 2:376–377; 1994:231–253). So we can now draw a conclusion regarding Apel's definition of the a priori of the community. He starts with the hermeneutic linguistic community, then considers the pragmatic definition of language games, and after discovering the different ways in which pragmatism makes use of this term, he arrives to the definition of an ideal and unlimited community of communication inspired on Peirce's semiotics.

What I take from Apel is that he starts with a concrete community, but then attempts to transcend it by means of a reflection on the meaning of discourses. All this applies solely to theoretical philosophy and entails a philosophical consideration of science. In each of the above-mentioned moments of Apel's philosophy there was not only an amplification of the idea of community, but also the progressive awareness of normative presuppositions. In an article entitled "The A Priori of the Communication Community and the Foundations of Ethics" [*Das Apriori der Kommunikationsgemeinschaft und die Grundlagen der Ethik*], he turns his attention to practical philosophy and applies these ideas in the area of ethics. He summarizes the challenges in this area as follows: there is a central paradox that concerns the necessity but apparent impossibility of a rational justification of ethics in the age of science; this implies the complementarity between value free science and an individualistic ethical decisionism, which are incapable of addressing contemporary global challenges (1973 2:359–360, 376). In this passage, we have a proposal for the transformation of Kant's practical philosophy, that is, of the attempt at a deduction of the moral law and establishment of a "categorical imperative" in Kant's *Critique of Practical Reason*. Using the same elements he had applied in theoretical philosophy, Apel now transforms ethics by affirming that morality should not be based on a soliloquy, as Kant had, but rather on the necessary "recognition of persons as the subjects of logical argument" (1973 2:401). This limitation of recognition to "subjects of logical argument" is surely controversial. What about those forms of communicative expressions that do not fall into the category of logical arguments? A cry for help, for example, would have to qualify as worthy of recognition, although crying is not necessarily seen as a rational argument. The difficulty here concerns the need to consider persons as both factual and virtual; persons who express themselves in several communicative forms that need to be taken into account. For Apel, this recognition should not be defined in empirical terms, but in terms similar to Kant's "fact of reason" [*Faktum der Vernunft*] (1998:221–222). Here we find another perspective on the transcendental, which now refers to an implicit view of solidarity and responsibility based on two basic principles that translate and upgrade Kant's categorical imperative in communitarian terms: to act in such a way as to guarantee the emancipation and survival of humanity; and to realize the ideal community of communication in a real situation. This is

the point of departure for a new transcendental-pragmatic Discourse
Ethics [*Diskursethik*] (1973 2:358–435; 1988:38–39; 1992:29–61).

In a series of studies (1980; 1984a; 1984b) and in texts brought
together in his book *Discourse and Responsibility: The Problem of a
Transition to a Postconventional Moral* (1988), Apel maintains the
tension between the factual "real community of communication"
and the counterfactual anticipation of an all-inclusive "ideal unlimited community of communication," in which communication is
free. He also adds a historical difference [*Differenz*] between the two
instances, thus indicating the gap between facts and norms, which is
the object of argument and critique (1988:141–147). By pointing
to this difference, we can always indicate how far our contemporary
society is from a just, free, symmetric, interactive, and emancipated
society (1973 2:423–424; 1988:9–13, 110–122). The point of this
differentiation is to establish a principle through which individuals can
be recognized as equal as they engage in communication and criticize
society whenever this ethical desideratum is not accomplished. This
need for normative principles is the point I would like to insist on!
If, on the one hand, we need a bold ideal to motivate our hopes and
projects, on the other we need a principle to orient action in the same
way as Kant's categorical imperative did. And here we find a certain
deficiency in Apel's proposal. It is not enough to have a norm telling us what we should aspire to do (the ideal community), but also a
norm that is applied *in concreto* and helps us to implement this in reality, otherwise we would simply be satisfied with a critique of our society, but have no incentive to fix the problems we identify. At a certain
point Apel recognizes this problem and argues that it is not enough to
have a principle for testing norms [*abstrakter Normenprüfungsprinzip*]
(1999:14). A *Principle for Action* [*Handlungsprinzip*] (Uh) is necessary as well, which includes the consideration of the probability of
actually applying ideal norms with success [*Zumutbarkeit*] (1988:123–
124). For instance, it would be naive or irresponsible to act according
to ideal norms in contexts that are totally adverse. One example would
be trying to present rational arguments against the strategic actions
being performed in an armed robbery. Another example would be a
situation of war in which many accepted norms are suspended. But
even this proviso is not enough because we still need to add an extra
step in order to think of the consequences of our actions. But before
we get to this point, Apel adds another step to differentiate between
mere strategic actions and morally strategic actions that are supposed
to be reconciled in what he calls the *Principle of Supplementarity*
[*Ergänzungsprinzip*] (1988:142).

The problem now, however, is that we have a series of new steps and principles that try to administrate the overall tension between universality and the particularity of an individual action within the transcendental-pragmatic framework of a Discourse Ethics of (collective) responsibility. To show the interplay among these aspects, Apel speaks of a "dialectical *a priori* of a real and ideal community of communication" (1973 2:428; 1975/1981:341–345) in order to have both dimensions simultaneously, but now we have a very complex structure that still does not seem to do the work required of an ethics, that is, to guide one's action and its consequences. Moreover, new issues arise such as the tension between ethics of conviction [*Gesinnungsethik*] and ethics of responsibility [*Verantwortungsethik*] (Apel 1988:141–142, 178–179). The point I accept as important and less controversial in all this is the basic principle that an individual decision to join the ongoing debate in a community of communication discussing social, scientific, or political issues is not a matter of faith, convenient private choice, or ideological imposition but rather a quest of collective moral responsibility (1983:375–434). Because we cannot abstract from other persons—otherwise we would not even have a sense of ourselves being born out of human relations—this unavoidable recognition of our interdependence in terms of reciprocity and universality is also valid as an ethical principle that substitutes the solipsism of the golden rule or Kant's categorical imperative (Apel 1990:10–40; 1993:16–54). This recognition of collective responsibility is important also because individuals cannot be made responsible for global problems beyond the scope of individual actions or problems whose solutions require collective initiatives such as the mitigation of climate change. This argument, however, would correspond only to the justification of ideal ethical norms. For example, collective actions need institutional frameworks, which Apel adds according to the *Principle of Supplementarity*. This supplement is obviously very important, but exactly at this stage we arrive to a central problem of the transcendental-pragmatic version of Discourse Ethics, that is, it is difficult to arrive at the application of discourses and the concrete engagement in the factual world, as well as the establishment of practical conditions based on existing institutional frameworks and their constraints. Such structures do not fall from heaven, but need to be built. Beyond that we also need to consider the historical application of norms, which demands that the previous views about the factual community be made visible again in the architectonics of Discourse Ethics. Apel reintegrates this factual dimension as the a priori of facticity—which functions as the dialectical counterpart to the ideal community of communication (1988:45–55, 453–459). But again, new issues arise. Although I am describing the complex structure of the a priori dialectics of the real and ideal community of communication in sympathetic terms, we need to note that as Apel touches matters of application, he brings a series of issues that cannot be dealt with so formally and now the question about the difference between universal norms and particular facts arise.

Apel's solution is to propose more principles for the "historically related transition [from questions of justification of a deontological ethics] to the application of discourse ethics" under distinct conditions. In the end he holds a realistic position of an ethics of responsibility that ponders the reasonable expectations concerning an action (1973 2:171; 1988:123–130, 144), but then he is forced to add more elements to the structure of the Discourse Ethics in order to prepare the possible application of ethics in history, politics, economics, science, and law: he defines a part "A" for the ideal ultimate justification [*Letztbegründung*] and a part "B" for a specific justification [*Begründung*] and application [*Anwendung*] of ethics guided by a teleological *Principle of Suplementarity* [*Ergänzungsprinzip*] that mediates moral and strategic rationality and supplies or reflects upon the conditions for such application (1988:141–153; 1999). Moreover, he adds two internal parts defined as the *Principle of Change* [*Veränderungsprinzip* bzw. *Emanzipationsprinzip*] and the *Principle of Preservation* [*Bewährungsprinzip*], which guide the consideration of history. Finally, there is a division of part B into two sections: a realm in which questions concerning morality are to be dealt with, independent of the coercions from law, economics, and politics, and another realm the institutional frameworks of politics, science, economics, and law are taken into consideration (1988:453–454; 1992:57–61). With all this, the architectonics of Apel's transcendental-pragmatic version of Discourse Ethics gains different contours (see figure 3.1).

Apel himself realizes that this is still somewhat abstract and does not fulfill the task of responding to the fundamental question of

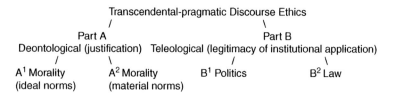

Figure 3.1   Transcendental-pragmatic version of Discourse Ethics.

ethics—what should I do?—in a realistic and consequential manner, so he retrieves his early theoretical discussion of Heidegger in his affirmation that "the Dasein can deliver or also recollect itself simultaneously" [*Das Dasein (kann) sein eigenes Seins sich selbst vorweg überbringen oder auch nur gleichsam "einholen"*] (Apel 1950:76–77) and connects it to the "implicit and self-referential philosophical claim to universality" in his argument for the "ultimate grounding" (1976b:66) in order to propose the *Principle of Self-Retrieval* or *Principle of Self-Recollection* [*Selbsteinholungsprinzip*] (1994:56–58; 1996a:311–312; 1998:602–607). This principle would guarantee a process through which the individual reflects and reconstructs from an internal perspective the historical horizon in which Discourse Ethics is applied, avoiding objective externalism or a metaphysical point of view. This is very interesting, but we need to recognize that there are now too many steps and principles inserted between justification and application, without a clear or single criterion for action.

This leads to my conclusion. Although I centered my attention on some basic aspects of Apel's philosophy, we can have a glimpse of the very complex structure of his *Transcendental Pragmatics* as well as of at least two basic problems that compromise the application of *Discourse Ethics*. First, after having said that we always presuppose a community that can be criticized by the projection and anticipation of a counterfactual ideal, Apel needs too many steps to be able to come to the application of norms—with parts A and B, plus complements and conditions—to arrive to a given case amid this machinery, postulating an individual capacity of reconstruction through reflection and an implicit variety of communities. He affirms that the conditions for actions based on discourse-ethical considerations are not always given and never may be completely given, so we learn a lesson: we need to "think twice" by means of strict reflection. But in cases of urgent and immediate action, this might be one thought too many. I wonder if these various steps could be synthesized in a pragmatic maxim of action or a rule, even if provisional, but effective. Second, it must be seen that although the different aspects are dependent on the ultimate grounding and find a synthetic formal point in the concept of communication community, there is still the need for a clarification of one's individual situation amid the various processes and the spatial plurality of communities: an individual can be a member of several communities, one aspect of the ideal community of communication such as the existence of democratic institutions can be given in a community, another aspect such as the openness to distinct cultural forms can be given in another. This plurality is already at play in overlapping forms of community mentioned by Apel, but seems to be shadowed by a Hegelian interpretation of history and culture as temporal progression that is oblivious to the simultaneity of diverse historical experiences (1988:468–474). Nonetheless, we can take Apel's emphasis on the dialectics of community as a positive aspect as well as his references to a "community of communication." He also uses terms such as "community of argumentation" and "community of interpretation," an ideal community for the solution of problems [*Problemlösungsgemeinschaft*], and "community of solidarity" [*Solidargemeinschaft*] (e.g., 1988, 1998), but, most importantly, this can be seen as a "community of discourse" [*Diskursgemeinschaft*] (1998:7–8). Having seen how various steps lead to a community of discourse based on ethics, we can now turn to Habermas's philosophy and observe how he develops a different approach based on his definition of discourse.

PRACTICAL DISCOURSES AND INSTITUTIONAL FRAMEWORKS

Habermas's initial definitions of discourse arise from his debate with sociologist Niklas Luhmann. He starts by seeing discourse as an ordinary form of communication that is free of constraints, but progressively changes his views (1971b/1982:418). Despite these changes, it is possible to observe a consistent effort to offer a strong definition of discourse and a typology classifying various applications of discourses. In this process, there are subtle differences. One of his first attempts to define a typology of discourses mirrors his argument in *Knowledge and Human Interests* (1968a), where he defines three types of cognitive interests: technical, hermeneutical, and emancipatory. In his Christian Gauss Lectures of 1971, he slightly expands this by proposing a division between hermeneutic discourse, theoretical-empirical discourse, and practical discourse [*hermeneutischer, theoretisch-empirischer,* and *praktischer Diskurs*] (1984:11–12, 115–116). Shortly thereafter, in his article on "Truth Theories" published in 1972 (1984), his starting point is the idea of *discourse* as a form of communication through *arguments* in which specific validity claims are raised in relation to given forms of knowledge: truth, correctness, authenticity, and sense. Consequently, he concludes that "the idea of truth can be developed only in reference to the discursive redemption of validity claims" while moral and subjective ideas imply other validity claims, which need to be brought up by means of a discursive argumentation process (1984:130,136; 1981a 1:48–49). Also in this context he holds that the redemption of claims through discourses demands the counterfactual anticipation of an ideal situation of speech [*ideale Sprechsituation*] ([1972]/1984:172). It becomes obvious that his point of departure is an interplay between a normative ideal and the specific applications of discourse.

Out of these initial definitions Habermas redefines his typology. Although he maintains the tripartite division of discourse [*Diskurstypen*], he proposes a subtle modification in the third type as he classifies discourses in the following terms: theoretical discourse, practical discourse, and therapeutic discourse. This is explained by his move from hermeneutics to pragmatism as well as by his turn to psychoanalysis as a therapeutic practice that deals with the individual sphere and the process of socialization, which require a form of critique of subjectivity. But this is only an initial move. After this first step, Habermas divides his concerns into two main areas:

The first area is linguistics, which leads to a definition of discourse according to the speech acts theory of John Searle and a proposal for his own *Universal Pragmatics*. "What is Universal Pragmatics?" This is the title of an article in which Habermas explores the double structure of speech [*Doppelstruktur der Rede*]; it includes propositional and performative parts in relation to which he explores assertions corresponding to different modes of communication—cognitive, interactive, expressive—various types of speech acts—constative, regulative, representative—and plural validity claims—truth, correctness/appropriateness, sincerity (1976b). All these types fit nicely into three corresponding realms of reality (1976b:246). The good thing here is an attention to plurality, but critics have also noted an insistence on a tripartite view of parallel modes of communication, types of speech acts and validity claims, which is definitely Hegelian. I will not dwell on this issue, but simply say that this scheme expands on Habermas's earlier definition of modes of experience between empirical experience [*Erfahrung*] and subjective life experience [*Erlebnis*] while emphasizing the normative role of communication.

The second area is sociological and leads to Max Weber. Weber had developed a typology of social spheres such as art, law, and politics, which become autonomous from religion and constitute their own forms of rationality. Accordingly, Habermas explores types of social action in a paper on "Aspects of the Rationality of Action" (1984:464), arriving to correspondent forms of knowledge that are related to social discourses and institutions (1984:469–471). This is explained as a result of the following process: we ascribe rationality to assertions, opinions, and actions insofar as they presuppose a learning process related to meaningful actions in these contexts of meaning; these three contexts are nothing but the systematization of our reference to external nature, society, and internal nature. The tripartite Hegelian scheme is now applied to ways of referring to reality and corresponding triad of social spheres: science, society, and art (1984:445–447). Based on this, discourses are defined in relation to institutions that provide a rationalization and systematization of contexts of meaning. This indicates a relevant change, since discourse is related not only to the normative ideal structure of communication processes oriented toward agreement and consensus and its implicit ethical claim but also to concrete social institutions.

Now there are two types of discourse at play: a philosophical discourse in relation to ideal norms with a correspondent typology according to validity claims and a sociological discourse in relation to systematic actions with a correspondent typology of institutional realms. How does this relate to the Kantian approach privileged by Apel? Habermas's *Theory of Communicative Action* (1981a) integrates all these elements in a complex framework.

The first volume, focusing on a philosophical theory of rationality, arrives to a new typology of discourses that still keeps its ideal, albeit detranscendentalized. He thus arrives at a new definition of discourse as a process in which participants in the argumentative process can presuppose that "in principle it is possible to pursue an agreement motivated rationally, whereby 'in principle' expresses an idealized reservation: only when the argumentation can be continued open and long enough" (1981a 1:71). The important point is that discourse has an ideal dimension and, therefore, cannot be reduced to empirical terms. Yet, it can be related to institutional frameworks of argumentation in which specific problems can be discussed. At this point, however, the talk is about five forms of discourse and critique corresponding to several social practices (1981a 1:43–45) as shown in figure 3.2.

The second volume is more sociological in nature, as it presents Habermas's view of institutions in relation to practical discourses.

Types of discourse and critique	Social actions
- Theoretical discourse	Argumentative
- Practical discourse	Dialogical
- Explicative discourse	Reflective
- Aesthetic critique	
- Therapeutic critique	

Figure 3.2   Forms of discourse, critique, and social action.

Aware of the vicissitudes of practical life, he adds a proviso that an argumentative discourse presupposes adequate practical conditions beyond the contingences of action that are not always fulfilled. The demand for a concrete context as point of departure has support in hermeneutics, in the speech acts pragmatics, and in semiotics, for all these theories affirm that language is based on either logical presuppositions, social institutions, or cultural conventions. That is the reason why Habermas speaks at first of "modes of experience" (1967:208) and progressively defines other forms of contexts such as hermeneutic fore structure, the scientific functional system [*System*], and the phenomenal lifeworld [*Lebenswelt*] that provides the background knowledge always implicit in speech acts (1984:404–405). This contrast between lifeworld and system is central to Habermas, also because based on this contrast he denounces the rationalization and "colonization of the lifeworld." This continuous need to refer to a common contextual and sociological background is defined by Habermas according to the semiotic model of the three functions of language corresponding to three forms of referring to the world—objective, social, and subjective worlds, which he develops by taking Karl Bühler's tripartite "Organon-modell" of language. Bühler describes how a sender's expressions and a receiver's attention relate to objects and their representation during a communicative process (Bühler 1934).

The central point around which the topics discussed in the two volumes of *Theory of Communicative Action* converge is Habermas's typology of discourses. He settles on three corresponding claims to universal validity—truth, correctness, and veracity—that orient his theory of communicative action: if one affirms that there is something in the objective world, a claim is simultaneously raised that this statement can be accepted as *true* and responded to either positively or negatively; by referring to another person and her behavior in the social world, one expects that actions in this realm are morally or legally *correct*; and by expressing feelings and symbolic actions in the subjective world, there is a mutual expectation of *veracity* or sincerity in such expressions. These tripartite schemes have architectonic consequences as well, for they motivate a separation between *Discourse Theory* and *Discourse Ethics* (1981a 2:137, 141–147; 1983; 1991b). The differences and affinities to Apel's philosophy are obvious!

Now that we have the "core" of Habermas's theoretical view on the universal-pragmatic conception of discourses, let us see how he develops a universal-pragmatic version of Discourse Ethics or, rather, a Discourse Theory of Morality. In 1976, in *Toward a Reconstruction of historical Materialism*, he published "Moral Development and Ego-Identity" in which he not only continued his dialogue with Apel's first writings about communication ethics but also expanded his dialogue with Marx, Jean Piaget, and Lawrence Kohlberg (1981) in order to "apply" a cognitive approach to ethics without losing sight of the sociohistorical context. This requires the collaboration with empirical sciences. Based on this insight Habermas develops his project of a reconstructive social science, leading to another tripartite scheme, now inspired by Kohlberg's theory of moral development, which classifies moral behavior according to three stages of moral judgment—preconventional, conventional, and postconventional—that go from particularity to universality. Later, in *Moral Consciousness and Communicative Action*, especially in the chapter "Discourse Ethics: Notes to a Justification Program" (1983:53–126), a further step is taken: in dealing with issues of justification and application, Habermas insists on a division of labor between philosophical and empirical research, goes on to question contextualist approaches in ethics, and departs from the idea of an ultimate justification [*Letztbegründung*] of ethics proposed by Apel (1983:93–94). Nevertheless, Habermas maintains the question concerning the motivation for moral action, which prompts him to include the expression of personal wishes or will in discourse while keeping the condition and presupposition of an "unlimited community of communication" as proposed by Apel (Habermas 1983:99). His universal-pragmatic version of Discourse Ethics stresses both individuality and universality. He consequently arrives to a definition of the *Universalization Principle* [*Universalisierungsgrundsatz*] (U), according to which a norm could be taken as valid only if it fulfills the condition that all individuals affected by such norm accept its consequences and side effects by means of "the power of the best argument"—instead of being forced by violence, coercion, or imposition (1983:103).

As we can see, there is no "ideal speech situation" anymore, but an implicit ethical *presupposition* revealed in the normative demand that only valid arguments accepted consensually by participants in discourses should be accepted. This ethical presupposition is also built-in in the formulation of the Discourse Principle [*Diskursprinzip*] (D) that functions as regulator of practical discourses and social institutions:

> Only the norms that are accepted by all those affected as participants of a practical discourse can claim validity [*nur die Normen (dürfen) Geltung beanspruchen, die die Zustimmung aller Betroffenen als Teilnehmer eines praktischen Diskurses finden*]. (1983:103)

Some criticism has been made against this formulation because it seems to say that only those in condition to participate in a practical discourse could be relevantly affected, but not necessarily other potentially affected persons such as those who are members of other communities, future generations, or who are incapable of participating in discourses as "competent speakers." In reaction to this point, new subtle differentiations emerge, including Habermas's proposition that this principle be translated into the language of specific social institutions. In fact, this challenge offers a good reason to keep a strict differentiation between an *argumentative discourse* that has a more ideal and theoretical character and the different *practical discourses* that are always contingent on the institutional context and the concrete situation of people participating in them. Habermas stresses the inevitability of recognizing particular contexts and institutionalizing practical discourses (1983:102, 115). Nevertheless, another critique can be made here because social institutions are systems notorious for their exclusionary character. In response to this challenge, another internal differentiation is proposed in relation to a practical discourse: this form of discourse is not free of the burden of conflicts or the challenge of strategic rationality, but legal and political institutions unburden individuals from having to worry about all these issues. Aware of this necessary facticity, Habermas is led to reintroduce some "functionalistic" aspects he had rejected before in his debate with Niklas Luhmann and to explain that his theory was not "blind to the reality of institutions" but rather applicable to spheres such as law, politics, economy, and morals. Here we detect a change of position and the question concerns how this affects his overall theory. This small but significant adaptation changes the status of what he had defined earlier as practical discourse and opens new venues for a *Discourse Theory*: now the discursive norm has specific institutional applications as Discourse Theory of Morality, Discourse Theory of Law, and Discourse Theory of Politics.

This move is made clear in *Remarks on Discourse Ethics* (1991b), where Habermas starts by defining four basic characteristics of Discourse Ethics—deontological, cognitive, procedural, and universal. However, he then comes to question the very term "Discourse Ethics" because the notion of a practical discourse in relation to rationality "refers to moral, ethical and pragmatic questions" (1991b:101): the "pragmatic discourse" justifies technical and strategic applications; in the "ethical-existential discourse" reason and will influence each other; and in the "moral-practical discourse" one has to go beyond the concrete conventions of a form of life by means of an enlargement of our community of communication to include the interests of all affected partners (1991b:111–113). What difference does this make in the typology we saw before? Some elements remain, but others are shifted and bring new challenges. For example, "ethics" now refers to the particularity of individual and group identities. Also, the claim to "authenticity" that was related to aesthetics is now seen as related to this conception of ethics while adequateness or appropriateness is related to law and universalization is related exclusively to morality. Anyway, the main difference requiring attention is the fact that now discourses are not seen in a vertical hierarchy anymore, but defined as specific co-original [*gleichursprünglich*] realms in horizontal inter-twining relations that sort out given tasks according to appropriate types of rationality, as displayed in figure 3.3 (Rehg 1994:219–220; Habermas 1999:102–103).

These types still maintain a triadic view (1999:105–106), but differences emerge: What happened to empirical discourse and aes-thetic-therapeutic critique? Do they become irrelevant or are they subsumed under the pragmatic discourse? Habermas clearly lacks a systematic approach to these subjects and it seems to me that "ethi-cal discourses" becomes a paper basket where unresolved issues are lumped, but I will not delve into this issue. Instead, I turn to a sec-ond question, more relevant to our present discussion: How do these two different sets of types of discourse include issues of justification and application and relate to one another, internally and externally? In *Between Facts and Norms* [*Faktizität und Geltung*] (1992), the book in which Habermas systematizes his Discourse Theory of Law and Politics, (D) is taken as a general norm that conditions the valid-ity of three types of practical discourses—technical-strategic, ethical, and pragmatic—and the status of (U) is changed (1992:196–197; Baxter 2011:65–66; Forst 2011:100–101). Prima facie, in his discus-sions on morality at this time, Habermas simply puts a softer load on (D) and concludes, "There is no meta-discourse which we can draw upon to justify our choice of different forms of argumenta-tion" (1991b:117–118). Even if we take this for granted, questions remain: What is the difference between ethics and morality? How are his views on discourses, which were once connected, now separated? How can we account for their relationship or unity? In an attempt to

ETHICAL-EXISTENTIAL ◀━━▶ PRAGMATIC ◀━━▶ MORAL-PRACTICAL

Figure 3.3   Horizontal intertwining of practical discourses.

answer these questions, Habermas starts from the premise that (U) and (D) are too abstract to touch the ground and need an institutional complement in order to be applicable to reality. Precisely for this reason, *Between Facts and Norms* introduces an institutional mediation and proposes that principles for Morality and Law are complementary and equiprimordial, since both are to be understood as aspects of practical discourses that cannot be imposed from the top to the bottom, but emerge in relation to one another at the ground level. Consequently, Habermas arrives to a new explanation on how practical discourses are applied:

> In my research to Discourse Ethics published so far I do not have sufficiently differentiated between the Discourse Principle and the Moral Principle. The Discourse Principle simply clarifies the point of view under which norms for action can be grounded at all impartially; and I assume that the principle itself is anchored in the symmetric relationships of recognition among forms of life structured communicatively. The introduction of the Discourse Principle presupposes, however, that practical questions may be impartially judged and rationally decided at any rate. This presupposition is not trivial; its justification awaits a research in argumentation theory…This leads, according to the logic of questions and corresponding varieties of reasons, to a differentiation between different types of discourses (and procedurally ruled transactions). Indeed, it must be shown in each type what are the rules according to which pragmatic, ethical, and moral questions can be addressed. (1992:140)

Habermas goes on to say that while in moral discourses (D) takes the form of a Principle of Universalization, in juridical discourses it appears as a Principle of Adequacy or Principle of Appropriateness and in political discourses it becomes a Principle of Democracy. In all these cases, the application and institutionalization of practical discourses is enhanced, but now practical discourses are less related to what he previously called universal discourse (1981a 2:147) and even to the general norm expressed in (D), which becomes "neutral" and is now limited to providing guidelines for the practical "self-organization of a community" in moral, legal, or political terms. What about the ethical community, that is, what Habermas defines as the context in which individuals raise their concerns and develop their discourses about preferences, choices, and purposes in life? Habermas isolates this aspect from law and politics, but this aspect keeps resurfacing. Independently of this issue, he holds on to these different types of discourse and arguments as well as to the assumption that "as long as

(D) is applied to norms of behavior guiding simple interactions in an unrestricted circle of addresses, then there are questions which correspond to a specific type of discourse, namely the form of moral argumentation. When (D) finds its application to norms of action that appear in the form of rights, political questions of different kinds play a role as well. Different discourse types and forms of transaction correspond to the logic of these questions" (1992:196). An advantage of this approach is that individuals are free from the heavy burden of applying abstract principles because well-ordered societies have institutions that take care of several aspects of social life. However, the disadvantage is the case in which neither society nor institutions can be trusted—as in the case of dictatorships, situations of war, and other cases that cannot be simply defined as "exception," as Carl Schmitt would have it. (D) is now limited to the expression of an implicit moral content and is used as a tool to sort out differences among discourses and to motivate collective participation, but becomes weaker as an instance for normative justification for action because this role is transferred to social institutions. As a result, there is a new architectonic structure guiding Habermas's "application" of discourses, as displayed in figure 3.4 (1992:196–201).

Differently from functionalism, these institutional areas are not necessarily closed in themselves but influence each other through intertwinements [*Verschränkungen*] and complementary relations. Moreover, Habermas goes in more details into the pragmatic discourse in order to show that there is a network of discourses in interaction and reference to different contexts, which are eventually submitted to the scrutiny of morality and justice. An illustration (figure 3.5) provided by Habermas gives the best view of this "process model of reasonable political will formation" (Habermas 1992:207).

This is definitely an improvement regarding the application of discourses; yet, there are tensions within this new architectonics. Habermas defines as "ethics" the *quasi*-existential individual or

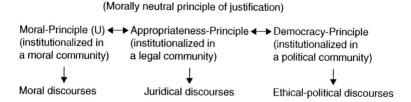

Figure 3.4   New architectonic structure for the "application" of discourses.

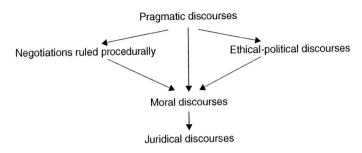

Figure 3.5 Habermas's "process model of reasonable political will formation."

collective answer to questions such as "Who do I want to be?" or "What should I do?," which should be answered intersubjectively, but in relation to one's contingencies, including the cultural and historical conditionings at play in educational processes (Habermas 1991b:115). Therefore, what he refers as ethics could be called more adequately an embodiment of morals, virtues, or civility in light of procedural discourses at the level of formal and informal institutions such as therapeutic practices and educational structures (Habermas 1983:127–128). However, the basis for a normative ideal beyond this somewhat limited perspective seems unclear. How can we have differentiated discourses and still insist that their applications occur under the guidelines of the same moral norm? Appealing to patriotism, for example, is compatible with the affirmation of a particular *ethos*, but when this value collides with the affirmation of a *different* culture, the appeal to a higher instance may be necessary. However, at this point there seems to be no provision of this kind in Habermas's model. All we can do is plea for participatory discursive practices and expect that institutions enable and respect them. Which measure do we have to judge and address the functioning or malfunctioning of a given institutional discourse? To answer these and other questions I have asked above, Habermas adds new components to his theory: he differentiates between ethics and morality; in the case of law, he adds that laws can "claim legitimate validity if they 'can meet the approval of all legal subjects in a legally constituted discursive legislative process'" (1992:141); in politics, he includes complementary conditions such as the exercise of communicative power and the adherence to a constitutional state through principles such as popular sovereignty, guarantee of ample individual protection, legality of the administration, and separation between state and society (1992:209–217). All this adds to the complexity of Discourse Theory and its applications to law, politics, and morality, but now we find the same problem we encountered in Apel: once Habermas arrives at the institutional level, there are many principles inserted as conditions—not vertically, as in Apel, but horizontally. In his view, institutionalization helps community members to figure out which kind of normative behavior they should expect from each other in particular settings that have their internal logic. This covers one part of the problem, but then there is still the issue of addressing the limits of institutions, their exclusionary character, and the possibility of moving in and out of them (Ingram 2010:153–191).

All this should suffice for now, for my main point should have become evident. Habermas proposes a more plural and horizontal approach in his *Universal Pragmatics* and *Discourse Theory*, contributing to the task of defining and applying practical discourses. Hence, his views are important, unique, and surely relevant to our task. However, in this process the dimension of moral justification is downplayed in favor of more realist institutional procedures. Is it possible to have both? My goal is to take a wider conception of *Discourse Philosophy* that integrates the points presented by Habermas and Apel and makes sure they are compatible and coherent with the general framework I have been outlining. This leads us to the next section.

DISCOURSE AND COMMUNITY AS ETHICAL NORM AND SOCIAL INSTITUTION

Now that I have differentiated between the two main contributions to a Critical Discourse Philosophy, I need to integrate them. I hope to build a case for the articulation of their positions as complementary dimensions of a wider critical framework, but before I get to this point, it is important to go into another level of details. When considering the architectonic differences within Discourse Philosophy, subtle distinctions should be considered carefully, including those related to their methodology and the meaning of important terms: "ideal," "metaphysical," and "transcendental" sometimes appear erroneously as synonymous or are understood negatively as mere abstractions; "lifeworld" and "worldview" are often deemed too contingent or biased. By considering the dissimilarities between Habermas and Apel, we can do justice to their respective positions instead of just taking their commonality for granted or just citing them without accounting for specificities. Next, I pose some questions that help me define which points to take from each of them.

What are the key architectonic differences between Habermas and Apel? The previous section has already answered this question, but the main points can be summarized here: Apel pursues a strong justification of Discourse Ethics; he insists on the transcendental-pragmatic dimension as the medium to reach this goal; he designs a more hierarchical architectonic project; and he develops a definitely more abstract approach that proves to be too far from a more immediate practical application of normative principles. Apel requires too many steps to get back to the realm of social action, so his architectonics appears as counterproductive at the institutional level, although he is very consistent in affirming the need to stress the critical self-referentiality of discourse. Habermas is more interested in social processes: he accounts for the reality of institutional structures in society; detects the subtle facts that underlie the exercise of scientific knowledge and political power; proposes a critical alternative guided by the normativity of a participatory and more inclusive form of communication oriented toward agreement and consensus; and he translates all this in terms of daily communicative actions defined in terms of plural practical discourses. Habermas recognizes that normativity implicitly demands a more detachable and impartial standpoint, but his conclusion that this impartial standpoint can be achieved by a neutral principle and universal-pragmatic reconstruction of lifeworld processes weakens the dimension of justification. The differences are clear! Habermas sees Apel's architectonic expansion of the transcendental-pragmatic Discourse Ethics as foundationalist and as a top-down approach that demands too much from individuals and does not account for the complexity of modern multicultural societies. Apel, in turn, accuses Habermas of relying too heavily on the structures of a contingent lifeworld for the task of justification, in a strategy that runs the risk of simply mirroring the vicissitudes of the empirical life, which a moral discourse is supposed to criticize. In my view, they are both right! But it all depends on the task they are addressing: justification or application. Apel provides a better answer to the question about the justification of ideal ethical norms while Habermas is surely more compelling in questions regarding the application of such norms. These differentiations will be relevant to my discussion on community, human rights, and cosmopolitan ideals, but before I address them, another question comes to the surface.

What are the main commonalities and contentions in their methodical approaches? Both Apel and Habermas share a turn to hermeneutics, pragmatics, and semiotics, but at each of these turns, Apel insists on the transcendental dimension, which is rejected by Habermas, who insists on social practices. Here are three examples of this tension:

First, at the time Habermas published *Knowledge and Human Interest* (1968a), he and Apel were in a fruitful dialogue and shared many of the same assumptions regarding the importance of language, especially the turn to hermeneutics. Although they were already discussing the importance of pragmatics and semiotics, they had not yet come to terms with Wittgenstein and Peirce, whose pragmatism is identified by Habermas as a form of scientific discourse and who Apel later relates more explicitly to semiotics. The unique contribution Habermas provides at this time is his definition of discourse, as he searches for an alternative between objectivity and subjectivity, accepts the fundamental importance of linguistic meaning [*Sinn*], and proposes a division between hermeneutic discourse, theoretical-empirical discourse, and practical discourse (1984:11–12, 115–116). Already at this point, he holds that redeeming claims through discourses demands the anticipation of an ideal speech situation [*ideale Sprechsituation*] (1984:172), a point seen by Apel as a transcendental element necessary for an ethical ideal, since it implies values such as justice, nonviolence, symmetry, and others that are not easily identifiable with empirical conditions. However, because Habermas does not develop this point, the ethical dimension remains only implicit and a strong justification is not deemed as needed.

Second, another commonality is the turn to pragmatics as they both notoriously identify problems with hermeneutics, especially in their critique of Hans-Georg Gadamer, whose hermeneutics did not give the necessary weight to universality and justification. However, Apel maintains the emphasis on the transcendental and defines his position as "Transcendental Pragmatics." In 1976 he defended his new approach in two directions: he followed Habermas in taking Searle's "speech acts theory" as a way to deal with the "naturalistic fallacy" in ethics—when one attempts to derive a moral and transcendental "ought" from the empirical "is" represented by conventional and institutional facts of language (1976a [reprinted in 1998])—; he questioned an argument advanced by Hans Albert against the justification of ethical norms—namely that they unavoidably lead to a trilemma—a *regressus ad infinitum*, a *circulus vitiosus*, or the avoidance of these two by means of a *dogma*. The answer in both cases is a self-referential method of strict reflective reasoning based on the transcendental role of language as a *metainstitution* or *metanorm* as opposed to the empirical linguistic approach privileged by Habermas. However, also in 1976, in his groundbreaking article on "What Is Universal

Pragmatics?" (1976b [1984:379–385]), Habermas distanced himself from the position defended by Apel and questioned the actuality of Kant's architectonics. Defending a weaker form of transcendentalism, he said explicitly that "the expression 'transcendental,' with which we associate the opposite to empirical science, is therefore not appropriate to clearly characterize a research orientation such as Universal Pragmatics" (Habermas 1976b [1984:385]).

Third, there is yet another commonality at a deeper level. One of the innovations of Habermas's Universal Pragmatics is the radical difference between the propositional and performative parts of speech, and Apel not only adopts this point, but also expands it to define a performative self-contradiction—that is, when the implicit and explicit content of the propositional and performative parts of speech do not match. One example is when a living person says, "I do not exist," which is a perfectly sound statement contradicted by the fact that the person is speaking and, thus, existing. This point was accepted by Habermas. However, Apel went one step further to reaffirm that it is possible to justify ethics "transcendentally" by applying this same test to identify performative contradictions in the following way: since ethical norms are always presupposed in the very propositional part of language and this can be revealed or shown—but not necessarily "derived" or logically deduced from something else—through strict reflection on the very fact that communication implies the tacit acceptance of certain unavoidable moral obligations, then we have enough evidence for a rational and transcendental justification of ethics. A simple example would be a statement such as "I do not recognize you," which implies that this statement is being addressed to someone who ought to be recognized as a human partner in conversations. If we take both examples—that is, statements such as "I do not exist" or "I do not recognize you"—they are compelling enough as a test to help us identify performative contradictions. However, the point of contention is Apel's insistence that they have a "transcendental" character.

Why is this question about the "transcendental" so important and contentious? The answer to this question leads us to both semiotics and ethics. Indeed, in his semiotics Peirce defines ethics—and even aesthetics—as a norm attached to anything, including science, because even the performance of an operation such as "$2 + 2 = 4$" presupposes the previous agreement and commitment of a community to the "law-likely" behavior of performing an addition whenever one sees "+" (unless there is a new agreement that changes the function of this sign and obligates people to a different behavior). This point is taken by Apel in his groundbreaking article "The A Priori of the Communication Community and the Foundations of Ethics" (1973 2:358–435). Expanding on Peirce's point, he defines "transcendental" as the reflective awareness of particular boundaries represented by conventional languages, allegiances, institutions, or cultures, which prompts the process of questioning such boundaries through philosophical arguments, until we can arrive to a point in which an argument and its validity cannot be doubted without a performative self-contradiction. He defines this final point as the "ultimate grounding" [*Letztbegründung*] of ethics. Why should we bother with such level of abstraction? Initially, Apel does not spell out very clearly the motivation and justification for such endeavor, but in his debates with Habermas on the justification of Discourse Ethics, he identifies this as a necessary condition to reveal, motivate, and justify any valid critical intention. For him, such an ethical justification is the very condition for a new Critical Theory. Herein lies the most contentious point between Apel and Habermas, and I want to discuss this point in more detail.

The main difference between the two philosophers can be traced to around 1983, when Habermas criticized Apel's insistence on a transcendental-pragmatic grounding of ethics. According to Habermas, this justification cannot have the status of an "ultimate foundation" or ultimate grounding because it does not stand against the skeptic's resistance to moral arguments. Moreover, this task is too demanding for both philosophy and individuals. For instance, it is pointless to deliberate rationally whether it is fair or not to drive on the right lane of a road, when everybody in a particular country drives on the right and the entire transportation system relies on conventions based on this practice. To question this practice in the United States would be pointless, but there is always the possibility of moving to England, where traffic rules are different. Thus, Habermas proposes a division of labor between empirical research—which provides these facts— and philosophical reflection—which reconstructs the background assumptions implicit in such practices (1983:93–94). In fact, he says that the foundationalist attempt should be left behind in favor of conventional morals and customs of a daily ethical life that cannot be rejected by skeptic arguments [*Er (der Skeptiker) kann, mit einem Wort, Moralität verleugnen, aber nicht...Sittlichkeit*] (Habermas 1983:54–55, 96–108, and 110). In other words, Apel's strategy cannot respond to the question "Why be moral?" and thus convince any skeptic to enter into a discussion about the validity or foundation of ethics, but the skeptic would recognize the rule of certain contingent games. Apel, however, replied that simply turning to the particular conventions represented by the *Sittlichkeit* would not work for either Habermas—at the theoretical level—or the skeptic—in the practical level of argumentative discourse. In an article for Habermas's *Festschrift* in 1989 he concludes,

> Unclear and contentious between Habermas and myself is probably the answer to the following question: is it sufficient (or at any rate necessary) for a *philosophical discourse* to rely on those background resources of mutual understanding that are already taken into account in any agreement within the lifeworld? Or again, could we base it [a *philosophical discourse*] on certainties that are *factually* indubitable (not even possible of becoming objective) and insofar uncircumventionable in *practical life* because such certainties—like those of a "form of life" in Wittgenstein's sense—are the ones that make possible a concrete doubt of this or that conviction as well as of any concrete, theoretical or practically relevant form of accord (consensus, agreements) beyond controversial questions? (Apel 1998:652)

This dense passage needs to be spelled out. The point here is that one cannot search for critical resources in the very cultural customs that need to be criticized, but can "transcend them" by means of reflexive processes that are uncircumventionable by any other means, not even by skeptic doubts. Why not? Because in order to question the transcendental importance of discourse, the skeptic would have to use language, acknowledge that others exist, assume that his or her point has meaning, and expect—counterfactually—that this meaning would be understood and taken seriously, and eventually accepted. Still, we can interpret Habermas's argument as saying that the skeptic does not even need to enter into this conversation, so these charges would not be applicable. For example, if the skeptic says "I doubt the this discussion is relevant," we could ask for reasons, and he or she would have to continue to engage in communication, thus acknowledging the communication is relevant; if the skeptic avoids this trap by remaining silent, then we would not know what the skeptic thinks and, therefore, his or her position would be irrelevant to our discussion. Still, Habermas goes on to stress the factual dimension of the lifeworld and to identify the different kinds of discourses with which we can clearly engage. Apel, in turn, reaffirms his position, summarizes the points of agreement—especially Habermas's differentiation between the propositional and performative parts of speech—and reiterates the main difference:

> I do not doubt that these and other findings of a universal-pragmatic interpretation of the speech-acts theory, as developed by Habermas, are

the conditions of possibility of valid argumentative discourses and have insofar a transcendental-pragmatic status...At the same time I want to add that the principle of a "counterfactual anticipation"—which is simultaneously and implicitly presupposed in a transcendental-pragmatic sense in all communication among mature speakers and hearers with "communicative competence"—can be convincingly shown as a necessary assumption only by means of a transcendental-pragmatic reflection on the conditions of possibility of valid discourses. (Apel 1998:394–395)

This language is cryptic and does not clarify much. Also, neither of them seems to be willing to give up on their views regarding the transcendental. As a result, their respective philosophies began to focus on different aspects that are constitutive of a Critical Discourse Philosophy. While Apel puts more weight on the question regarding the justification of moral norms, Habermas gave more importance to practical discourses and their social application. Yet, they are working with the same material. Hence, I believe they are actually talking about different aspects of the same critical endeavor. There is a division of labor between the justification and application of norms with profound implications for Discourse Philosophy.

What are these implications? In my view, the focus on justification leads Apel to be more concerned with Discourse Ethics, while the emphasis on application prompts Habermas to work on a Discourse Theory. This can be seen in the internal differentiation of practical discourses that Habermas describes in *Remarks on Discourse Ethics* (1991b). He starts by defining four basic characteristics of a Discourse Ethics—deontological, cognitive, procedural, and universal—then questions the very term "Discourse Ethics," since according to him the notion of a practical discourse in relation to rationality could "refer to moral, ethical and pragmatic questions" [*der* Name *Diskursethik (mag) ein Mißverständnis nahegelegt haben. Die Diskurstheorie bezieht sich in je anderer Weise auf moralische, ethische und pragmatische Fragen*] (1991b:101). Moreover, Habermas rejects his original idea of an "ideal speech situation" and suggests a detranscendentalization of the "ideal community of communication" proposed by Apel (1992:34–35), so that (D)—which had already only an implicit ethical content—is used merely as an impartial tool to sort out differences among discourses and "suggest" collective participation, but becomes weaker as an instance for normative justification for action because the burden of establishing rules and norms is now transferred to institutions that have the power to exercise sanctions and make things happen. (D) serves only as a test to determine if there is enough participation and other democratic procedures to render an action valid and legitimate. As a result, there is a new architectonic structure and corresponding typology of discourses in *Between Facts and Norms*, which provides a good horizontal model for a principled "application" of discourses to different institutional settings (1992:196–201).

In three essays published in *Contentions in the Assessment of the Transcendental-Pragmatic Approach* [*Auseinandersetzung in Erprobung des transzendentalpragmatischen Ansatzes*], Apel criticizes this move (1998:759–760; 1999:28) and requires a more explicit ethical justification or principle that orients the application and mediation between (U) and (D). He demands that (D) be conceived as a principle that is not so dependent on the internal categories of the institutional frameworks in a given culture, so that the very institutional frameworks can be criticized on morally justifiable grounds (1998:776–777). According to him, once we enter the language games of these particular settings we are bound to their internal logic and the only way to escape would be by appealing to transcendental standpoint that is external enough, so that we can criticize institutions (1993:162–163; 1998:729–730). Habermas has not provided a systematic answer to this criticism yet, but expressed a few reactions. In the introduction of *Truth and Justification*, in 1999, he limits himself to a footnote, saying that he is not yet ready to answer the points raised by Apel:

> K.-O. Apel has pursued this interest more decisively because his program of a 'transformation of philosophy' still envisions the architectonics of Kantian transcendental philosophy. The deep reasons for differences, which K.-O. Apel expresses in *Auseinandersetzungen in Erprobung des transzendentalpragmatischen Ansatzes* [1998:609–837], would lie in my option for a "weaker" naturalism. (Habermas 1999:13)

In fact, Habermas wants to show that the fundamental point of divergence between him and Apel concerns the very function of the (D) as an "anchor" for *practical discourses* within institutional realms:

> Karl-Otto Apel pleads for an expansion of the Discourse Principle based on an ethics of responsibility. This term is related here not to the deontologically obvious consideration of consequences which, according to my suggestion, are dealt with in the very formulation of the Principle of Universalization and are of great importance for the application of norms; rather, this term refers to the process of establishing of relationships that make possible both an involvement in practical discourses and a plausible moral action. Apel introduces a basic norm of responsibility

that requires as the duty of any political actor, that they take into account the plausibility of legitimate self-interests and act in such a way as to promote the progressive institutionalization "of a practice of moral reason free of violence." Apel himself realizes that the "moral responsibility for the institutionalization of law and moral" indicate a specific goal and cannot be justified as a general norm by itself—or in light of a norm already recognized as valid. The "complement" to the Universalization Principle that he suggests has a teleological character that escapes the perspective of a deontological explanation. (Habermas 1999:60–61)

Then again, in 2005, in his book on *Between Naturalism and Religion*, Habermas dedicates a whole chapter to explain his divergences with Apel and suggests that his own architectonic project offers better results because Apel burdens the moral principle with too many concerns that should be left to law, politics, and other institutionalized areas (2005:84–105). Moreover, Habermas identifies the main contention as being the difference between transcendental and deontological views on normativity and adds that the uniqueness of his approach is to be able to capture how law "represents an action system infused with political power," which helps us to domesticate political power in areas in which the appeal to morality cannot go very far (2005:90–94). Although he is right, Apel does have a point when he says that law and politics have their limits in relation to areas of moral concern. As a matter of fact, Apel adds, law and politics are themselves matters of deep ethical and moral concern.

Why does Habermas want to detranscendentalize Apel's views on community and ethics and maintain a more realistic view of individuals? It is easy to see his motivations. In the *Theory of Communicative Action*, he insists from the beginning that the unity of collectivity by means of a sacred force like a community of faith should be secularized by a rational and consensual "unity of a communication community" (1981a 2:126, 139). This is particularly important, since this religious conception of community can be coercive. Surprisingly enough, the fact that religious references could be used as metaphysical ways to escape reality may explain Habermas's attempts at detranscendentalizing Apel's concept of community in the program for a postmetaphysical thinking that proposes a "transcendence from within" (1988:35–36; 1991a:110–156; 1996:16–17; 2001c). This reveals also a point of divergence with Apel that becomes more evident in several instances (Habermas 1983:10; 1991b:100–108; 1992:378; 1996:50–55). As synthesized in *The Inclusion of the Other*, "the attempts to explain the 'moral point of view' remind us that moral commandments cannot be justified publicly anymore from a God's eye view, after the breakdown of a 'catholic' cosmovision that unified everything and the transition to the worldviews of pluralist societies" (1996:16). What I have just described is another moment in which Habermas substitutes transcendentalization for social institutionalization. Altogether, Habermas presents a compelling argument that Apel simply wants to justify too many things in a single move—recognition of the norms guiding argumentative discourses, moral commitment to communication, obligation to pursue policies, create institutions, and oversee their roles.

At this point, another question arises: What can be considered the minimal consensus between Apel and Habermas? To a certain extent, on the one hand, the very difficulties we have seen as Apel tries to arrive at a historical application of Discourse Ethics point to the plausibility of Habermas's views of institutions and practical discourses. On the other hand, the limitation of discourses to particular settings may limit their critical potential, as Apel notes, so we need to find ways to transcend these constraints. In my view, this is nothing but the necessary tension between facts and norms. Let us then turn to both philosophers to address the limits and possibilities of Discourse Philosophy in a double role of justifying and implementing general norms. Next, I will discuss three positive aspects that can be integrated in a wider critical framework.

First, it is evident that *discourse* is emphasized by both philosophers and that both share the premise of a *(D)* as basic ground to their philosophical endeavors. The main question dividing them concerns whether a philosophical discourse can either aspire at a "fundamental" role and transcend social constraints in such a way that it provides a secure and ultimate grounding for ethics without losing contact with the reality in which it has to be practically applied; or have institutional, social, or historical constraints that tie it to specific circumstances that make a universal claim untenable. In other words, we need to know how strong the *(D)* should be and how far should it reach. I believe we can at least agree on having *discourse* as a point of departure, as a category that has a systematic role in both their specific programs. Independent of the strong or weak reading, there is a common base on the *philosophical argumentative discourse*, out of which they establish their respective discussions on the application of *practical discourses*. For this reason, I propose the general denomination *Discourse Philosophy* for both positions and consider these two positions as constituting the critical framework guiding my views.

Second, there is an implicit historical and evolutionary element at play, which is well expressed in the way Apel and Habermas identify three various worldviews that orient historical and philosophical evolutionary process: ontology or metaphysics, epistemology or science, and communication or discourse. This assumption of historical evolution implies a teleology that allows them to claim a certain consequentialism in the discursive approach and its corresponding advantage over metaphysical or positivistic views. In fact, they use the term "paradigm" to identify these worldviews and propose terms such as "postmetaphysical," "postconventional," "postnational," and "post-Kantian," among others that denote a certain advantage of Discourse Philosophy over positions that do not make the linguistic turn. The turn to this factual historicity and parallel transcending character of discursive procedures becomes, therefore, the condition necessary for the upgrading of the critical tradition.

Third, I believe that the assumption that discourses require the context of a *community* is consensual among both philosophers. Community is not necessarily a particular group of people, but it is an open concept conceived in the widest way so as to include as many participants as possible. This is what Apel defines as the dialectics between a real and an ideal community and that Habermas makes more precise in his definition of an ongoing tension between facts and values. For Apel, the ideal community provides us with a normative reference; for Habermas, claims for justice are to be redeemed in history and this calls for reliable social, political, and juridical institutions that free the individual from too many worries that are many times unnecessary. Both arrive at different views of a *community of communication* or *discursive community* with a very complex internal logic that functions as a regulator of interactions among community members at different levels. Apel insists on the counterfactual anticipation of an ideal community of communication as the very "condition of possibility of valid discourses" and for the necessary engagement in discourses. Habermas criticizes Apel because "the ideal community of moral capable subjects—the unlimited community of communication from Royce to Apel—enters into the limits of the historical time and the social space by means of the law and gains a concrete, spatio-temporal localized form as a community of rights" (1992:136–137). Clearly, we need both dimensions. Therefore, I suggest that the concept of communication community can be used as both an ideal ethical norm and as a real institution, but we need to be more precise about the usage of this concept in such differentiated roles.

I hope to have been fair to both philosophers, having arrived at this conclusion after discussing their views in detail. On the basis of the discussion developed thus far, I also need to bring two critical points.

First, I need to point out the issue of *individuality*. Generally, questions about morality and responsibility stress an individual rational decision, but this approach is criticized by Apel and Habermas because they see the danger of moral decisionism and require an intersubjective approach to moral reasoning. However, we cannot talk about community without explaining how an individual relates to other persons or to a collectivity. Habermas and Apel address issues of individuality in terms of an existential reference to personal identity, based on their reading of Kohlberg (Habermas 1983; Apel 1988:348–349). The question we need to ask is, if we cannot escape from the presupposition of an ideal community already anticipated in the real community whenever one engages in discourse, how can we affirm individual autonomy, singularity, or personal identity? Apel does not offer an adequate answer to this question. Habermas tries to address this issue by defining "ethical" discourses not as related to matters of universal morality but to matters of individual and collective identities and life experiences (1991b). Through a reconstructive procedure he distinguishes between volitional and rational aspects involved in the individual decision to belong to a community and shows that individuality implies a collective and evolutionary learning process. Adding Mead's views on linguistic community and role taking, he gains a dimension of reciprocity and complementarity in the construction of individual and collective identities (1981a 2:47–48), which enables him to affirm that to understand a person is not only to take the role of the other and anticipate responses—what is compatible with instrumentalization—but also to share a common ground, "being member of the same linguistic community" (1984:157–203, 311ff.; 1971b/1982). One may ask how to ascribe responsibilities, identify errors and mistakes in personal choices, or sort out the issues involving solipsism, individualism, or decisionism. Such questions need to be answered by a more explicit reference to individuality, building on what Habermas has already developed on this theme.

Second, there is the issue of *plurality*. Apel insists much more on the temporal evolutionary dimension that includes the counterfactual anticipation of an ideal community by members of a real community, but he does not seem to recognize the existing interplay among plural real communities. For him, a critical impetus can be derived from our reflection about the ideal standards, but a critical standpoint can emerge also when one takes the perspective of another person

or another community. What about the discourses and intersubjective relations that involve other individuals and communities beyond
one's own collectivity? In the conclusion of his essay "Transcendental
Semiotics and Hypothetical Metaphysics of Evolution" and in texts
on multiculturalism (1996b), he touches on this issue recognizing a
variety of good for persons and different forms of life, but he avoids
the question concerning the simultaneity of intersubjective relations
across communities. Also, his approach is more vertical and misses
important aspects of horizontal relations. For instance, it would be
important to identify the ways in which people transcend their particular community by taking the standpoint of a different community
in order to criticize their own society. One example in German history
would be the case of Dietrich Bonhoeffer, a Lutheran pastor who
worked with excluded Black communities in the United States in the
1920s and, upon his return to Germany, applied this experience to
daily life, participated in the plot to assassinate Hitler and justified this
as a moral act—which not only disrespected the constitutional power
established during the Nazi times in Germany, but also the sensibilities
of Bonhoeffer's own Christian tradition. This example, which brings
a complex relation between issues of individuality and plurality, provides a good challenge to Discourse Philosophy because Bonhoeffer
transcended his condition and justified his actions not only by means
of postconventional ethical and theological reflections, but also by
referring to cultures beyond Germany. In my view, it is necessary to
go beyond the impression that there are only two communities—the
one that prevails in one's historical, cultural, and linguistic horizon
and an ideal community in opposition to it—to acknowledge differences and simultaneity in relationships with individuals, institutions,
and communities among which we can move by means of practical
discourses. This cannot be covered by a general teleological principle,
as Habermas correctly points out. However, Habermas does not offer
much guidance in this regard either. In his references to the inner
plurality of modern and multicultural societies, he seems to use this
term as a description of the various worldviews that need to be accom-
modated within a particular nation by means of liberal measures. But
plurality goes beyond this. He neither affirms the value of differences
within and beyond the framework of a community nor extracts more
systematic consequences from the plurality of worldviews. Therefore,
our critical framework needs to make room for a more radical affirmation of plurality as the dimension that allows us to move between
plural language games and communities, while maintaining the presupposition of an ideal community of communication. It is by moving

between interpersonal interactions and the plurality of language games and communities that one is prompted to ask questions concerning universality. In this sense, one could speak of fragments of an ideal that might be brought together by means of intercultural communication.

Once we acknowledged these points—which I derive from my initial criticism of the critical tradition—we can also see how this lack of a systematic approach to plurality affects the understanding of globalization. To address this issue and propose a framework for the subsequent discussion, I would like to propose the concept of a *multidimensional community of communication* or a *multidimensional discourse community.*

A MULTIDIMENSIONAL DISCOURSE COMMUNITY IN A CONDITION OF GLOBAL PLURALITY

Thus far, I have accepted the framework of Discourse Philosophy. First, from an internal perspective, I reconstructed the philosophies of Apel and Habermas to highlight different emphases in their projects and use them differently for different purposes: justification or application of norms. In this process, I added the missing dimension of plurality that is both internal and external to a community. Second, I want to relate this internal critique to my overall point—at the end of the first chapter—that there is a need for a truly participatory and inclusive global approach in theory and in practice. These two conditions can be defined in terms of a "global plurality": a view of globalization that is not imposed upon others but recognizes internal differences and is constructed from the bottom up. This plurality is not limited to a conception of multiculturalism or a merely internal difference to a given community, institution, or society, but it is rather "global" because it goes beyond such constructed boundaries by means of intercultural communication (Habermas 2009 5:387). Discourse Philosophy is taken here as a dual project that includes a Discourse Theory and a Discourse Ethics that offer alternative but complementary approaches to foster and enhance the tradition of critique in relation to intercultural discourses. But the question we need to address is, where do we get the resources for critique?

One possibility is to turn to critical *individuality.* Habermas clearly inserts the concern with the autonomy of individuals in his systematic consideration of "ethical discourses," while Apel's views on this issue are more limited to a reference to the individual certainty implicit in the "Principle of Self-Recollection." I would suggest that an individual's claim within and beyond a particular framework not be taken necessarily as solipsistic, decisionist, or outside the realm of rules guiding a particular community of discourse, but be considered as part of a process in which a free and autonomous subject observes and learns from other persons that come in and out of particular communities. Individuals are not detached from communities, but rather have the possibility to participate in and move in and out of different communities that may overlap. By sharing the personal experiences within and beyond a particular community, a critical comparative distance may be gained. The condition to move among these different realms without necessarily having to turn to a metaphysical point of view is a way of correcting the limitation we saw in Habermas's initial version of (D), which did not account for forms of being an "outsider" who can have a voice. This means that an individual who has a question or claim—even the skeptic—has the potential of bringing a critical point that should be taken as relevant by the community— according to (D).

Surely, individuality has its limits as well. As Habermas suggests, individuals may be part of *social institutions* by means of communicative processes within civil society. Although he previously criticized the functionalistic view of an internal autoregulation of institutional frameworks, he later came to affirm that discourses are regulated according to their "internal logic," so that practical discourses are regulated by historical institutions in service of a "reduction of complexity" and individuals need to know which rules to follow whenever they enter an institution or a community. Many reliable institutions have been established which free individuals from unnecessary deliberations, empower individuals to participate in communication and argumentative discourses, establish basic democratic procedures to guide practical life in real communities, make room for subjective rights and cultural specificities, and avoid arbitrary changes or abandonment of rules agreed upon consensually. In this way, institutions are very important and contribute to democracy and the rule of law. However, a crystallized institution may abstract from daily experiences, negate individuality, and exclude the plurality of expressions beyond its reach, so that a constant critique of institutions is needed. There must be a different instance for appeals or claims of validity that cannot be reduced to a limited institutional level or particular situation that contradicts these values or is not open to other values not yet recognized within its framework. What about the situations in which social institutions are not given or do not work? What about situations in which an immigrant to a particular community is not recognized as bearer of rights or as citizen, and thus limited in his or her basic rights? The critical source of answer to these questions is often found beyond particular institutions.

This source can be found in a *real community of communication*. Following Apel, I believe that the critical impetus provided by the participation in overlapping discourses in a community helps us move beyond institutional limitations. In this regard, he offers a stronger view according to which argumentative practices can be described in the dialectics of real and ideal community of communication or community of discourse. Before we jump into universality, however, we need to spell out what is involved in a real community. Here Habermas has a point! Having the view of real communities with their respective relationships among individuals and institutions, we can better account for systemic interrelations, references to the lifeworld, sharing of cultural and linguistic assumptions, and the concrete conditions under which communication is realized on a daily basis. For this reason, I suggest that we expand our framework in order to include an ethical element that can guide us to criticize communities. In my view, it is possible to maintain the emphasis on the integrity of institutional discourses as structures that are given in society, but with the proviso—somewhat implicit in a stronger reading of (*D*)—that their legitimacy and acceptation by others must be grounded on and controlled by stronger and ethical standards that emerge through the commitment to plurality in a global context.

A window for *plurality* is the necessary complementary answer to the limits of community. Plurality is not only a description of existing personal, social, and cultural differences—the "fact of pluralism"—but above all a normative aspect that "demands" our recognition of other individuals, institutions, or communities as possible critical resources. An important critical resource is learning from a plurality of communities and putting our own community into question. However, neither Apel nor Habermas offer a more systematic consideration of plurality because they seem to be speaking of plurality more as a problem to be solved than as a perspective from which we may learn. Therefore, the process of questioning the real community by appealing directly to an ideal community needs to be corrected by including the dimension of plurality in relation to a global and intercultural context. This plurality has an important normative dimension, but it also can be considered at the level of application. If we take the different architectonic systems suggested by Apel and Habermas, we can then ask about where this suggestion ought to be integrated. While Apel could include plurality according to his Principle of Supplementation in part B[2] for the application of ethics, Habermas would probably suggest that it is within pragmatic discourses that this type of issues should be addressed.

After these revisions, we can finally consider the other aspect of Apel's dialectical a priori of the real and ideal community of communication and include a *universal* dimension that is not simply an abstract ideal, but a norm informed by global plurality. By considering universality in this way, we can have a structure that accommodates the complementary proposals by Apel and Habermas. Habermas's Discourse Theory is inserted here as an orientation to social, juridical, and political action while Apel's Discourse Ethics can provide a strong ideal or universal *justification* or *grounding* of norms. In this way, Discourse Ethics backs the structures provided by Discourse Theory, but is complemented by the elements of plurality and global universality, which I have included above. The structural result of my proposal articulates the vertical and horizontal approaches by Apel and Habermas and includes them in the idea of an integrative *multidimensional discourse community* as displayed in figure 3.6.

This schematic, nondualistic view surely needs to be worked in more details, especially in relation to the gap and mediation between real and ideal levels of justification, which is a theme of ongoing debate. The point is that individuality does not get lost in a community, but is put in relationship with several dimensions that can be transcended, going from the interpersonal or intersubjective relationship with other *individuals,* which is then transcended at the level of *institutions* and *communities,* to the dimension of *plurality* that prompts us to search

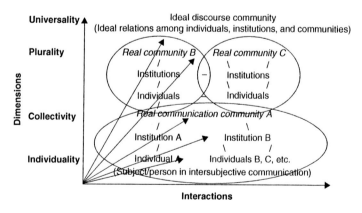

Figure 3.6   An integrative multidimensional discourse community.

for the normativity of truly ideal *universality*. This process occurs in the context of a *global plurality*. Although this is only a schematic summary of what I have been discussing so far, I hope this suffices as a synthetic architectonic proposal for a division of labor and complementarity between Discourse Theory and Discourse Ethics, taken as two proposals within a general Discourse Philosophy. In the next chapters, I will test and apply this conception to the analysis of different issues related to the normativity of community, human rights, and cosmopolitan ideals.

II

COMMUNITIES, HUMAN RIGHTS, AND COSMOPOLITAN IDEALS

4

INDIVIDUALITY AND COLLECTIVITY IN CHANGING CONCEPTS OF COMMUNITY

Cosmopolitan discourses are often conceived as a way of transforming and expanding traditional conceptions of political community. While this reference to community may be a helpful guide to the discussion, there is both ambiguity and potential in this concept. The contemporary quest for community includes many perspectives with their corresponding values, which often collide with each other because the meaning of community is informed by particularities and references to specific contexts, local challenges, cultural experiences, and social differences. Building on the point stated in the previous chapter about the requirement to uphold global plurality, I now argue for a reconsideration of the contemporary call for community in light of a multidimensional reinterpretation of this concept, so that we can differentiate between particularistic and universalist approaches as well as between conservative and critical views. This shall help us to better qualify the kind of structure at stake when we talk about the possibility of building cosmopolitan communities.

In the next section, I want to show how conceptions of community are continuously changing and updating themselves—in the same way, the critical tradition underwent important transformations. In fact, the observed changes within the critical tradition are consequences of social, cultural, and political challenges that require specific responses and, therefore, call for a continuous adaptation of our theoretical perspective. It is important to sort out a series of questions often attached to the idea of community: the tense relationship between individual autonomy and belonging to a collectivity; the plurality within and beyond particular communities; the conflict that may arise among different communities; and the possibility of transcending the limits

imposed by individual and collective dimensions without losing positive and important aspects at each of these levels. In addressing and
articulating these concerns, I shall use the wider and multidimensional
structure suggested earlier to question the limits of individualism and
at the same time move beyond a collectivist particularism in order to
address issues regarding the recognition and interdependence of individuals, include the plurality of cultural and ethnic identities inherent
to multicultural societies, and uphold the promotion of human rights
as a universal standard that guides us as we navigate global challenges.
One of the advantages of considering plurality at the outset is the possibility of acknowledging from the beginning the ways in which one
individual can move in and out of specific communities. This undertaking is central if we want to grasp better the relationship between
community, human rights, and cosmopolitan ideals. In this chapter, I
therefore propose to apply the idea of a *multidimensional community*
as a tool to articulate these various issues.

OLD AND NEW VERSIONS OF THE
QUEST FOR COMMUNITY

The idea of community is old, multifarious, and broad (Nisbet
1976:445–447). Its common appeal lies precisely in its ambiguity.
What is meant by community? What is the motivation behind the
quest for community? I want to avoid the simple equation of community with metaphysical assumptions, particularist communitarian
values, or progressive movements without further clarifying the relationship between this concept and many possible political practices
informed by a critical perspective. Many assumptions are at play in
the call for community values, which need to be understood in light
of a wider social and historical context. Therefore, before applying
Discourse Philosophy to interpret this concept, I need to review various notions of community. Based on this review, I will be in better
condition to propose a critical way of identifying moral, social, legal,
or political issues at stake whenever we talk about communities.

    First, there is a metaphysical sense of this concept, which can
be traced to the Greek concept of *koinonia*, which—according to
Morgen H. Hansen—denotes a political community in its more
abstract sense. Accordingly, in Book III of the *Politics* (1276b1–2),
Aristotle understands the *polis* as a "community" [*koinonia*] of citizens [*politai*] with regard to a constitution [*politeia*], that is, a *koinonia politon poiliteias* (Cohen and Arato 1992:83–86; Hansen 1993;
2006:57–61, 110). A similar meaning was translated in Latin in the

Roman concept of *communis* that later became central to Christianity. Key theological discourses define the processes of belonging or ostracizing as directly related to this term, in concepts such as *communio* and *excommunication* (Niebuhr 2004; Rahner 2010; Stowers 2011). Let us define this particular perspective as that of a "religious community" informed by metaphysical views. So understood, this term would apply to any group of believers united around a common faith from members of a Jewish synagogue to those of a Yoruba divination house (Apter 1992; Nascimento [with Sathler] 1997b; Nascimento 2012). Examples about these various forms of religious communities abound, and refer to varied situations, with differing histories and contexts.

Second, beyond the religious and theological perspective, the very same concept has had political applications. In political theories of early modern Europe, the concept of *communis* was widely used to imply the connection or union of the political body (B. Anderson 1983:5–7). The transition from the early republican concept of common interest [*communio utilitatis*] to *commonwealth*, as seen in the British context, brings us to the beginnings of the modern nation-state and the principle of separation between church and state as a way of creating a radical gap between the religious community and the political community. For instance, the political community defended by Thomas Hobbes and John Locke was based not on faith but rather on the argument that common interests, common good, and common law could bring unity to the political body (Hobbes 1640, 1651; Locke 1689, 1690). In France, Jean-Jacques Rousseau used the French equivalent, *communauté*, to talk about a social contract in which citizens symbolically give away their individual rights—but maintain their freedom—as they constitute and submit themselves to the general will of a larger sovereign community (Maus 1992:117). While Hobbes started with the assumption of a natural state in which individuals are intrinsically egoistic and in continuous conflict with each other—the *bellum omni contra omnes*—so that a contract with a sovereign power becomes necessary, Rousseau argued that humans are born in equality and solidarity, and need to be suspicious of forced coalitions. Because modern society turns persons into individualistic beings hostile to others, he conceives of sovereignty as the collective will of the "people" (1975). As we can see, there are variations in regard to this particular application of community.

Third, there is yet another meaning that refers to the idea of an economic community related more directly to the advent of modern, economic liberalism as seen in Hobbes and Mandeville. While economic liberalism stressed individual freedom, there were groups who criticized liberal economic individualism to propose communitarian alternatives to laissez-faire such as libertarians, communists, utopians, and conservatives. These positions became very influential in Europe and the Americas during the nineteenth century. For example, Pierre-Joseph Proudhon, Ettiene Cabet, Robert Owen, Charles Fourier, Karl Marx, Friedrich Engels, and Comte de Saint-Simon, all elaborated projects for the implementation of utopian communities in the United States that would promote different kinds of collective economic practices (Quint 1964). It is not a mere coincidence that Marx spoke of a "community of producers" [*Produzentengemeinschaft*] in *Das Kapital* (Marx and Engels 1958; Dussel 1988; Kymlicka 1989). There is, therefore, an obvious connection between community, communism, and the critique of liberalism that helps us to understand an internal tension in the meaning of "economic community." This view of economy is clearly opposed to religious metaphysics and economic individualism, but it has been criticized for the contradiction it presents between individual freedom and authoritarian imposition of centralized policies.

Fourth, there is the concept of a scientific community. One of the most complex philosophical initiatives at the end of the nineteenth century is related to the concept of community in the works of pragmatists like Charles S. Peirce, Josiah Royce, William James, Herbert G. Mead, John Dewey, and W. E. B. DuBois (West 1989). Peirce spoke of a "scientific community," and Royce coined the term "community of interpretation," while Mead emphasized the "moral community" (Apel 1975), and DuBois focused on the sociology of the "Negro community," that is, a "social community." They were influential philosophers whose discourse is implicitly appropriated today whenever we use the term "scientific community" and promote practices such as peer reviews and academic evaluations. For these pragmatist philosophers, science is based on a concrete problem whose solution requires cooperation among different experts who present their hypotheses and submit their views to verification (Menand 2001; Mendieta and Kautzer 2009). This verifying process aims at assuring that there is no individual or group bias influencing the outcome, so that the individual contribution and participation is rescued, but at the same time submitted to collective scrutiny. In this sense, the scientific community functions as a kind of legitimizing procedure to guarantee the effectiveness of scientific research as it pursues a final truth that may be attainable, according to Peirce, only in the long run.

Fifth, I would like to connect this concept to some other views on social and cultural communities that can shed light in the plural applications of this term today. Sometimes it is difficult to differentiate the utopian and communist groups from anarchist and libertarian initiatives that proposed communitarian alternatives to a central government and promoted civil disobedience. At any rate, what I want to highlight is their cultural impact. These groups created niches where certain cultural values would be abolished, such us Victorian morals, patriarchal structures, sexual taboos, and legal requirements. The United States was a fertile ground for these initiatives in the nineteenth century. One example would be *Icaria*, the famous "community of love" that anteceded the hippies a century later. Other examples are the communities of *Hopedale* and *Oneida* as well as models of community inspired in Henry Thoreau's *Walden* and in many other initiatives focused on erotic, esoteric, and naturalistic experiences that were later revived by environmental movements (Hine 1953; Berry 1992).

With these brief examples, I hope to have provided enough evidence to justify the title of this chapter: changing concepts of community. Thus far, all I have done is to review a series of conceptions, very briefly, without even arriving to the twentieth century. What do these initial descriptions tell us? First, there is a plethora of perspectives on community throughout history. Second, they are not frozen in the past, but are still available and can be revived at any moment. Third, each of these conceptions has theoretical assumptions and specific practical applications that can be identified. Fourth, we can also observe how new concepts of community partially overcome older ones, as seen in the idea of a political community clearly differentiated from the religious community and the economic community becoming autonomous from political control. Fifth, concepts of community have been a steady counterpoint to many forms of liberalism: while personal salvation is a doctrine of liberal theology and freedom and equality are individual rights for political liberalism, private property is key to liberal economics and privacy is a value fundamental to cultural liberalism. Finally, therefore, we find corresponding political, economic, social, natural, scientific, and artistic conceptions of community that diverge on how to understand the primacy of the individual sphere. In my view, they may rightly question problems of *individualism* such as the exacerbated possessive tenet, selfishness, or altruistic tendencies, but cannot contradict the moral demands for freedom, recognition, and equality stemming from the dimension of *individuality*.

Based on this short historical overview and preliminary conclusions, we could simply deduce that the idea of community is open enough to be operational in many ways. However, we need to be vigilant regarding its ambiguity because it allows for this concept to be applied in ways that contradict the critical intention. Let me provide examples and definitions that show that it is precisely in notions of "political community" that we find the most dangerous appropriations of the term. Therefore, I will argue for a careful analysis and a parsimonious use of this word. Let me simply mention a few cases that reveal how this concept has been appropriated politically, before I delve into a more systematic discussion.

Community has been used by conservative opponents of liberalism. For instance, one of the main German conservative thinkers in the twentieth century, Ernst Jünger, considered the German army during World War I as "the community on the front" [*Frontgemeinschaft*] (Nevin 2003). A similar slogan was used by the national-socialist regime as it promoted slogans such as "blood and soil" [*Blut und Boden*] and "folk community" [*Volksgemeinschaft*] to affirm an ethnocentric model (Bruendel 2004). It does not take a stretch of the imagination to see possible uses of the same strategy today. This appropriation of the term shows that it can have theological and political meanings, as well as authoritarian, fascist, and racist connotations. This view of community aims at defining a model—for example, the Aryan race—and excludes whoever or whatever does not fit into this model, thus contradicting the dimensions of individuality and plurality I have now inserted as criteria components of a critical approach. In contradistinction, however, the philosopher Emmanuel Mounier led a movement during the period of the German occupation of France, based on resistance as well as on a combination of Christian ethics with socialist ideals. These ideas were very influential among French priests and intellectuals who supported the *communauté* pacifist movement in France. Here we have another appropriation of the concept, this time influenced by Mounier's philosophy of *personalisme* that leads to a radically different sense of community (Mounier 1950). Based on the motto "community, life, and communication," the personalists expanded existentialism beyond the individual to include the collective dimension of daily life. They were very influential not only in Europe, but also in Latin America and Africa, especially in areas influenced by the Catholic Church (Maritain 1947).

This ambiguity is apparent in another example. An interesting political initiative that appeals to religious discourse and ethnic identity can be seen in the United States (Hudson 2002). We can start with a movement influenced by W. E. B. DuBois, who was not simply the first African American to receive a PhD from Harvard, but also a pioneer of American philosophy and sociology who studied with the pragmatists at Harvard and with Max Weber in Berlin. Therefore, he was surely informed about the pragmatist conception of community and the German discussion on the difference between community [*Gemeinschaft*] and society [*Gesellschaft*]. He applied this conception loosely in his study of an urban "Negro Community" in Philadelphia to contrast it to the "white world." More important, however, is how he was later involved in the foundation of the National Association for the Advancement of Colored People (NAACP), which was crucial to the development of the civil rights movement in the United States (DuBois 1899, 1995; West 1989:138–150; Schäfer 2001; Chandler 2006). Also here we find complex perspectives on community that go from Martin Luther King Jr. and his Roycean view of the "beloved community," which he probably received through E. S. Brightman (Genovese 1995; Herstein 2009), as well as the religious practices of the African American churches through the political references to Black liberation to the affirmation of an ethnic identity by means of artistic expressions—especially in the tradition of *spiritual* and *gospel* music—and the pursuit of social and economic goals through grassroots initiatives defined as "community organizing" (Cone 1972; Hudson 2002:141–166). The dimension of individual freedom and search for liberation is central here as well. Moving beyond Frederick Douglass's conceptions of the "self-made man," DuBois revealed concealed forms of exclusion and added the concept of an individual "double consciousness" of being "out of place" in a given community due to the belonging to different contexts: Africa and the Americas (Gilroy 1993). The African experience in the Americas offers a different insight into the tension between individual and community, which is to be contrasted with the European interpretations.

A similar strategy can be found in a series of liberation movements in Latin America, such as the movement for popular education and liberation theology that use the concept of Base Christian Communities (C. Boff 1981). This is related to a series of initiatives such as the theory of economic dependency, the pedagogy of the oppressed, and the aesthetics of hunger and Augusto Boal's "theater of the oppressed," as well as the liberation philosophy (Freire 1970; Dussel 1986, 2000, 2009). These liberation movements struggled for years and were victims of military repression, but in the end they played a very important role in the democratization of Latin American countries. The election of new presidents in Argentina, Bolivia, Brazil, Chile, Venezuela, and Paraguay at the beginning of the twenty-first century who had affinities to liberation movements are evidence of the impact of these grassroots initiatives in various countries (Car and Ellner 1993; Castañeda 1993). The base church communities inspired by liberation theology are a clear example of a grassroots movement. Their social relevance is evident not only in the term "base," which refers to a social pyramid in which the majority at the bottom are poor, opposed to and oppressed by the rich, but also in its connection to the word "church." The church in certain areas—and oriented by specific theological views—was the space where groups at the periphery of society in Latin America could bring their claims to the public sphere, express a critical intention, and motivate critical political action (Gutiérrez 1971; Libânio 1976; L. Boff 1981). However, this reference to church and theology complicates matters for us, since we now have an association between religious and political action that cannot be rejected by simply applying the negative labels "metaphysical" or "conservative." Instead, wider critical criteria are needed to locate and define this form of "church community."

This is not an easy task because religious discourses are also used for other political purposes. The conservative movement in the United States needs to be differentiated from the fascist movement in Europe, but there are some common points among them. Since its origins in the eighteenth century as a movement against liberalism, the conservative movement in the United States has renewed itself, going from a traditional conservatism of the 1920s through the new conservatism and neoconservatism between the 1950s and 1990s to the contemporary compassionate conservatism that is now called social conservatism (Gottfried 1988; Olasky 2000). Political conservatism is a movement in flux, but as Russell Kirk argued in *The Conservative Mind: From Burke to Elliot* (1953), there are some core conservative values such as the emphasis on family, church, corporation, and the nation that are loosely defined as part of community values. In fact, Robert Nisbet articulated these conservative ideas in two of his books: in *The Quest for Community*, he argued that totalitarianism and the postwar "loss of community" would prompt a search for of belonging, intimacy, and cohesion that needed to be guided by an "ethics of order and freedom" (1953:63, 229) and in *The Social Philosophers: Community and Conflict in Western Thought*, he rearticulated this "quest for community" in more philosophical terms as he criticized Rousseau's political ideas (1976:249). Similar views were espoused by Daniel Bell, who saw the erosion of American values as a result of the industrialization, urbanization, and consumption of the postwar period (Bell 1976). For these thinkers, social problems could only be adequately addressed through a return to family values, the solidarity provided by traditional institutions, the virtues of loyalty and patriotism through education, and the maintenance of the status quo ante (Nash 1976).

What can we learn from these examples? First, it is important to recognize that the concept of community is plural and can be manipulated and imposed according to hidden, particular agendas. Second, grassroots movements in several countries were able to reinvent this concept and ascribe a new meaning to it by supporting impoverished and oppressed groups in their struggle for recognition, equality, and justice. Third, in the cases of the African American civil rights movement and the Latin American liberation movement, the idea of community combined religion, politics, and economy in a critical way, guided by ethical and moral concerns. Fourth, the conservative concept of community changed steadily in the twentieth century, but core ideas remained constant, such as the connection to specific social institutions represented by a particular family model, the official church structure, a cultural association, or a political party. Finally, we are now confronted with a problem of interpretation, because these groups seem to be combining views that seemed incompatible. For instance, they contradict the liberal separation of religion from politics or affirm community to promote ethnocentric values, and conflict with the emphasis on individuality. In view of these ambiguities, what can be critical in a critical conception of community?

This question may be spelled out in other terms: What can we make of a concept that can be related ambiguously to religion and theology, politics, economy, art, and many other areas? Should we give up using this word at once, find something better, or work on providing a better definition of its meaning? This latter option is seen in several initiatives that characterize a new "turn to community," especially regarding the debate between liberals and communitarians in North America. This debate can offer a deeper insight into analytical differentiations in a variety of issues related to the quest for a critical concept of community.

THE DEBATE ON COMMUNITARIANISM AND LIBERALISM

Philosophers and political theorists aligned with liberalism have always been suspicious of the link between community and conservatism. This is actually the underlying assumption of the debate between liberals and communitarians. John Rawls is surely the main representative of the liberal position as well as the main target of communitarians.

Since there are many interpretations of Rawls's work and his debates with communitarians, I will provide a brief introduction of the positions involved in this debate (Kymlicka 1989, 2002; Pogge 1989; Rasmussen 1990; Mulhall and Swift 1992; Bell 1993; Chapman and Shapiro 1993; Forst 1994).

From today's perspective, it is important to acknowledge that Rawls's initial views can be traced back to his senior thesis presented at Princeton University—published only posthumously in 2009—whose title speaks directly to the topic of our discussion: *A Brief Inquiry into the Meaning of Sin and Faith: An Interpretation Based on the Concept of Community* (2009). This text was subject to analysis in an introduction by Thomas Nagel and by other authors who reveal the likely religious roots of his deontological approach (Gregory 2007; Habermas 2012:257–276). However, an important point in his view on community at this stage is the definition of an ethical standpoint. This includes the recognition of the interdependence between individual and community and the critique of an egotistical "bargain-contract society" that uses other people as means and creates a state of fear and distrust (Rawls 2009:110–113, 229). Based on this assumption, Rawls affirms the importance of a religious community—inspired by Christian teachings—by stating that "Christian morality is morality in community, whether it be the earthly community or the heavenly community...This fact means that man can never escape community, and therefore is always responsible and always under obligations" (Rawls 2009:122). This point of departure appears to be in radical contrast with the framework Rawls established in *A Theory of Justice* (1971) and *Political Liberalism* (1993), but as Thomas Nagel recognizes, there is a common thread in all these projects, which is the search for a comprehensive outlook about the social world (in Rawls 2009:5).

In *A Theory of Justice*, this comprehensive outlook is provided by a procedure similar to Kant's criticism, as Rawls identifies utilitarianism and intuitionism as two extremes he wants to avoid and proposes a form of ethical and political constructivism as an alternative between both (1971:39). It is out of this perspective that he advances a "general conception of justice" that is not blind to social reality, but upholds the need of both a guarantee for basic liberties and a fair distribution of social goods. Within his principles of justice, Rawls develops the idea of an "original position" and the requirement that individuals abstract from their contingent situations by making their choices behind a "veil of ignorance" (1971:11–12). With these theoretical tools, he hopes to establish equality among moral persons and get a result that might be accepted by each individual, especially the least fortunate, as fair enough (Rawls 1971:102). Rawls starts with individuality and concedes that one must eventually explain the value of community, but instead he goes directly to a conception of a "well-ordered society" defined as "a social union of social unions, [where] the members of a community participate in one another's nature" (1971:264–265, 495). Such views are later expanded and made more explicit in his affirmation of Kantian constructivism and of justice as fairness (Rawls 1980, 1985), but because his views on justice demand impartiality and neutrality, disregard personal differences, and give no consideration to particular conceptions of good that emerge in community relationships, Rawls was criticized by the so-called communitarians. They questioned his views on the person, community values, conceptions of good, and universalism and often used the example of religious communities to raise their point. This explains why Rawls was prompted to advance beyond his early notion of justice as fairness to react to communitarian critiques, review some of this initial concepts, and defend a *political liberalism* while rejecting religious metaphysics (1987, 1993:xix–xx).

Rawls's *Political Liberalism* offers an important counterpoint to his previous publications and views on community. After having delineated a normative theory of justice, Rawls found it necessary to develop a purely political conception of justice that could be accepted generally without falling into the consensus of Catholic universalism or the intolerance of religious wars after the Reformation (1987:13). As alternative, he not only accepts the "fact of pluralism" and postulates the possibility of an "overlapping consensus" (Rawls 1993:36–37), but also insists that a "well-ordered democratic society is neither a community nor, more generally, an association," since, in his view, the notion of community would apply either to a church or medieval society that could be "more or less united in affirming the catholic faith" guaranteed by the Inquisition (1993:36–43, 146). Moreover, in order to come to terms with religious pluralism and question sectarian relativism, he upholds a principle of toleration (Rawls 1993:xxi; Macedo 1995:474; Forst 2003:615). This consideration and critique of religious and metaphysical assumptions in the political realm is seen in his debate with Habermas and generated a new debate on religion and politics (Rawls 1995:133, 134, 136, 137; Habermas 1996:65–127; 2012:257, 277. See also Forst 1994:152–161; 2007:127; Macedo 1995; Baxter 2011:193; Finlayson and Freyenhagen 2011:1–21).

It is in the context of this debate between liberal and communitarian positions that the concept of community reenters the political debate and gains newer dimensions (Mulhall and Swift 1992; Kymlicka

2002). In reaction to the abstract individualism implicit in the liberal conception of rights, a number of people opposed Rawls's ideas. I shall only mention briefly some communitarians who argue that the liberal emphasis on a general concept of justice leads to an inadequate view of community that, in turn, jeopardizes a socially oriented politics derived from grassroots initiatives (Nascimento 1995, 1998a, 1998b).

In *After Virtue* (1981), Alasdair MacIntyre raises a sophisticated and controversial position in opposition to Rawls. He turns to a conception of virtue that goes back to Aristotle and Thomas Aquinas and, based on this Aristotelian tradition, he points out that important traditional values have been forgotten in modern liberal democracies. His views were labeled conservative due to his turn to religion and his emphasis on liturgical traditions, but he also operates with comprehensive views of morality, culture, and politics to show the limits of liberalism. For instance, in his early writings in the 1960s, he had already discussed morality, Marxism, and theology, criticizing Engels for his view that secularization would prevail in England and asking which authority could challenge the power of the Church in providing morality for a community (MacIntyre 1967:21, 51). But in *Whose Justice? Which Rationality?* (MacIntyre 1988), he advances similar points by questioning the very concept of ethics, defending the heterogeneity of morals, and claiming that morality "presupposes a sociology" that relates values to concrete communitarian contexts (1981:23; 1988:370). Also here, MacIntyre reaffirms that a particular community is determined by a cultural tradition that provides identity for its members and a set of virtues that guide individual actions (1981:140; 1988:146–240). Michael Sandel takes an analogous approach, first raising sociological objections to liberalism, and then expanding them into a rather anthropological critique (1982:11, 48). But his most salient point is based on the claim that justice must be linked to what can be justified as morally good. Thus, he criticizes Rawls's theory of justice and political liberalism for pretending to be "universal" and for relying on an essentialist and individualist concept of "person" that ignores how humans shape and are shaped by a plurality of moral, cultural, and political understandings (1982:50, 212). In his opinion, Rawls's project is doomed to fail because the liberal view of the person proposes an "unencumbered self" that consequently leads to an impoverished view of the political community (1982:186).

Charles Taylor shares many perspectives with MacIntyre, including an early interest in the debates on Marxism and secularization (Taylor 1958, 1960) and a recent reappraisal of religion, as exemplified in his

book *A Secular Age* (Taylor 2007). The deep roots of his communitarianism are also related to an hermeneutic tradition that goes from
the so-called three H's—Johann G. Hamann, Johann G. Herder, and
Wilhelm von Humboldt—to the theories of meaning in Wittgenstein,
Heidegger, and Gadamer (Taylor 1985a). These philosophers provide
him with a tool to question the overly individualistic and instrumental
views of modernity, which occlude the anthropological conditionings
of the self, forget how individual agency and identity depend on the
particular language and culture of a localized historical experience,
and lead to a loss of meaning, loss of cultural expressivity, and loss of
freedom (Taylor 1991:1–12, 25–30). Because liberalism is the political
heir of these modern views, it becomes the target of Taylor's critique
as well: he questions liberal "atomism," rejects ethical subjectivism,
and opposes the primacy of individualistic rights over collective goods
(1985b:187–209; 1995:181–202). Moreover, Taylor takes the concepts of freedom and "recognition" [*Anerkennung*] from Hegel to
develop a proposal for identity politics and group rights (Taylor 1975;
Taylor and Gutman 1992). With this move, his communitarianism is
expanded into both *multiculturalism* and *interculturalism*, inspired
in the particular case of Québec and the constitutional debates for a
multicultural Canada in the 1960s (Taylor and Gutman 1992; Taylor
2012). For Taylor, "equal recognition is not just the appropriate mode
for a healthy democratic society. Its refusal can inflict damage on those
who are denied it" (Taylor and Gutman 1992:36). Therefore, the
antidote to liberal impartiality is a "politics of difference" that recognizes distinctions, opposes assimilation, and creates affirmative policies to avoid or rectify oppression (1992:58). This, however, is not
simply internal to the Canadian society or the North American context. Because "some of the reasons that make interculturalism right
for Quebec apply also to some European countries" (2012:422),
Taylor amplifies his communitarianism to the international level. For
example, the Turkish guest workers [*Gastarbeiterinnen*] not only
want to be integrated in terms of citizenship but also want to maintain
their cultural and religious identity. This can be observed especially
in his discussion about an intercultural "consensus on human rights
(1999:124–144).
    Another communitarian critique is provided by Robert Bellah,
known for his sociology of civil religion and his plea for community values (1967, 1970, 1975). In his research on the problem of
individualism in the United States, he rescues the values of mainline
Protestant theology and the prophetic tradition personified in Martin
Luther King Jr. to propose a social realism in which a good community

would not be a particular church but rather a civil attitude of upholding values "common to the biblical and republic nations" (Bellah et al. 1985:223). According to Bellah, the biblical and republican language demands an individual commitment to social justice locally, so that "the community of memory that ties us to the past also turns us toward the future community of hope" (Bellah et al. 1985:153). A similar appeal to community was made by Michael Walzer in his book *Spheres of Justice* as he observed the need for communal solidarity, attention to different "shared meanings," lower indexes of social disintegration, and a respect for the values and conceptions of good in different communities (1983:10). Using the example of Medicaid, he showed the failure of liberal distributive justice and argues that the members of different local communities should decide about what is good for them, instead of reducing their values to a single standard (1983:89). One point I would like to highlight is that Walzer also identifies a clash between values and the religious implications of such a clash. For instance, in the chapter "Divine Grace" in *Spheres of Justice* (1983:243–245), he criticized the Protestant emphasis on the individual's affair with God to show that such an individual grace does not play any role in communion or communication with others. Accordingly, he stressed the need of a wall between church and state. Yet, in his discussion of social criticism, Walzer searches for a model of societal critique in the Jewish prophetic tradition, taking the paradigmatic image of the Exodus as reference and establishing a dialogue with Liberation Theology (1985, 1987). Therefore, it is fair to see that religious values seem to play an implicit role in his and in many other communitarian positions.

Finally, we should also include the feminist position in this debate. For example, Iris Young, Susan M. Okin, and Amy Gutman criticize the ideal of community in neoconservatism, romantic feminism, and communitarianism while raising questions concerning liberalism. Amy Gutman provides an account of the communitarian critique of liberalism and a defense against Sandel's attacks, but maintains that liberal theories still need to address issues regarding the subordination of women (1985:309); Susan Moller Okin criticizes both liberals and communitarians for their gender bias in failing to recognize structures such as the family or women's roles, but defends the possibility of combining liberal and communitarian values in terms of a "liberal community," provided that liberalism manages to accommodate some feminist concerns (Okin 1989; 1991:187). From a critical perspective, Iris Young proposes the normative ideal of "city life" as alternative to communitarianism (1990). In her view, the city and the urban centers are where we find most of the contemporary problems related to poverty, exclusion, and oppression that were not addressed by either liberals or communitarians. Similarly, the "city life" could be a public stage for social and political action (1990:227; 2011:43–52). Young also requires that we account for group difference and heterogeneity in order to avoid an "assimilationist ideal" (1990:118, 182). This alternative to communitarianism transforms the classic idea of *polis*, criticizes the utopia of isolated communities, and brings a strong argument for multiculturalism. However, the idea of a "city life" alone makes it difficult to account for the action of rural, ecological, tribal, and peripheral movements whose specificity lies on their situation beyond the urban context. Moreover, we can also recognize that some communitarians have critical intentions that are compatible with the feminist claim for attention to particularities. How can we make sense of this variety and identify the critical aspect?

One possible answer is provided by Rawls in his response to these critics. As we saw, he insists that a well-ordered democratic society is neither a community nor an association because such ideas apply either to a church or to a medieval society and have no place in a modern liberal democracy. This has been criticized, but he then came to acknowledge plurality and conceive of the possibility of an "overlapping consensus" among different comprehensive doctrines that would support the same legal or political principles for different reasons. This is a possible way to account for the plurality of meanings I described above. Another way would be to point to negative appropriations of the concept and abandon altogether any hope of giving new meaning to the quest for community. Beyond these extremes, there are alternatives. As a matter of fact, Rainer Forst has made a valuable proposal to integrate these approaches and mediate the levels of individuality and collectivity qua person and community in four "contexts of justice" represented by the practical realms of ethical, political, legal, and moral discourses defined by Habermas (Forst 1994:51–54, 131–142, 205f., 347–437). Moreover, Habermas himself became involved in this debate and was prompted to review his position, acknowledge multiculturalism, and reconsider the role of religion in postsecular societies (2005, 2012). Therefore, instead of siding with positions I just reviewed, I want to retain some aspects of this debate—such as the need to affirm individual freedom in ethical and political terms as well as the need to recognize contexts and differences—and go back to the critical tradition and the multidimensional conception I developed in dialogue with Discourse Philosophy.

PLURAL PERSPECTIVES FOR A CRITICAL
CONCEPTION OF COMMUNITY

A critical perspective on community needs to take the above-mentioned plural contexts into account, refer to the tradition of critique, and uphold global plurality. I have already anticipated this need in the very structure of the multidimensional community of communication, so all I need to do now is to explore this model more deeply in a dialogue with Habermas and Apel and see if it can address the issues discussed above.

First, let us consider how Habermas's understanding of community helps us to address issues of individuality and plurality within Discourse Philosophy. He conceives of individuality as the subjectivity implied in intersubjectivity—as defined by George H. Mead—and makes room for expressivity in individual intersubjective articulations while recognizing a plurality of social spheres. In light of his institutional approach, he offers a more sociological and political view that does not lose sight of practical tasks. He also provides details about how a real community can be described and guided by a communicative principle. This empirical interest on the internal structures of a community is at play already in *The Structural Transformation of the Public Sphere* (1962), in which Habermas holds on to Kant's idea of a "public use of reason" [*öffentlicher Gebrauch der Vernunft*] and works out the differentiation of public and private spheres to consider intrinsic elements of modern liberal societies—such as the ideal of democracy, the forms of publicity, and the different channels of civil and political expression. In fact, he begins this book with a consideration on the meaning of the word "common" and its variables in the German and British political traditions (1962:18–19), and concludes by mentioning Wright Mills's view of a "community of publics" (1962:293). What he finds as problematic is that the original function of publicity as means of criticizing the lack of transparency of the state disappeared as publicity became a product for private consumption due to the cultural industry. On this basis, Habermas concludes that a "critical publicity" is needed, which would establish "public communication" and guarantee free political opinion (1962:269, 287–294).

This point is maintained in later texts, but there are changes because Habermas progressively makes the concept of community of communication more empirical and less ideal. In his initial lecture in Marburg [*Antrittsvorlesung*], from 1961 and reprinted in *Theorie und Praxis* (1963), he mentions various concepts of community in the classic political doctrines of Thomas Aquinas (*civitas, societas, dominium*),

Thomas Morus (Utopia), Machiavelli, Hobbes (commonwealth), and Vico (*sensus communis*), but centers his attention upon the liberal *raison* of Hobbes's absolutist state (1963:48–49, 72), which is combined with Hegel's philosophy of right by conservative authors who insist on the primacy of an ethnic community [*Volksgemeinschaft*] (1963:140, 150). Habermas clearly questions this political concept because its authoritarianism implies a rejection of individual freedom and autonomy, stresses a belligerent affirmation of territorial integrity, and imposes a conservative interpretation of collectivity as an ethnic collectivity [*Volk*]. These are very important points to keep in mind, for this critique remains a constant theme in his *Kleine politischen Schriften*, a series of articles in which Habermas intervenes in public debates in Germany whenever he sees the threat of conservatism. In these texts, his targets are intellectuals such as Arnold Gehlen, Joachim Richter, Carl Schmitt, Helmut Schelsky, and Ernst Nolte as well as neoconservative authors in the United States. I cannot go into details at this point, but we should keep in mind that this critique of a conservative *Volksgemeinschaft* is a very strong motivation in Habermas's political philosophy, which reappears in several moments. The question is, how could we differentiate the fascist affirmation of ethnic identity from the affirmation of identity by oppressed minority communities? This leads us to a discussion of multiculturalism (Kymlicka 1989, 1995, 2001).

Habermas is clearly aware of these ambiguities. What is the alternative he offers? He attempts to articulate a political view of community that is more strictly tied to a normative framework of communicative actions. For example, after observing the connection between work and interaction in Hegel and Marx, and having made the point that language is the condition for reflection (1968b:10, 13, 16–17), Habermas defined communicative action [*kommunikatives Handeln*] as that kind of interaction which does not abstract from human interests, is more participatory, and promotes emancipation (1968b:22, 62–65). As he insists on the primacy of the emancipatory interest, he adds, "The unity of knowledge and interest is guaranteed in a dialectics that reveals what was oppressed in the historical traces of a repressed dialogue" (1968b:164). I can only note en passant that this political demand is definitely based on an implicit ethical or moral concern that is not spelled out. At this point, Habermas is more concerned in saying that the social and political issues at the community level have an epistemic character that cannot be left without scrutiny. However, when he tries to address this epistemic issue in *Knowledge and Human Interests* (1968a), he identifies new challenges represented by positivism and historicism. Also here, his answer refers to the social primacy of a collectivity that has a universal character, as expressed in Mead's notion of a "community of all beings" (1968a:139, 192; Joas 1980:125–128) and Dilthey's view on the "commonalty" of human interests [*Gemeinsamkeit*]. It is from this insight that Habermas proposes communication as the "ideal regulator" of human emancipation, later expanded in the concepts of "ideal speech situation" and "community of communication."

Other political implications of this move are sketched in *Legitimation Crisis of Late Capitalism* (1973), where Habermas postulates a normative ideal based on reason in order to define Critical Theory (1973:192–196). Also here, he is trying to avoid two problems. First, although he does not seem to differentiate clearly enough between legitimacy as a normative outcome and legitimation as a factual political process, his concern is to question the traditional faith in the legitimacy of domination [*Herrschaft*] described by Max Weber and the mechanic solidarity and stress on social facts defined in Émile Durkheim's sociology of religion. Second, he criticizes Luhmann's functionalist and objectivistic view of legitimation through systemic operations because this abstracts from the constitutive commonalty of lifeworlds and from the process of individual identity [*Ich-Identität*], thus leaving issues of normative justification and particularities aside (Habermas 1971b:221, 239; 1973:16). As he challenges Luhmann's system's theory for its focus on an administrative system that leaves no room for subjectivity, the earlier motives of *Structural Transformation of the Public Sphere* reappear (1962:66, 106, 126) and the need for an articulation between community and individual in terms of socialization processes emerges. In looking at how an individual person joins collectivity, we can also observe a reconstructive procedure at work, as Habermas reassesses historical materialism in light of Lawrence Kohlberg's levels of moral development (1976a) and distinguishes between volitional and rational aspects in an individual decision to belong to a certain community. This occurs by means of an evolutionary learning process in which an individual not only develops a discourse that provides meaning to his or her personality, but also takes the role of the other—as Mead proposes—and shares a common ground as "member of the same linguistic community" (1967:157–203, 311–315; 1971b). It is clear, therefore, that Habermas proposes an important critical normative reference to avoid the problems we saw before. He is adamant in upholding the dimension of individuality as a fundamental criterion: if a community disrespects this dimension, it ought to be criticized.

This process is summarized in the second volume of *Theorie des kommunikativen Handelns* (1981a 2:42, 77–88), when the idea of a (real) communication community is consistently applied to show the communicative interaction in the lifeworld, inner world, and external world corresponding to a personal relation with the social world, the objective world, and the subjective world (1981a 2:182–217, see 193). Turning to Durkheim, Habermas insists that the unity of collectivity by means of a sacred force like a community of faith [*Glaubensgemeinschaft*] is not critical enough and should be secularized by a rational and consensual "unity of a communication community" (1981a 2:79, 126, 139; Matuštík 1993:97–104). He does not view a religious conception of community as the proper place for an articulation between individuality and collectivity because this form of community can be authoritarian and coercive. Instead of the Durkheimian anomie or Luhmann's substitution of subjectivity by a cybernetic unit, Habermas follows Mead in order to establish the immanent "appeal to a larger community" as the rational ground for a Discourse Ethics [*Diskursethik*] of Kantian inspiration (1981a 2:119, 141ff.; 1983:45; 1991a:25, 142), but the concept of community is now transformed through a reassessment of Kohlberg, Rawls, and the communitarian debate (1981a 2:429–431; 1983:127; 1992:78–90; 1996:11–64, 65, 237–276). As a result, the pragmatic notion of community starts to play different roles (1983:10; 1991a:147; 1991b:100–101, 155–159; 1992:378; 1996:50–51). In *Between Facts and Norms*, Habermas maintains the idea that a critique of meaning presupposes people communicating and sharing the same "linguistic community" (1992:26), but adds the need to situate such community in daily life, independent from a mere public of experts, and anchored in specific settings. On the one hand, this distances Discourse Philosophy from religious and metaphysical worldviews on community; on the other, it specifies more clearly how Discourse Philosophy relates to legal, political, and moral settings (1992:29–35; Günther 1994:486–487; Höffe 1996:146–147; Baxter 2011:60–70).

A first moment of this strategy is to be found in his remarks on sociology and philosophy of law. After summarizing his critique of Rawls, Habermas considers three legal views on community: the idea of a "liberal community" developed by Ronald Dworkin (Dworkin 1981; Habermas 1992:87), Max Weber's consideration of rationality in terms of "communitarian action" [*Gemeinschaftshandeln*] (Habermas 1992:94, 97), and Talcott Parsons's definition of "societal community" as the nucleus of societal organization (Habermas 1992:99–101). With these three authors, Habermas concludes that a system of law is a legitimate component of the *Lebenswelt*, as it becomes a part of the social integration process, which runs parallel to cultural reproduction and socialization (1992:107–108). In effect, in the reconstructive consideration of the system of rights, law is defined as an abstract system under which individuals are free and equal, and this yields a specific view of a legitimate community as the one based on popular sovereignty and political autonomy—which needs to be distinguished from the popular self-affirmation of a majority. At the same time, he criticizes Apel because "the ideal community of moral capable subjects—the unlimited community of communication from Royce to Apel—enters into the limits of the historical time and the social space by means of the law and gains a concrete, spatio-temporal localized form as a community of rights" (Habermas 1992:136–137). This means that the transcendental community of communication is substituted by the necessary concreteness of subjects acting in a real community of communication according to the prescriptions of legal or constitutional community [*Rechtsgemeinschaft*]. The question now is how to make sense of this new move in light of Habermas's previous views. For him, the moral or universal community of communication is different from but equiprimordial [*gleichursprünglich*] to both the empirical political community (1992:224–225, 263–264) and the legal community (1992:135–136, 181–187, 388–393, 396, 398. See Forst 1994:78–79, 131–132, 144, 395–396; Baynes 1992:215–225). There are many implications in this move. For instance, Habermas establishes forms to minimize ideological manipulation and avoid the limitation to a particular community, since he proposes a loyalty to the democratic procedures in terms of a constitutional patriotism [*Verfassungspatriotismus*] instead of the conservative emphasis on a *Volk*. Also, he stresses the need for concrete democratic institutions that uphold legitimacy standards through concrete participatory processes. Moreover, by stressing the political power of communication he brings communication closer to political practices of social agents in the lifeworld and away from a functionalist system that focuses on the administration of power, money, and other institutional media.

   In all this, Habermas maintains his critique of encompassing and authoritarian views of an ethnocentric, functionalistic, and conservative community—expressed in terms such as "*Volksgemeinschaft*," "*Glaubensgemeinschaft*," and "*System*"—while defending the affirmation of individuality in differentiated communitarian settings: the belonging to a cultural community is implicitly affirmed by means of ethical-existential discourses; the idea of individual autonomy in relation to a moral community is maintained and exercised through moral discourses; the subjective rights of an individual legal person and the corresponding freedom and autonomy guaranteed in terms of private law is acknowledged but at the same time contrasted and correlated with a Kantian definition of autonomy according to public law, which is to be expressed through juridical discourses; furthermore, there is room for the political autonomy of an individual citizen, but this is connected with and restricted by the collective dimension of popular sovereignty, affirmed democratically through political discourses (1992:124–135). Most importantly, however, these conceptions of community and discourse are not strictly separated in conservative or functionalistic ways but keep a certain porosity that allows for mutual influences. As a result, individual freedom, subjective rights, and political autonomy are capable of "transmuting" [*verwandeln*] according to the institutional context in which they are exercised (1992:134–135; Forst 1994:289–306). Most importantly, a democratically conceived political process turns moral conceptions of freedom into "human rights" and makes them compatible with popular sovereignty. Prima facie, it seems that Habermas avoids metaphysics and conservatism by affirming individuality and implicitly including plurality and multiplicity regarding communities (1992:135).

Nevertheless, this empirical point of departure is still limited by a particular nation-state at this stage and does not spell out the encompassing normative ideal that makes it possible for critical norms to be generalizable. This would be the role of a moral discourse with reference to a moral community, but because Habermas has changed his position on this issue, new questions arise. He seems to equate plurality with an internal "problem" that emerges in modern multicultural societies, which requires an internal political solution, not necessarily an asset regarding the plurality of worldviews. Therefore, in *The Inclusion of the Other*, he limits the acceptability of moral foundations on religion because they are associated with forms of religious or metaphysical fundamentalism, nationalism, or ethnocentrism, which are often used by conservative positions (Habermas 1996:11–64, 154). This seems to reduce universalization to an inductive process that could lead to the projection of one community over the variety of communities (1996:284). Due to this problem, a criticism must be brought up. The proposal for constitutional patriotism—that is, the allegiance not to simple historical or cultural contingencies but to democratic procedures—permits a non ethnocentric justification of our belonging to a legal or political community (1990:149), but Habermas then generalizes it to the postnational level (Müller 2007:32), in a move that opens his position to many charges (Fine

2007:44–55). This points to another issue: although Habermas still refers to a moral community in terms of a community of communication, the original universal character of this concept seems weaker now. Therefore, other ideal norms, maxims, or principles are needed, so we can judge this particular move. There is not only the danger of assuming that one specific form of rights or law is crystallized as a representation of the ideal, but also of generalizing the specific result of an internal process of cultural reproduction and socialization over other forms of life and lifeworlds. In the same way that Apel's ideal community cannot be empirical, Habermas's empirical community cannot replace the ideal!

Second, let us turn to Apel's program to transform Kant's philosophy by means of a linguistic conception of community. In light of his transcendental approach he proposes an "*a priori* dialectics of real and ideal unlimited community of communication" that may complement and correct the problem we identified above. In his earlier writings, Apel takes a hermeneutic point of view and criticizes methodical solipsism and individualism, uncovering the "*a priori* commonalty" of Being-with-others (1950:59–64) and stressing the role of language in this process (1963:318–380). At this point, differences become visible: while Habermas is adamant about the importance of *individuality*, Apel seems to give more attention to a critique of *individualism*. Furthermore, Apel considers the question about *community* with an emphasis on a transcendental point of view. On the one hand, he recognizes the hermeneutic "corporeal and historical being-in-the-world of a linguistic community" (1973 1:122, 132, 137); on the other, he complements it with an ideal, based on the fact that the language of such communities already provide the medium for a transcendental reflection on the very conditions of their existence. With his "transcendental hermeneutical" concept of community, he hopes to avoid that a conventional community simply projects its culture without recognizing others.

As we examine the development of the concept of community in Apel's thinking, we find a threefold critique of a hermeneutically oriented philosophy that amplifies the reach of this concept. He recognizes the social dimension—that is, the articulation of individuals in society as shown in Hegel's triadic scheme—agrees with the conditional facticity of hermeneutics, and accepts the multiplicity of forms of life. But in each of these cases, he sees the problem of the crystallization of a particular mediation, the projection of its biases or the problem of ethnocentric self-affirmation, and therefore he insists on the need of constantly "transcending" conventional self-understanding by means of discourse and strict reflection on the ideal conditions of communication and consensus formation [*Konsensbildung*]. Again, he insists on the "transcendental" as a way of promoting the reflective awareness of particular boundaries that must be overcome in order to reach universal *consensus*. In *Transformation of Philosophy* (1973), he establishes the priority of language as the medium for reflection in hermeneutics, pragmatics and semiotics (1973 1:225–377) and works on the idea of the "*a priori* of a community of communication." He insists that the importance should be given not to a particular or conventional language game of a specific community, but to communication as a presupposition to logic and enquiry and as a reflective medium through which a person interacts with nature as well as with other humans. Note that there are two implications of communication in his concept of community: one is more logical qua criteriological, functioning as an ideal norm for discourses in general; the other is more social and implies a critique of political institutions. As mentioned before, these two dimensions correspond to the division between theoretical and practical philosophy, inspired on Kant.

Let us first consider more details about Apel's theoretical philosophy, which takes the *Critique of pure reason* as point of departure and transforms it by appealing to a transcendental semiotics based on the philosophy of Peirce. Here we have a level in which the pragmatism and the semiotics of Peirce in the idea of a "Critical Common-Sense" and a "community of inquirers and interprets" are worked out, as registered in Apel's German edition of Peirce's *Schriften* and in a series of writings (Apel 1967; 1973 2:121–137; 1975/1981:84–85, 134–135; 1994:95). The basic insight taken from Peirce is that the search for truth in science presupposes a community and is open to question and verification, although it cannot be put into question by a simple doubt. It is the process of argumentation that presupposes a wider normative context. In relating Peirce's indefinite community of investigation or inquiry (Peirce 1931 [*CP*] 2:655, 5:356), Royce's community of interpretation, and Mead's universal community of discourse with Peirce's transformation of Kant's universalism and transcendental logic, Apel comes to a synthetic point (Apel 1973 2:157–177, 208, 223–224; 1981:35) and meets the nucleus of the pragmatic maxim: we not only "perceive" and conceptualize but also "interpret ideas with the members of a historical 'Community'" (1973 2:114).

Here we have the transformation of Kant's theoretical philosophy, that is, the *Critique of Pure Reason*. To summarize his lengthy considerations, we can go directly to the central point: the pragmatic-semiotic concept developed first by Peirce allowed Apel to go beyond the mere assumption of a cultural and linguistic community to define the a priori of an intersubjective interaction of real human beings projected toward the future. What is this view of the future? The collective anticipation of an "unlimited community of communication" [*unbegrenzte Kommunikationsgemeinschaft*] (Apel 1973 2:376; 1994a:231–253). This shows a move from solipsism and particularism to a formal universal standpoint based on discursive reflection and interpretation. So now we have a progressive line in the definition of the a priori of the community by Apel: he goes from the linguistic community [*Sprachgemeinschaft*], through the community of communication [*Kommunikationsgemeinschaft*], to the unlimited community of communication [*unbegrenzte Kommunikationsgemeinschaft*] proposed by Peirce, and arrives to the ideal community of communication [*ideale Kommunikationsgemeinschaft*].

Now we have to see how the concept of an ideal and unlimited community of communication is applied also to Apel's practical philosophy. His communicative ethics is anticipated early enough in his writings (1950:123) and then developed jointly with Jürgen Habermas, but articulated in more detail in the essay "Das Apriori der Kommunikationsgemeinschaft und die Grundlagen der Ethik" (1973 2:359–363) and in *Discourse and Responsibility* (1988). Apel announces a central paradox that concerns the necessity but apparent impossibility of a rational justification of ethics in the age of science, rejects the complementarity between value free science and ethical decisionism, and reveals the social implications of this problem (1973 2:359–360, 376). He also proposes a turn to a sophisticated version of the hermeneutic circle as solution (1973 2:386), arguing first that even logic presupposes ethics, since it requires values such as coherence, truthfulness, or verification; and second, that we have to add the recognition of persons as cosubjects and members of a community of communication (1973 2:397, 405, 415, 423).

As he tries to relate these above mentioned aspects to Kant's second *Critique*, Apel bases his ethics on the principles of solidarity and responsibility, from which he derives two basic principles that mirror the a priori dialectics of community: to act in such a way as to guarantee the emancipation and survival of humanity, and to realize the ideal community of communication in a real situation. What he means by this is that the point of departure for a global ethics is not an individual's soliloquy but a dialogue and mutual recognition among members of a "real community of communication" that anticipates an "ideal unlimited community of communication" (Apel 1973 2:358–435; 1988:38–39; 1992:29–61).

Some problems can be mentioned in relation to this formulation: for instance, the dimension of individuality is downplayed and, although he does maintain the dimension of collectivity in the concept of a real community of communication, the spatial and plural dimensions disappear because he seems to operate with a dual view of community that goes directly from the facticity of one's contingency to the dimension of ideal universality—without any mediation. To be fair, Apel does propose the following dialectics as mediation: our participation in a "real community of communication" implies the counterfactual anticipation of an all-inclusive "ideal unlimited community of communication," in which communication shall be free and symmetric. He also adds that a historical difference [*Differenz*] between both needs to be recognized through reflection (Apel 1988:110–122, 141–147). With this dialectical differentiation, he establishes a principle through which individuals can be recognized as equal as they engage in argumentation and to critique society for not having accomplished the universalization of democratic ideals. This is his "dialectical *a priori* of a real and ideal community of communication" (Apel 1973 2:428; 1975/1981:341:345; 1988:141), a structure that administrates—so to speak—the distinction between particularity and universality within a communitarian realm: there is an ideal community of communication (anticipated counterfactually) as there is also a real community of communication (our particular social conditions), and the dialectical relation between both by means of our reflection leads us to recognize the difference and necessary mediation between both. Like Habermas, he insists on the tension between facts and norms (Apel 1988:45–55, 453; 1993:150–152, 167–170).

Apel's conclusion is relevant because it affirms that universal measures are needed for universal problems—that is, particularism is not the answer to totalitarian universalism. However, his dialectics remain somewhat dualist: he fails to acknowledge that between the factual linguistic community and the ideal community of argumentation there are many different language games and communities to be considered. It is necessary to go beyond the impression that there are only two communities—the one that prevails in one's historical, cultural, and linguistic horizon and the opposition to it in an ideal community. Rather, I propose that we recognize that there are different simultaneous communities that are in interaction and sometimes even in conflict, in such a way that they might mirror the universal in different aspects, but never completely. As I mentioned before, there could be fragments of an ideal that can be brought together by means of intercultural communication. An ideal universality can be conceived only as a consensual sum of these fragments. Moreover, there is also the need for the clarification of one's individual situation amid the plurality of communities: one aspect of the ideal community of communication, such as the existence of democratic institutions, can be evidenced in a real community; an additional aspect, such as the openness to distinct cultural forms, can be given in another.

It is fair to conclude, therefore, that there is an intrinsic plurality at play in overlapping forms of community and different lines of argumentation, but Apel and Habermas seem to neglect the dimension of plurality and fail to explore a more pluralistic conception of community. Habermas offers a strong and detailed articulation of individuality and collectivity while identifying what we need to avoid as negatively ambiguous and problematic and contemporary appropriations of community. He also maintains a somewhat weak reference to universality because he downplays the role of the moral community in complementing the legal and political order. Apel provides a much stronger view of ideal universality, which he connects dialectically with a concrete collectivity while maintaining the emphasis on the concept of a communication community. He rightly points out the universal character of communication but does not recognize sufficiently the plural perspectives involved in the claim to universality in a global context, which require a more explicit commitment to intercultural communication. While Habermas allows for plurality within particular multicultural societies and even considers the emerging postnational constellation, he does not work out in detail the implications of plurality at the global level. Community of communication or discourse community [*Diskursgemeinschaft*] is a common concept to both of them, but they fail to articulate the four dimensions I defined as necessary for a critical position: individuality, collectivity, plurality, and universality. Therefore, we need to make sure we affirm *global plurality* more vehemently.

GLOBAL PLURALITY AND THE MULTIDIMENSIONAL COMMUNITY

I began this chapter with some questions regarding the meaning of community. To answer these questions, I provided an overview of several historical definitions of community, as well as a typology of communities, moving from religious through political to economic and cultural versions of collectivity that have influenced Western history. The concept of community is definitely pluralistic. It has been used by different social, political, economic, cultural, environmental, and religious movements under a variety of meanings. I discussed several of these meanings, but also acknowledged that they are in constant flux. Among the main challenges, we found that new positions based on dogmatic metaphysics, authoritarian conservatism, functionalism, positivism, historicism, and communitarianism rely on particularistic notions of community that ought to be rejected.

The variety of meanings attached to community can always be revived, so it is important to keep in mind what their underlying theoretical assumptions are, what their specific practical applications could be, and how tensions internal to the idea of community surface in different areas. Within this analysis, I have argued that the most important resulting tension is between individuality and collectivity; the most important challenge is the recognition of plurality and differences; and the most important value is the pursuit of universality. Community is certainly opposed to individualism—especially in its egoistical economic form—but it cannot eliminate individual dimensions such as freedom and autonomy. This is the criticism that can be brought against totalitarian views of economic and religious communities, and other forms of authoritarian communities that exclude individuals based on taboos, behaviors, or ideologies. To avoid this problem, a critical and progressive concept of community needs to account for individuality without falling into individualism, collectivity instead of authoritarian collectivism, plurality rather than cultural relativism, and universality as the antidote to assimilatory practices characterized negatively as universalism. Let me just give a couple of examples to highlight this point.

A conservative concept of community has at least three basic characteristics: it is empirically defined, internally limited, and externally ambiguous—due to the rhetorical combination of different contradictory values. Community, in a conservative sense, is a closed social institution that can be defined in opposition to those who are considered external to these structures and thus seen as enemies or outsiders. This point was clearly defended by Carl Schmitt. The neo-conservative appropriation of this term, however, was able to provide a more sophisticated combination of social, cultural, and economic conceptions of community. But instead of questioning the exclusion, and imposition of power or authoritarianism, it promotes assertions of power both at the domestic level and in international relations. Therefore, conservative and neoconservative conceptions may contribute to the dimension of collectivity but do not pass the critical test implicit in a multidimensional conception of community.

Communitarians distance themselves from conservatism and question some liberal assumptions, especially the primacy of individualism in economic and political liberalism and its conceptions of justice, autonomy, and rationality. They value grassroots movements, have an open conception of community as a cultural marker, and show social concern for the situation of impoverished groups. However, these different authors and groups criticize various aspects of liberalism, but do not provide an analytical differentiation between forms of liberalism. There is a critical intention here, as communitarians emphasize community to criticize metaphysics and abstraction, reject perfectionism and neutrality, value a plurality of cultures, question individualism, and assess the negative impacts of these views on society. Nevertheless, communitarianism is not clear about the internal workings of communities. Here we find a lack of clarity on the dimension of individuality, so this position needs to be criticized on this point.

A critical perspective on community has to address these issues. First, we must understand, differentiate, and categorize our various conceptions of community. Second, it is necessary to understand their origins, intentions, and entailments so that we are able to understand what differentiates a religious community committed to a liberation movement in Latin America and a group of religious fundamentalists in Asia. Third, we do not need to remain "pure" in the definition of a community, but we can explore the combinations that are adequate to particular goals. What would be a possible good way of promoting a critical conception of community? It is important to identify and distinguish the plurality of meanings in such a way that we know what to expect, are open enough to include differences, allow for porous boundaries, and negotiate the articulation of these distinct elements by means of a participatory process. A new theory and practice of community should be based on the idea of a *multidimensional community*. By observing the strategies of those conceptions we are trying to avoid, we realize that it is possible to go beyond their strategies, thus enlarging its explanatory power and application. It is possible to avoid the negative ambiguity in the appeal to community by criticizing any process that maintains structures of exclusion in any of the previously defined dimensions. This means that we have to apply the test of *multidimensional community* constantly and permanently take four important dimensions into account.

First, we need to guarantee that *individuality* remains an important value, especially in the establishment of communities. This concern was particularly salient in our discussion of Habermas. By upholding this dimension, we correct a neglected dimension in communitarian thinking: individuality and individual choice. We need to recognize that a community is made up of individuals and groups that join together in a collectivity, based on choice and mutual recognition. If they share a common belief or a common interest, they might accept to form a collectivity based on different values such as religious, political, economic, or cultural references. Therefore, the definition of individual is central to the understanding of a community, as individuals and groups are the ones that form a collectivity. Individuality—not individualism—is the first dimension.

The second dimension is that of *collectivity*. Many conceptions of community equate a community to a collectivity, to a common public background based on a given value. This makes sense, because joining a community is not limited to individual choice. There is a collectivity that either accepts or rejects this individual. In a religious community, the individual must assume certain vows while a liberal political community is based on a balance between private and collective *interests*. An individual may seek the membership in a collectivity for reasons of safety, opportunities, refuge, and economic guaranties without being necessarily concerned about cultural issues or matters of faith. For example, ritual practices such as baptism, ceremonies, songs, and prayers may identify a Christian religious community while the allegiance to a nation, belonging to an ethnic group, acceptance of certain symbols, speaking of a language, belonging to specific organizations, and other external markers can provide a collective political identity. This means that a community not only accepts a particular individual, but also requires a certain behavior or external indication that he or she shares the values of that particular community. The collectivity exerts some pressure upon this individual and establishes conditions for belonging. In my view, this can be fair if individual rights are respected, but this needs to be evaluated in light of the other dimensions also. If we stop at the level of collectivity, we risk falling into a particularistic conception of community limited to a nation-state or similar structures. If a particular community identifies itself as the only community or the "chosen" community, integration process can well lead to repression, conflict, assimilation or exclusion. Therefore, referring to a combination of factors may provide an extra normative guidance to avoid these problems.

The third dimension is the recognition of *plurality*. It is obvious that there is a plurality of understandings of community, such as a communities based on faith, legal concepts, economic production, culture, and so on. This indicates already that community is partly defined in relation to a system or function within society and partly defined in relation to something external to it, and not only by its internal constitution through individual participation. For instance, by specifying political or cultural values, a given community differentiates itself from religious collectivities. Similarly, a particular political community establishes differences in relation to other polities. It is at this point that limits are defined. Anthropologically speaking, those who are outsiders may not share this common understanding, fail to grasp the shared meanings, and therefore be doomed to exclusion. In a political community, there is the noncitizen; in a religious community, the nonbeliever; and in a scientific community the limits are defined by technical expertise. Yet, the fact that someone is excluded from a religious group does not necessarily mean that she cannot be a member of a scientific association. Individuals can be members of several communities and move in and out of them. While a traditional view of community requires that a certain group views the "other" as radically different and inferior in order to affirm itself, the acceptance of an overlapping plurality of communities presupposes that within one particular community we will interact with those that may also belong to differing communities. The consideration of plurality allows us to recognize that there are others who move in and out of particular settings—freely or not. If we see this in light of systems and institutions, an individual may go to a religious community on Sunday, but then participate in an economic community on Monday and join a cultural group on Tuesday. These experiences can overlap. From the perspective of the lifeworld, other issues arise. One example is the "double consciousness" of African American ethnic and political identity in particular moments in the history of the Americas. Being excluded from citizenship in American nations by slavery and segregation, African descendants searched for their identity in a distant past and origin in Africa while being connected to a contingent location. Here individuality is a complementary dimension that helps us to make sense of individuals coming in and out of different communities. In conclusion, this internal plurality adds more complexity to our conception of community and indicates the availability of options and alternatives in a multicultural society.

I indirectly mentioned some external aspects as well, which go beyond a multicultural context and refer to an intersocietal realm that I define as *intercultural plurality*. The fact that communities include some individuals with their values and behavior and exclude others does not necessarily mean that they are impermeable. There are external communities in relations of mutual direct and indirect influence! For example, cultural meanings can be communicated or even appropriated, practices can be learned, and values can be expanded or changed. Thus, African American musical styles usually sung in a church can be learned by other groups and used in political campaigns—as the civil rights movement did. Marxist ideas about economic cooperation can be combined with Confucian ritual practices—as observed in the Cultural Revolution in China. European values have influenced Latin America as observed in the struggle against colonialism. Similarly, traditional ideas that seemed to be restricted to the United States can be learned by other cultures in the same way as other cultures now influence the United States. It is easy to conclude, therefore, that even though communities may seem closed at first, there are openings that permit the transfer of peoples, values, and practices, so that individuals excluded in a given collectivity may be accepted in another. The openings we see in certain communities may serve as entry points for excluded individuals and groups. This recognition of intercultural plurality has yet another consequence. At a more abstract level that corresponds to the complexity of our contemporary world society, we could say that individuals and groups may not only belong to a community of faith, but also express a political allegiance to a nation identified with a particular territory, participate in an economic community beyond the nation-state, and share cultural values that may correspond to regional frameworks—as seen in the case of the European Union.

It is at this point that we need to add *global universality*, a fourth dimension that can be called intercommunitarian, understood as the transcendence of given boundaries to search for an ideal space "in between," a consensus in which our perceptions of community may converge. This, however, needs to occur without giving up what is gained through multicultural and intercultural plurality. Today individuals have choices to leave or join several communities at the same time, precisely due to a plurality of communities and a space, an interstice, between them. The complexity of Western societies not only frees the individual from certain strict forms of belonging or defines new profiles of responsibility and leadership, but also opens the opportunity for plural memberships due to voluntary or even forced shifts that change traditional boundaries. Economic hardships, ideological differences, political persecutions, cultural affinities, cultural globalization, or human rights can serve as reasons for the questioning of one's own boundaries, so that we can go in and out of different communities and express our religious, political, gender, economic, cultural, or ethnic differences. Many contemporary communities seem to be able to allow this in and out movement of individuals and groups, although in most cases it is easier to let people out than welcome others in—immigrants, asylum seekers, refugees, and even tourists. The sensitivity to the threats of individual terrorists has made these systems of exclusion even more efficient. However, by upholding the normativity of globality, we can at least measure these movements, classify communities according to their level of tolerance, wellbeing, openness, or inclusiveness, and criticize their practices.

Surely, no community has been able yet to provide an ideal situation in which all these elements converge. For example, a given community may provide economic opportunities to outsiders, but exclude them from cultural participation or disregard their language and ethnic origin. This also means that this particular community may combine a series of elements that seemed contradictory, but still lack certain elements—or dimensions—that would transform it into a more democratic, just, or open community. Along these lines, it is possible to criticize this particular community because it does not fulfill all possible dimensions. Generally, the perspective of an outsider helps us to identify these shortcomings. This is how the encounter with the "other of global plurality" gains a normative significance. Yet, a question remains, why should we bother to work out a definition of multidimensional community if this seems like an unattainable ideal?

At this point, I need to reaffirm and redefine the multidimensional community. First, it is a community that is formed by individuals— thus recognizing certain values, such as freedom, creativity, singularity, and others, instead of imposing its values upon all its members in the same way. This proviso allows us to recognize some important values of individuality, freedom, and personal leadership or responsibility without falling into the trap of individualism. Second, it is a community that defines its values and provides a set of expectations in terms of behavior and concrete references, through which it judges, accepts, or rejects its individual members. By defining its values, such community also establishes what differentiates itself from other communities. A multidimensional community, however, adds a third condition as it recognizes an inherent plurality that seems to be neglected very often. This acceptance of plurality has many consequences: it shows that there are insiders and outsiders, recognizes that it defines itself in relation or opposition to other communities, and it includes channels for individuals and groups to move in and out of different communitarian experiences, thus allowing individuals and groups to express themselves in a variety of ways. The problem, however, is that this plurality may be seen as a form of relativism in which anything goes or also a form of power granted to gatekeepers who allow mobility to certain individuals and groups. Therefore, a fourth condition is necessary, which adds the universality of an ideal ethical community of communication in which the normativity of freedom, mutual recognition, justice, and other expandable and nonrestrictive initiatives can be promoted as global. It is in the light of these values that we can measure the porosity and flexibility of a community, its capability of accepting new members and of promoting inclusion instead of exclusion. Finally, all we would need is an open public field for intercommunitarian connections, in which we could participate in an open debate on community expectations. One could argue that this is only a dream of an ideal community. However, it also works as a model to integrate individuality, collectivity, and plurality as complementary to universality and as a criterion to criticize societies for not promoting these dimensions. Without these dimensions, universality could be an authoritarian imposition of global views that contradict freedom, diversity, mobility, and participation. Only when these different dimensions complement and correct each other in the space of intercommunitarian relations, we can have a glimpse of a *multidimensional community.*

Based on these points, I conclude this chapter by returning to my presentation and interpretation of a critical and multifarious concept of community in Discourse Philosophy. I am using the categories of both universal-pragmatic Discourse Theory and transcendental-pragmatic Discourse Ethics while adding my own considerations on *universality* and *multidimensionality.* The important point I want to emphasize is the need for criteria to differentiate between political imposition and cultural assimilation through the generalization of particular institutions and intercultural processes of agreement based on a pluralistic conception of community that includes a strong ethical norm.

In my opinion, we need to neither fall into metaphysical assumptions to assume an ideal position, nor consider ethics as intrinsically or necessarily utopian and intrinsically negative in order to affirm the possibility of a critical view as compatible with autonomy and sovereignty. Rather, we need to recognize the plurality of perspectives, the possibility of one being a participant in such a plurality, and the existence of channels of communication and publicity beyond crystallized institutions. The obvious formal question now concerns the relation of this multidimensional model to Discourse Philosophy in general. With Habermas, the issue of individuality gains a systematic place, as we saw above, but Apel indirectly allows an individual to put the conventional understanding of community into question on the basis of a reflection on common ethical ideals. One way of articulating these views is to say that individual claims are always expressed through processes—in the language of the Discourse Principle (D)—potentially "affect" or involve other persons and communities at different levels. Thus, the multidimensional test has a complementary normative function.

In the end, adding plurality more explicitly as an element of the multidimensional discourse community affects personal individuality, social institutional reality, and global universality. As I took the real and ideal community of communication into account as a wider normative basis, complemented it with aspects of social and political action, and insisted on the element of plurality, I reaffirmed the primacy of ethical and moral norms. Therefore, Discourse Ethics should guide us in matters related to a strong ideal or universal *justification* or *grounding* of norms while Discourse Theory provides internal specifications for matters of institutional *legitimation* and systematic *application* of such norms with regard to individuality and collectivity according to a socialization process. Therefore, despite the criticisms and changes I proposed, I also reaffirm my commitment to Discourse Philosophy and its definition of a discourse community.

5

FROM PLURALITY TO GLOBAL HUMAN RIGHTS DISCOURSES

Contemporary views on human rights are built upon deep foundations in shared community values that can be traced back to developments that occurred not only in the past decades, but also in the last centuries and millennia. Like the tradition of critique, the positions within Discourse Philosophy, and the notions of community I have reviewed, conceptions of human rights have undergone transformations as well. In the previous chapters, I accounted for the plurality of communities and applied the conception of a multidimensional discourse community as a guide for sorting out and criticizing various community concepts and practices. I will now expand the application of this framework and relate it to the global discussion on human rights. I understand plurality not simply as the inner variety proper of multicultural societies but also as the outer variety that emerges through intercultural relations. This recognition of intercultural plurality brings a new set of challenges and has been the topic of intensive debates regarding human rights discourses, especially because some cultural traditions charge that the repertoire of rights defined in the new paradigm established by the *Universal Declaration on Human Rights* reflects values that go back to the European Enlightenment or to Christianity, thus revealing a problematic Eurocentric bias. As a result, new regional cultural discourses have emerged and appealed to specific interpretations of rights and humanity, which are now being retrieved to orient and update discourses on human rights in particular settings.

Based on Discourse Philosophy and the proposal for a multidimensional understanding of plural communities of communication, I want to address this issue by moving in two directions: first, by stressing the differentiation between inner *multicultural plurality* and outer *intercultural plurality*; second, by connecting this plurality to philosophical paradigms that help us to differentiate, acknowledge, accept, or criticize the plurality conceptions of human rights presented in the global context. To introduce examples of this existing variety, I turn to Karl Jaspers's theory of the "Axial times" [*Achsenzeit*], which refers to the simultaneous and independent appearance of new worldviews that made a passage from mythical and religious perspectives to more elaborated ethical, political, cultural, and scientific systems a few millennia ago. The concept of axial times allows me to account for cultures and traditions as diverse as ancient Mesopotamia and Egypt, contemporary Asia and Africa, and modern Europe and the Americas as well as institutionalized religious systems that offer specific definitions of rights and humanity. Prima facie, these traditions remain opposed to philosophical conceptions that emerge out of "natural law" and "natural rights" tradition in Europe, which led to more secular and epistemic approaches to human rights characteristic of the European Enlightenment. I sort out these approaches by combining Jaspers's horizontal perspective on the plurality of cultures with Thomas Kuhn's description of scientific revolutions as "paradigm shifts." In so doing, I simply radicalize a move already made by Habermas and Apel in their postulate of an evolution from metaphysics to postmetaphysical thinking by means of a process that includes three comprehensive worldviews: ancient metaphysical traditions and religious views on humanity and law that are still influential today; natural and civil rights theories implicit in many European philosophies and explicitly made into positive law by national constitutional frameworks; and contemporary theories and practices that have emerged in tandem with the most recent wave of human rights documents, initiatives, global mechanisms, and institutions, which interpret human rights in light of contemporary discursive categories. Relying on these differentiations, I ultimately side with contemporary philosophical comprehension of human rights as discourses embedded in a community of communication. However, it is necessary to consider other worldviews in an effort to have a more contingent and cogent view of the universality of human rights without losing sight of their intrinsic inner and outer plurality.

Once the multicultural plurality of communities is expanded to the outer plurality yielded by intercultural communication, it becomes clear how paradigmatic understandings of humanity and rights are not simply abstract categories but also realities. The social, legal, and political experiments in the European Union and the Inter-American System as well as initiatives on human rights at the level of the African

Union, the League of Arab States, and the Association of Southeast Asian Nations are examples of this trend. I obviously draw more positive consequences from this plurality than the assumption that they lead to a "clash of civilizations"—as stated by Samuel Huntington. Based on the paradigmatic understandings of human rights and the model of a multidimensional community of communication I believe we can derive the resources and criteria to address the tension between plurality and universality.

THE CHALLENGE: A TENSION BETWEEN PLURALITY AND UNIVERSALITY

The emergence of contemporary discourses on human rights is traditionally characterized as the materialization of a *new paradigm* marked by the *Magna Carta* of the United Nations in 1945, the Nuremberg Trials between 1945 and 1949, the prosecution of crimes against humanity committed by the German National-Socialist regime, and the proclamation of a nonbinding *Universal Declaration on Human Rights* in 1948. This paradigmatic change involved the creation of other mechanisms such as the *American Declaration of the Rights and Duties of Man* in 1948, the *European Convention for the Protection of Human Rights and Fundamental Freedoms* in 1950, and many other instruments, culminating with the establishment of the International Criminal Court in 2002, which is the institution with authority to prosecute cases of crimes against humanity (Arendt 1959:188–199; 1977:253–279; Bassiouni 1999; Luban 2004; May 2005). Other initiatives resulted from this paradigmatic change, but because the *Universal Declaration* was nonbinding, some nations initially abstained from voting on it and many others continue to disrespect its contents. Consequently, several analysts have concluded that only the positivity of constitutional law at the level of the nation-state would be able to guarantee compliance with human rights norms. However, with globalization, the creation of international courts to prosecute "crimes against humanity," the organization of humanitarian interventions authorized by the United Nations and justified in terms of a "responsibility to protect," the establishment of regional mechanisms to promote and protect human rights, and the involvement of nongovernmental organizations and private corporations in human rights initiatives, there is now a multilevel approach to human rights beyond statecentric measures and a search for a justification of such approach in terms of both plurality and universality.

The Universality of "Humans" and "Rights"

Based on my introductory remarks, it can be suggested that a new normative reference to "humanity"—implicit in terms such as "laws of humanity," "crimes against humanity," or "human rights" (Bassiouni 1999:17–18)—provides the background to recent paradigmatic shifts that should be taken into account by human rights discourses. This fundamental, albeit implicit and vague conception of the quality of being human refers to the aggregation of humans that form humanity, the bearers of rights, and the jurisdiction of such rights, which shall not be limited to a particular national community or even to international law but refer to a universal dimension.

Humanity is a fundamental concept behind this radical shift (Bohman 2007:101–102). However, recent discussions about human rights have given much more emphasis on the meaning of *rights* than to the meaning of *human* because references to human worth, human dignity, human needs, or human capabilities are deemed too metaphysical or weak to provide a stable foundation for the universality of human rights. Bohman relies on Jaspers and Arendt to provide an insightful distinction between humanness and humanity as to better qualify the status of what is "human" in human rights. He also accounts for the plurality of political communities, which he identifies as *dêmoi*, but his focus is on the self-understanding of modern democracy. If we also include the plurality of paradigms, other distinctions may emerge. Furthermore, we need to include a discussion on universality. Justifying the inalienability or universality of human rights poses numerous challenges, so many philosophers prefer to leave this theme aside. As a result, the issue remains unaddressed and unresolved.

For instance, the General Assembly of the United Nations proclaimed the *Declaration* as "a common standard of achievement for all peoples and all nations," which was to be promoted by progressive national and international measures so that the rights it listed could receive universal recognition. Note that universality is aspirational; it is a normative goal to be achieved by national and international measures, so the *Declaration* is not describing how reality *is* but rather proposing how it *ought to be* and establishing a criterion based upon which we can judge how well these national and international measures may work. Also, among the rights that ought to become universal, the first article of the *Declaration* affirms unequivocally, "All human beings are born free and equal in dignity and rights. They are endowed with reason and conscience and should act towards one another in a spirit of brotherhood." If taken as a description, this statement is unrealistic and open to the attack Jeremy Bentham once brought against the first article of the French *Declaration des droits de l'homme* in 1789: humans are not necessarily born free or remain free, for a variety of reasons. In response to this charge, Thomas Pogge writes that this right can be analyzed in two components: "First, all human beings have exactly the same human rights. And second: The moral significance of human rights and human-rights violations does not vary" (Pogge 2008:63). It is fair to conclude that this article of the *Declaration* affirms, that *each* and *every* individual human being *ought to be* born under conditions of freedom, that is *equal* among all of them, and that this refers not to *some* humans or some *kind* of humans, but to *all* humans. It is upon this intricate and complex basis that the *Declaration* expands the repertoire of rights and describes a total of 30 articles with specific items to be respected and protected by the signatory countries.

One way in which these rights have been interpreted is as a series of six or more families of entitlements that can be claimed by individuals and groups according to the following categories: *liberty rights* that protect freedoms in areas such as belief, expression, association, assembly, and movement; *equality rights* that guarantee equal citizenship, equality before the law, and nondiscrimination; *due process rights* that protect against abuses of the legal system such as imprisonment without trial, secret trials, and excessive punishments; *security rights* that protect people against crimes such as murder, massacre, torture, and rape; *political rights* that protect the liberty to participate in politics through actions such as communicating, assembling, protesting, voting, and serving in public office; and *social (or "welfare") rights* that require provision of education to all children, protections against severe poverty and starvation, and promotion of environmental sustainability. Another family that might be included is *group rights* that include protections of ethnic groups against genocide and the external ownership of their national territories and resources. This last category of rights, including "self-determination," has emerged recently in human rights discourses, for although the *Universal Declaration on Human Rights* does not include group rights, subsequent treaties do (Hayden 2001; Donnelly 2003, 2007; Anaya 2004; Smith 2010).

A different way of understanding and classifying these rights is by defining "generations." Liberty rights, including civil and political rights, would correspond to "first generation rights" because they have a longer historical tradition and are seen as basic rights to be enshrined in modern constitutional frameworks. "Second generation rights" expand the repertoire of rights to include basic entitlements that should be equally available, such as the right to economic subsistence, education, work, housing, and health care (Cranston 1967:43–51; Waldron 1993:5–6, 339–369). Rights of the "third generation" include the recognition of minorities and other social issues not included in previous generations, adding another layer of "new" concepts. These brief ways of cataloging rights should be enough to imply that rights are not static but are always changing (Smith 2010:176). There are yet other ways of understanding and classifying human rights: protecting the "negative liberties" of the individual—that is, the actions that states should refrain from taking; promoting "positive rights" through agents such as states and other providers; and "solidarity rights" as recommendations for possible actions aimed at fostering human culture, institutions, languages, and traditions. Reflecting on the historical process through which these rights emerged and the existence of different normative frameworks erected to justify them, the articles of the *Declaration* have been understood in terms of "moral rights," "legal rights," or "political rights." Scholars have given considerable theoretical effort to define them according to structural, constructivist, cosmopolitan, and attributive approaches (Chwaszcza 2010). There is much controversy regarding this repertoire and many ethical, juridical, and political debates revolve around how to define, justify, and apply these rights (Talbott 2005:19–22). Certainly, they are plural, and open to interpretation.

Another characterization points out to a "human rights paradigm" that denotes the growing positive acceptance of these rights as legal norms that have a legitimizing impact on the international order (Teitel 1997:302–304). According to this understanding, human rights are a matter of international law, whose clauses might have been inspired by moral considerations but which are legally binding on nation-states and expressed through practical discourses (Beitz 2009:106–113; for a critique, see Lafont 2010:198f.). Abdullahi An-Na'im clearly defines this perspective in the following way: "By the term 'human rights paradigm,' I mean the articulation and application of the same norms to every human being everywhere, a standard that presupposes the validity of cross-cultural moral judgment and requires systematic efforts to influence state policy and practice in matters that were previously deemed to be subject to the exclusive domestic jurisdiction of the state" (2000:907). This focus on rights and functional institutions has many advantages, but reports on how states fail to protect or promote human rights in various regions and the role of nonstate actors allow me to question this optimist conclusion. An-Na'im insists that "due to the activism of civil society around the world, the human rights paradigm has become such a powerful legitimising force in national politics and international relations that no government in any part of the world today would openly reject or defy its dictates" (An-Na'im 2000:937). This consistent use of the terms "rights" and "paradigm" assumes that official governments and institutions delegated by them are ultimately the ones legally bound by the *Universal Declaration on Human Rights* and other instruments. In this view, it is this legally binding framework of rights, not duties or the implicit reference to humanity, that defines what is paradigmatic.

Beyond this interpretation, it is also possible to read the *Universal Declaration on Human Rights* and its corollary documents as providing a corresponding taxonomy of conceptions of humanity (Bohman 2007:101–134). In fact, the preamble of the *Declaration* affirms the "recognition of the inherent dignity and of the equal and inalienable rights of all members of the human family." Moreover, as the first article states, human beings are the bearers of both dignity and rights: "All human beings are born free and equal in dignity and rights." A recurrent accusation here is that this statement implies the acceptance of a metaphysical view of human nature. Yet, although what counts as human was expressed rather vaguely or made explicit only in general terms, humanity has been spelled out in a series of documents that specify who would count as humans and what would be considered as rights. Therefore, new documents came to complement the *Universal Declaration*, such as the *International Covenant on Civil and Political Rights* (1966), the *International Covenant on Economic, Social and Cultural Rights* (1966), the *Convention on Biological Diversity*, the *International Labor Convention No 169 Concerning Indigenous and Tribal Peoples in Independent Countries* (1989), the *Convention on the Rights of the Child* (1989), the *Declaration on the Rights of Persons Belonging to National or Ethnic, Religious and Linguistic Minorities* (1992), the *Convention Concerning the Protection of the World Cultural and Natural Heritage*, and the *Declaration on the Rights of Indigenous Peoples* (2007), among many others instruments that specify the rights of women, children, ethnic minorities, indigenous peoples, and other group identities (Smith 2010). There is no need to stress the plurality implied in these documents. *Women's rights* would address specific issues related to bodily integrity—that is, protection from violence directed specifically against women—protection against discrimination, access to democratic participation, education and professional opportunities, equal pay, reproductive justice, and others. *Children's rights* are implicitly expressed in the *Universal Declaration on Human Rights*, but because children are not always afforded full human status—on developmental, biological, legal, political, or cultural grounds—rights to nondiscrimination or abuse, birth registration, family and nationality, privacy as well as education, health care, and leisure—including the right to be protected from economic exploitation from their own families—needed to be reaffirmed and made explicit. *Ethnic minorities' rights* include the right to survival and existence, protection of identity, nondiscrimination, and participation in public life. *Indigenous peoples' rights* have some overlap with minority rights, but make specific the particular contexts of indigenous peoples. After centuries of oppression and the continuous threat to their existence as well as conflicting understandings of sovereignty, citizenship, and protection [*tutelage*] of indigenous peoples, specific documents affirm their collective rights to cultural development, to their own legal systems, to guarantees against genocide or assimilation, and especially to self-determination (Nussbaum 2001b; Anaya 2004; Bohman 2007; Archard 2010). This variety of human rights documents makes apparent the plethora of understandings of humanity and the rights asserted by or ascribed to various groups that claim recognition.

Based on what I have considered so far, it is possible to draw some initial conclusions. First, there is a plurality of normative instances as well as plural positive means to address, define, justify, implement, and guarantee the rights of different claims to humanity. Yet, in philosophical debates on human rights discourses, the human dimension that ought to guide the ascription of rights is rarely addressed. Second, in the drafting process of the *Universal Declaration on Human Rights* the specific and varied conceptions of humanity brought to the table by the committee members were bracketed out in order to arrive at a pragmatic agreement (Ishay 2004; Morsink 2009; Moyn 2010). Since then, an increasing body of literature keeps reminding us that human rights are not only international and national norms, laws, and rules but also expressions of biological and cultural assumptions on what counts as human. This is very important because a common way of denying rights is to deny humanity—so, for a long time indigenous peoples, peoples of African ancestry, women, and children were not considered fully human and the same can be said of people with disabilities and those who do not define themselves according to traditional gender definitions. Third, another implication of this initial discussion is that despite the tendency to see rights as absolute neutral standards, they are embedded in human cultures that influence the way we develop and interpret legal frameworks. Rights are not immune to political and economic policies but rather related with them in ways that can influence their effectiveness. This may explain the wisdom of placing humanity and rights together in the definition of *human rights*, for they critically complement each other.

The Quest for Plurality

The attempt to stress the intercultural plurality of humanity and rights as a way to affirm their universality is not free of risk. Historical research has provided much detail on the drafting of the *Universal Declaration on Human Rights* and the issues discussed among members of the committee established in 1947 and chaired by Eleanor Roosevelt. The drafting committee had intercultural representation and, already at that point, tensions between European and Asian worldviews as well as between Muslim and Christian beliefs emerged, which had to be put aside in order to achieve a wider consensus (Ishay 2004:218f.; Morsink 2009:92f.; Moyn 2010:84f.). Currently, however, these issues have resurfaced and this pragmatic solution appears as less compelling.

One particular tension refers to questions concerning what counts as universal in human rights. While those who emphasize legal rights assume that providing a legal foundation is a way out of the vicissitudes of moral conceptions and cultural idiosyncrasies, those who oppose such emphasis on legal conceptions charge that they are Western values in disguise, which are imposed upon other cultures (Bell and Bauer 1999; Langlois 2001; Sen 2003; Talbott 2005). In 1990, when the United Nations decided to convene a World Conference on Human Rights, the international environment seemed to offer a historical opportunity for giving human rights a central position in world affairs. The euphoria, however, was misplaced. Instead of focusing on further developments for a global human rights protection system on the basis of the liberal tradition, member states became engulfed in debates about fundamental and competing conceptual issues. Several Asian states questioned the applicability of universal human rights in different cultural, economic, and social settings and affirmed the specificity of a Confucian tradition in ethics and human rights (van Dijk 1995; Confucius 1998; de Bary and Weiming 1998; Chang and Kalmanson 2010; Yu, Tao, and Ivanhoe 2010). The Asian regional preparatory meeting that took place in Bangkok between March 29 and April 2, 1993, resulted in the *Bangkok Declaration on Human Rights* signed by over 40 Asian governments and provided an opportunity for Asian governments to put forward their definition of human rights on the global agenda. It did not reject universal human rights but its article 8 suggested that universality should be considered "in the context of a dynamic and evolving process of international norm-setting, bearing in mind the significance of national and regional particularities and various historical, cultural and religious backgrounds." The document also sought to link social and economic development issues with human rights questions and emphasizes the importance of noninterference (Bell and Bauer 1999:3–5).

A similar challenge has been brought against "Western values" in 1990 by Middle Eastern cultures and countries identifying themselves as Muslim states, which affirm that they already have a set of human rights, which was established in the seventh century of the Common Era (Bielefeldt 1998). As An-Na'im concedes in his discussion about human rights and Islam, the philosophical point supporting these initiatives is the assumption that it is not possible or desirable "to identify a set of neutrally formulated human rights. Any normative regime, which justifies a set of rights and provides or informs their content, must necessarily represent a commitment to a specific value system" (1995:229). Based on this conviction, the *Cairo Declaration of Human Rights in Islam* formulates a set of specifically Islamic human rights defined in terms of Shar'ia law (An-Na'im 1990, 1995, 2008, and 2010; Dallmayr 2002; Scott 2009). Thus, its article 24 states, "All the rights and freedoms stipulated in this Declaration are subject to the Islamic Shari'ah," creating an immediate conflict with human rights norms because practices such as stoning, amputation, or restriction of women's accessibility to public areas as defined in Shar'ia law are not subject to hermeneutic interpretation. An-Na'im has championed an approach to make these normative claims compatible and the Organization of Islamic Cooperation (OIC) has established an Independent Permanent Human Rights Commission in 2011 with the objective to "advance human rights" and "support the Member States' efforts to consolidate civil, political, economic, social and cultural rights." But even within this tradition there is little consensus on what counts as human rights (Khan 2003). There is, however, a common assumption that human rights can be interpreted in relation to particular development goals.

Even within the Western context, there are internal criticisms to the claim to universality. For instance, there is a suspicion that human rights represent a mere political strategy elaborated in the nineteenth century for colonial reasons, influenced by the Cold War between the United States and the Soviet Union, or designed as a device to allow the questioning of German constitutionality after World War II. (Koskenniemi 2001; Morsink 2009; Moyn 2010). Also, there are traditional debates discussing whether moral, legal, or political rights should have priority and what should be the criteria to justify them as universal (Talbott 2005). Moreover, recent philosophical positions are more concerned with the logical structure and practical application of language and communication in our understanding of human rights.

With the globalization process and the relativization of national borders, structures, and legal arrangements, a clear consequence is a postnational situation that turns many national frameworks partially obsolete, so that new mechanisms are created to affirm human rights at a regional level and in accordance with these cultural and geographic markers. Examples are institutions and frameworks such as the *European Charter of Fundamental Rights* (Di Federico 2011), the Inter-American Court on Human Rights and the Mercosur Institute of Human Rights in Latin America (Nascimento 2007a), the *Arab Charter on Human Rights* (Bielefeldt 1995; An-Na'im 2001), and the *African Charter on Human and Peoples' Rights* in the African Union (Nmehielle 2001) as well as the *Bangkok Declaration on Human Rights* and the ASEAN Intergovernmental Committee on Human Rights in Asia (Bell and Bauer 1999; Seah 2008). Therefore, when we consider these intercultural discourses we are not simply dealing with abstract worldviews but also with real institutions. This also means that by questioning the exclusive focus on discourses on rights and demanding a simultaneous attention to discourses on humanity a subtle transition is performed that reveals metaphysical implications of our legal frameworks, tensions with our conceptions of law as positive science, issues of cultural poliversity, and political issues that are always implicitly at play when we talk of human rights. Therefore, I want to recall Jaspers's definition of the axial times and propose a reflection on the intrinsic plurality of perceptions about the *humanity of human rights*, which is always presupposed but rarely spelled out (Bohman 2007:105).

Despite the critique that Jaspers's approach may be Eurocentric, his definition of axial times performed a decentering of perspectives that is helpful today. In his book *Origin and Goal of History*, he defined an axis out of which "a common framework for the historical self-understanding" of humans evolved and characterized a time around 500 BCE as "an age in which the basic categories emerged, based upon which we still define our thinking" (1949:19–20). This he describes as a move from myths to a more abstract and speculative process [*Vergeisterung*] that led to the origins of philosophy. Jaspers does not see this process as a necessary development, but rather as a rupture that could be observed simultaneously and independently in several high cultures [*Hochkulturen*] and geographic regions. This idea of an "axial age" [*Achsenzeit*] has been reassessed in several ways: Shmuel Eisenstadt led a series of initiatives to study the presupposi- tions and current impact of the axial civilizations and other civiliza- tions in the preaxial times—such as Egypt and Mesopotamia (1986); Samuel Huntington recognized the plurality of civilizations and their role in a multipolar world, but then concluded that this plurality would lead to a "clash of civilizations" (1996:28, 41–55, 183–184); many sociologists are reassessing the axial age to make sense of the tensions between secularism and postsecular societies (Bellah and Joas 2012). Considering the axial age helps to draw attention to specific traditions and their impact on various views on human rights.

I am not alone in this approach. Many authors defend the possibility of recognizing this plurality and the move toward an understanding of universality as an "overlapping consensus" that articulates these differ- ent traditions. An-Na'im suggests that by encouraging cross-cultural conversations there is a possibility of arriving to universal agreement on the meaning of human rights (An-Na'im 1992). Charles Taylor argues that the implementation of human rights in non-Western soci- eties requires an appropriate philosophical justification that recog- nizes the historical and cultural context in which human rights are being applied (1999). As Taylor researches the sources of the "Self" in modern Europe, he reveals a particular conception of the human being that places higher value on individuality and defines society in terms of a contractual agreement among individuals who are endowed with rights (1989), but at the same time he recognizes that the goal of having an individual as the subject of rights and of establishing the foundations of society on mutual cooperation and a legal order has been achieved in other societies by other means (Taylor 1999:134). I believe it is possible to advance these ideas in order to observe and sort out metaphysical and religious conceptions, scientific and epistemic categories, and more recent symbolic and discursive ways of under- standing human rights in distinct cultures. For example, the ancient thinking of Confucius in China or the pre-Socratics in Greece was def- initely metaphysical, but implied some notions of humanity and rights and duties. Modern European philosophy was influenced by scientific naturalism and defined humanity and rights in a more positivist fash- ion. Recent philosophical studies are more concerned with the logical structure and practical application of discourses in human rights. How can we explore this perspective without falling into the problems of particularism and relativism that in fact contradict universality?

In order to address this question, I would like to refer to Discourse Philosophy. Despite its European origins, I believe that Discourse Philosophy can offer a framework that makes sense of the variety of positions on Human Rights. While acknowledging the positions above, I follow the views proposed by Habermas and Apel in order to characterize some of the geopolitical and cultural-regional contexts of Europe, Asia, Africa, North America, and South America beyond the corresponding traditional national boundaries within these geographic markers. I consider especially the idea of differentiating these perspectives in terms of paradigms. At the same time, however, I distance myself from the Hegelian tone that Apel and Habermas give to this discussion.

DISCOURSE PHILOSOPHY AND ITS INTERPRETATION OF HUMAN RIGHTS

Discourse Philosophy makes an effort to establish a framework for human rights that is compatible with a critical tradition transformed by the linguistic turn. Hence, human rights are discourses and norms that require the deliberation and consent of *all* humans, not only the members of a particular community or citizens of a given country. It is fair to say, therefore, that they are *moral rights*. However, Habermas seems more concerned with making room for institutional realms in which such rights can be implemented, so that they can also be guaranteed as *legal rights* or *political rights* of individual citizens. In view of various possibilities, how should we conceive of human rights? To address this question, I want to explore the inherent plurality in conceptions of both humanity and rights as I continue my dialogue and counterpoint with Habermas and Apel. I begin by indicating six steps that mark the evolution of Habermas's views on human rights. He has undergone a process of continually transforming his conception of human rights and oscillating between ethical, legal, political, and moral definitions (Flynn 2003; Abdel-Nour 2004; Ingram 2009; 2010:175–189).

First, Habermas's point of departure for a discursive conception of rights can be identified already in *The Structural Transformation of the Public Sphere* (1962), where he shows that the public use of reason prompts a change from an aristocratic representation based on secretive dealings to a new bourgeois "public sphere" [*Öffentlichkeit*] based on free and nonhierarchical human interactions. This shift is due to the role of the liberal state in establishing rational norms and laws that guarantee the "humanity" [*Humanität*] and basic rights of bourgeois and *citoyens* (1962:117–121). For Habermas, the claim that private owners were recognized as humans and constituted a public has many consequences: while "liberal human rights and democratic citizen rights are at first separated" (1962:328), the *Universal Declaration on Human Rights* and a few constitutions came to "guarantee a sharing of social services and participation in political institutions" for all (1962:330). This historical understanding of the emergence and evolution of civil rights and human rights as well as their institutionalization through law in liberalism remains a consistent point in Habermas. He briefly reiterates this in *Reconstruction of Historical Materialism* (1976a:26–30, 260–267) and in *Theory of Communicative Action* (1981a 2:257–265). However, this point is later overshadowed by his accent on juridification.

Second, in his magnum opus, Habermas accounts for human rights only indirectly, but the pendulum is on the side of morality. He starts by referring to the normativity of *communicative rationality* in terms of Discourse Ethics, then deals with the ethical implications of claiming rights for *all*, and finally analyzes juridification trends [*Verrechtlichungstendenzen*]. He provides a detailed critique of four waves of juridification—represented by the bourgeois state, constitutional state, democratic constitutional state, and the social-democratic welfare state—and ultimately opposes them because they are interventionist, contribute to the colonization of the lifeworld, and lack moral justification (Habermas 1981a 2:522; Erman 2005:69–81). Let me spell out some of the aspects involved in his considerations. Since claims to universality are connected to moral discourses, Habermas explains them in reference to Mead's concept of the "generalized other" and the necessary appeal to a larger community: "If we assert our rights, we are calling for a definite response just because they are rights that are universal—a response which everyone should, and perhaps, will give. Now that response is present in our own nature; in some degree we are ready to take that same attitude toward somebody else if he makes the appeal" (1981a 2:61—quoting Mead). Combining this with a reading of Durkheim and Kohlberg, Habermas then arrives to the conclusion that such rights evolve according to preconventional, conventional, and postconventional levels applicable to both ethics and law, and then become institutionalized [*institutionalisiert*] (1981a 2:259–262). If these rights are anchored in legal and political institutions, what is the role of morality? Habermas does concede that because morality is universalized at the postconventional level it becomes deinstitutionalized once again [*entinstitutionalisiert*]. Therefore, *Theory of Communicative Action* seems to understand human rights definitely as universal moral rights, to which he refers explicitly only once, when he presents new potentials for social protest (1981a 2:575–577). Yet, the reference is clear enough to show that human rights are based on the moral appeal to a larger community beyond institutions. Hence, they are anchored in the formal-pragmatic version of Discourse Ethics and implicitly related to the various formulations of the Discourse Principle (D) (Habermas 1981a 2:144; 1983:132–133; 1992:138; 1996:59).

Third, however, Habermas seems to change his views regarding juridification. In his *Tanner Lectures*, he states that juridification is the best way to justify human rights because "processes of moral argumentation get institutionalized by means of legal procedures," which remain permeable to moral reasoning (1986:220, 230–233; 1992:541–570). This shows an oscillation between moral and legal conceptions of human rights, which, far from being resolved, is intensified later. *Between Facts and Norms* makes a definite shift toward legal rights, based on Habermas's realization that (D) can be applied differently and horizontally to moral, political, and legal systems, so that a normative relationship among the moral principle of universalization, the principle of law, and the principle of democracy can be established [*das Verhältnis von Moral-, Rechts- und Demokratieprinzip*]. Based on this tripartite view, Habermas is then able to articulate "private and public autonomy, human rights, and popular sovereignty," whereas human rights are located between moral and legal norms (Habermas 1992:112, 118, 123). By establishing this parallelism Habermas now proposes that these three dimensions are co-original and complementary. Human rights are understood as basic rights whose status is defined within a particular legal framework: "Liberal (in the narrower sense) basic rights make up the core of human rights declarations. From them a system of rights justified rationally and juridically [*vernunftrechtlich*], has emerged," so that "their constitutionality allows individual legal subjects (in some cases also associations) to use the means of constitutional complaints if the Executive Power interferes in their basic rights" (Habermas 1992:214–215; Ingram 2010:170–171; Baxter 2011:68). Noticeably, Habermas's references to human rights in *Between Facts and Norms* are more explicit than in *Theory of Communicative Action*, but still very abstract. Human rights are seen as a legal by-product of liberal policies that ought to be generalized while the moral dimension is clearly downplayed. Moreover, human rights claims are now bound to the jurisdiction of a nation-state and gain more applicability but lose in universality. Many arguments can be brought against Habermas's conclusion, which can be seen as variations of Apel's critique of his approach (Apel 1998:649–837). One point is that a legal institutionalization of popular sovereignty needs to be "secured via human rights," not the other way around (Flynn 2003:438); another is that this "juridical conception of rights is relatively impotent in remedying the cultural causes that contribute to the insecure enjoyment of subsistence" (Ingram 2009:195; 2010:175f.); yet another is the charge that this view may reflect a certain ethnocentric or Eurocentric limitation (Erman 2005:19, 69–81); and finally, we can refer to Koskenniemi's argument that through similar procedures the European legal system justified colonialism (2001). To these I would add that Habermas's conception of human rights at this point is too limited to address the intercultural issues I introduced initially.

However, this is not the last definition we find in his writings. In a fourth step, Habermas takes into consideration criticisms, including Dieter Grimm's diagnosis of a crisis of constitutionalism at the national and supranational level (1991, 2011), Ingeborg Maus's remarks on the meaning of popular sovereignty (2011), and Gunther Teubner's proposal for civil global constitutions beyond statecentric approaches (1996; Teubner and Fischer-Lescano 2006). So, he recognizes that human rights have a Janus face that refers to either internal legal rights or external moral rights, so he expands his definition to include multicultural societies and their claims. Actually, this is not new because this element had already been affirmed by him in the first place. As we can see, he is not necessarily introducing new material, but rather accentuating different aspects. Anyhow, in *The Inclusion of the Other*, he clearly not only takes multiculturalism into consideration, acknowledges the rights of minorities, identifies differences beyond the nation-state, and tries to avoid the problems of Eurocentrism; but he also rejects those comprehensive views that appeal to religion because they fail to adopt a *postmetaphysical thinking* and transition from an ethical to a legal understanding of rights (Habermas 1996:239–251). Despite Taylor's proposals for the recognition of the equality of cultural forms of life and for the possibility of an overlapping consensus on the definition of human rights, Habermas asserts that claims in a struggle for recognition have legitimacy only in a formally democratic context (1996:239). Otherwise, he says, there would be an "ethical impregnation of the constitutional state [*Rechtsstaat*]" with particular interests that could include fundamentalism (1996:255). He offers a double alternative: first, the only allegiance within a democratic society should be to a democratic constitution; second, he sees the possibility of defining human rights in light of Kant's idea of "Perpetual

Peace," but with a few corrections (1996:192–236). In reassessing Kantian cosmopolitanism, Habermas acknowledges Kant's brilliant anticipation of current trends such as a global public sphere, the establishment of institutions such as the United Nations, the changes in the sovereignty of nation-states, and the existing declarations to protect human rights. Still, he asserts that "the weak link in the global protection of human rights remains the lack of any executive power that could secure, when necessary, the General Declarations of Human Rights through interventions into nation states, despite their 'supreme power' over their territory" (1996:212). This requires a revision of both Kant and contemporary theory of international relations, which shall lead ultimately to the "improvement of an institutional framework necessary for a feasible politics based on human rights" that serve "humans," not merely citizens of a particular state (Habermas 1996:217, 223). Based on the above, we should expect an expansion of his conception of human rights to accept plurality and universality. However, he maintains that it is a mistake to conflate human rights with moral rights because "they have a positive form in national constitutional frameworks, possess weak validity in international law, but can still become institutionalized with the establishment of a cosmopolitan order" (Habermas 1996:226). Obviously, the oscillation I pointed out remains unresolved, but the concept of human rights is "thicker."

In "The Multicultural Discourse on Human Rights" originally published in 1996 and later republished as "Remarks on Legitimation through Human Rights" in *The Postnational Constellation*, Habermas insists on this double character of human rights and accepts that a multicultural discourse has progressively led to the recognition of "workers, women and Jews, gypsies, gays and refugees as 'humans'" in the same way as the bourgeoisie once claimed humanity (1998:171). With this statement, the pendulum definitely swings back to the moral side of the discussion. Moreover, as he reacts to the *Bangkok Declaration* in 1993, he defends human rights as an answer to claims to difference (1998, 1999) and affirms that this debate opens the possibility for the participation of other cultures in the pursuit of a consensus regarding human rights (1998:181–192). Reflecting on the reprinted version of this text in 2009—in the *Studienausgabe* of his selected texts—he adds that this multicultural discourse includes strong traditions that go back to the axial times, but inserts the proviso that they need to acknowledge the democratic channels constituted by the secular democratization processes in liberal and social-democratic societies (2009 4:29). This is definitely an opening to a more robust account of human rights that could address the challenges I introduced at the beginning of this chapter, even though Habermas does not seem to explore this topic systematically.

Fifth, in *The Divided West* (2004), Habermas presents more detailed arguments for the globality of human rights, building on a series of elements he had explored before: the role of the United Nations, changing practices of war, threats of neoconservative and neoliberals positions, recognition of multicultural societies, and many forms of globalization processes that reveal a "postnational constellation." In view of all these challenges, he still maintains the need for a juridification of procedures, now at the level of international relations [*Verrechtlichung der internationalen Beziehungen*]. This should occur by means of concrete legal norms and the coupling of these norms not with morality but with concrete sanctions that respond to the claims of emancipatory movements around the world (2004:104–105). Now, after a detailed reading of Kant's project for a condition of world citizenship as a set of rights for individuals, Habermas rejects proposals for world republic or world governance [*Weltrepublik, Weltregierung*]. Instead, he adds, what is needed is a kind of nonstate constitution for a plural global society [*entstaatliche Konstitutionalisierung*]. He concedes that the United Nations is a legitimate "community of states and citizens" and, as such, it could be the formal instance to fulfill two important innovative tasks in relation to a global society: to guarantee global security and promote human rights globally (2004:122–123, 131–133, 157–161). This admission of a global dimension is surely different from what he had affirmed in *Between Facts and Norms*, where he was open to the charge that he did not provide an instance beyond the nation-state to which individuals could appeal when states fail to protect them in cases of dictatorships, in failed states, or in the situations of expatriates and refugees. Now he corrects this gap by including a clause defining a wider community through which national citizenship might be transferred [*übertragen*] to the global level. This does not address the problems of refugees or stateless persons (Bohman 2007:103), but in advancing this suggestion, Habermas is more concerned with avoiding several other challenges such as comprehensive metaphysical worldviews, the cultural particularity of conservative and communitarian claims, the imposition of unilateral measures by a powerful state, and other hegemonic strategies. However, it is in Carl Schmitt's legal theory that we find one of the most subtle challenges. Against him, Habermas reaffirms the Kantian project, insists on constitutional patriotism, and updates his views in a program for a new world order (2004:160–165). The relevant point in all this is double: on the one hand, we can see that human rights are seen as positive rights guaranteed by a coercive legal order at the national level and expandable to the global level, a move that requires both existing democratic states and a reformed United Nations; on the other, despite juridification Habermas is not ready to give up the moral dimension implicit in human rights because he recognizes that humans are capable of claiming universal validity beyond the limited frameworks of existing institutions. This explains why he comes to recognize that philosophical discussions on human rights in the liberal tradition have focused largely on rights and neglected the discussion about human dignity.

Finally, Habermas introduces yet another subtle change. He now says that *human dignity* is co-originary [*gleich-ursprünglich*] with *human rights*. This is a radical move, but it should not come as surprise. In fact, it is anticipated by his previous reflections on human dignity [*Menschenwürde*] in relation to religion and genetic engineering (2001b, 2001d). In *The Future of Human Nature*, his concern is with medical practices such as preimplantation genetic diagnosis, genetic interventions, and embryo research, which, in his view, affect the authentic self-understanding of autonomous persons and create a conflict between Christian metaphysics and natural science (2001d:60). To respond to these challenges Habermas develops a proposal for "species ethics" [*Gatttungsethik*], thus expanding a definition of ethics that he had previously limited to individuals and groups. With this reformulation, he relates human rights not only to the universalization proper to morality, but also to a person's self-understanding as a member of a community of the human species (2001d:60). After considering several possible situations concerning the impact of biotechnological enhancements of humanity, Habermas ultimately concludes that human dignity is both a fundamental ethical value prior to moral deliberations and a legal right enshrined in the German constitution. His intuition is that human dignity applies even to prepersonal entities such as embryos because they are potential humans capable of full development. As such, they would eventually elaborate their own ethical self-understanding through intersubjective relations (2001d:59, 66, 99). Habermas's reflections on genetic engineering were received with certain skepticism, but beyond his controversial points I want to highlight that this subtle change corresponds to a profound review in the very meaning of Discourse Ethics: in considering the theme of human dignity, he adapts his understanding of ethics and now relates it more directly to morality. It is this change that allows him to affirm that no one would have the right to affect the future autonomy of another person, except for therapeutic purposes, otherwise we would be using other humans as means, not ends. This conclusion opens the way for his statement in the article "The Concept of Human Dignity and the Realistic Utopia of Human Rights" (2011), where he affirms that "'human dignity' is not only a classificatory expression, an empty placeholder, as it were, which lumps a multiplicity of different phenomena together, but the moral 'source' from which all of the basic rights derive their sustenance" (2011:16). While in his discussion on genetics he addressed the complementarity between species ethics and constitutional guarantees to the integrity of humanity, in this article he focuses on the complementarity between legal and moral precepts. This allows him to reiterate that moral elements are transferred to rights discourses and become positive law through democratic political measures that recognize all humans as possessing the same status (2011:23–27). For sure, he continues to say that law adds a further step to guarantee individuality and the absolute value of the person [*der absolute Wert der Person*] (2011:33), but for me, in this strategy Habermas finally establishes a stronger *internal link* between the moral and legal dimensions of both rights and humanity, which are expressed in the very indisociability of the terms constituting the concept of *human rights*. He therefore provides us with a tool to address the challenge I presented at the beginning: to find a way of upholding both humanity and rights in plural contexts and in light of a communicative approach.

It is easy to see that Habermas oscillates between various aspects, but in the course of these internal transformations, human rights clearly become coupled not only with human dignity but also with a more plural and realistic global or cosmopolitan outlook. This opens a window of opportunity to reconsider human rights and discuss certain limits of both metaphysical worldviews and biotechnological definitions of *humanity* as well as conservative and liberal conceptions of *rights*. Further, this allows us to see *human rights* in their global dimension as a result of social and political processes—including struggles for recognition—that have occurred in different parts of the world. Many details remain to be interpreted, but by articulating the "indivisibility of human rights" internally, in the very structure of human rights discourses, Habermas provides us with a tool to deal more directly with a variety of issues such as the guarantee of individuality, respect for the political will of a collectivity, recognition of plurality in multicultural societies, openness to intercultural dialogue, and search for global universality.

Looking back, it is clear that Habermas makes room for the human dimension I discussed at the beginning and progressively begins to address the various levels of the multidimensional discourse community. Nonetheless, Apel, Forst, Pogge, Ingram, and many others have reacted critically to his emphasis on *juridification* and his downplay of morality in human rights by insisting that moral arguments are still very relevant at the level of *justification*. Apel proposes Discourse Ethics as a critical instance above legal institutions (1998, 1999); Forst goes as far as to propose a "human right" to justification (2007); Pogge argues that the fulfillment of many human rights—such as the access to medicine—does not necessarily require juridification (2008); and Ingram adds that juridification fails to address structural or institutional injustices and does not provide tools to motivate the pursuit of human aspirations in political or economic terms (2009). They all agree that there is also a need to consider *concrete implementations* of human rights and address material issues such as poverty, human subsistence, and access to common goods.

What is Apel's contribution to our understanding of human rights? I have already described the content of his critique to Habermas. Although he does criticize Habermas directly for not giving primacy to the moral justification of human rights and for identifying a particular form of political legitimation of rights with human rights at the global level (1998:745; 1999:36), his contribution to the discussion on human rights is more indirect because he focuses on the paradigmatic preconditions for the justification of human rights. His definition of paradigms provides us with a perspective to advance two other points I indicated at the beginning: history is not necessarily linear (situations can suddenly change, regress, or progress rapidly) and our historical reflection needs to account for plurality (a variety of historical events occur at different paces in different locations and may influence each other). Based on his views on "paradigms" we can affirm that the *Universal Declaration on Human Rights* and other documents derived from it represent a "paradigm shift" in our understanding of both "humanity" and "rights." Let me add a few comments regarding Apel's views.

First, a good summary of Apel's position can be read in his lectures in Louvain, published as *The Response of Discourse Ethics* (2000). He starts with the "human situation" as a challenge for ethics and provides an overview of cases of exclusion and negation of rights, from the cultures of the "axial times" to contemporary politics. With the broad perspective of an intercultural anthropology of human evolution, he reconstructs history and concludes that modernity seems to have exhausted its resources to deal with the variety of global challenges that emerged after 1945 (1988:373–385; 2000:12). He partially agrees with Habermas that we must work toward the juridification of human rights, but he also realizes how often such systems have been either corrupted or become exclusionary (2000:63). Therefore, he proposes a transformation of Kantian philosophy in terms of a "discourse ethics of global co-responsibility" [*globale Mit-Verantwortung*] that deals with questions of law, economics, and politics. Differently from Habermas, however, he concludes that the legal codification of human rights is not enough because global challenges cannot be addressed by simply focusing on positive law and abstracting from moral justification (2000:83–90). In his view, an ultimate justification of ethics is required, which is intrinsic to human communicative interactions. Accordingly, the right to participate in a communicative process is the foundation to both human rights and cosmopolitan ideals (1997:79). This position has been rejected as too abstract by Habermas. Apel himself concedes that in order to avoid the problems of metaphysical assumptions he must think of human rights as "regulative ideals" and leave their realization open to the practices of particular communities. Nevertheless, he insists that *human* interactions oriented by (D) should have primacy over institutions.

Second, Apel shares with Habermas a conception of paradigms. Before I explain how I take this concept, it is important to recognize that paradigm is a *terminus technicus*. The initial reference is Ludwig Wittgenstein (1937 II:31, 41), who defines paradigm as standards or agreements underlying daily practices or implicit general views bound to "forms of life" [*Lebensformen*] that cannot be reduced to particular statements (Luckhardt 1978:245). The second reference is Thomas Kuhn, who borrowed this term from Wittgenstein in order to identify the hidden assumptions of scientific theories and practices. For him, a "global paradigm" is the implicit framework orienting a mature science while a "community paradigm" is the set of rules and practices accepted and followed by a given professional group (Kuhn 1970:10, 43, 119). When faced with new and persistent problems that are fundamental to their field, scientists may try to go beyond their specific community and search for a different worldview to guide their actions. This "paradigm shift" requires a radical break with tradition and this demands a transition to a new worldview. A third reference is Talcott Parsons's "interchange paradigm," which explains the relationship and adaptation of functional subsystems within a society. This model is related to his AGIL scheme of four systemic aspects he finds in every social system: Adaptation, Goal Attainment, Integration, and

Latency (Habermas 1981a 2:360–361). In the chapter "A Paradigm of the Human Condition" of *Action Theory and the Human Condition* (1978:352–433), Parsons expands this model to consider more general norms for social actions. Finally, we have the interpretation that Apel and Habermas offer of these views. They critically appropriate the term "paradigm" to identify the main worldviews that orient historical and philosophical endeavors: ontology or metaphysics, epistemology or science, and communication or discourse (Apel 1977, 1994, 2011; Habermas 1981a 2; 1988). While Habermas describes current programs in more detail, Apel centers his attention on main positions that represent varieties of a *prima philosophia*.

In his "Ernst Cassirer Lectures" of 1977, Apel turns to Plato and Aristotle to identify their views as representing the first paradigm, which relies on ontology or metaphysics to determine the essence of reality; he then characterizes the trend that goes from René Descartes through Immanuel Kant to Edmund Husserl as critique of knowledge or philosophy of consciousness [*Erkenntniskritik oder Bewusstseinsphilosophie*], which relies on an abstractive conception of a reasoning subject who is capable of transcending given objects (2011:65, 151). Based on the traditional triadic scheme of Peirce's semiotics, Apel explains how the linguistic turn overcomes these previous paradigms by correcting their corresponding perspectives and integrating them into a larger framework that stresses the intersubjective conditions of both subjectivity and objectivity (2011:148–159). Apel not only extracts a series of consequences from this scheme—including references to logic, semantics, scientific development, history, and anthropology—but also attempts to avoid problems such as the relativism of Kuhn's assumption of incommensurability among paradigms as well as the empirical reductions observed in Carnarp and Morris. Nevertheless, he does maintain an explicit Hegelian approach based upon which he claims not only the primacy and superiority of the last paradigm—that is, the intersubjective conception of discourse and community—but also a necessary evolutionary and "revolutionary" process that leads to the progress of human rationality (2011:66). There are many details to Apel's approach and many possible criticisms, which I cannot describe in detail. For my purposes here, suffice it to say that he follows Habermas in describing a "postmetaphysical paradigm" (2011:165), but then moves on to defend his transcendental-pragmatic approach in a Hegelian way that implies a metaphysics of evolution. Although this might be acceptable as a device for historical reconstruction, projecting it toward the future and giving it a certain directionality brings the danger of metaphysics; also, an optimistic

view of evolution does not account for setbacks or the emergence of
something new; finally, by imposing one view, one leaves no room for
plurality and contingency. Therefore, the only point I want to take
from this "historic-hermeneutic reconstruction of epochs in the history of philosophy" is the corresponding mapping of plural cultural,
scientific, and social revolutions that remain available for contemporary reflection and practices (2011:7, 358–361).

Habermas shares these views with Apel. In *Theory of Communicative
Action*, he not only shows the transition from the philosophy of
consciousness to communicative action as a paradigm shift (1981a
1:518), but also adds that the difference between lifeworld and system
correspond to a conflict between two paradigms (1981a 2:9, 122).
His assessment of systems theory is largely based on Talcott Parsons's
text, "A Paradigm of the Human Condition," from which Habermas
extracts a series of characterizations of "paradigm shifts" (1981a
2:297). In *Between Facts and Norms*, he uses a similar strategy, but
now speaks more specifically of "paradigms of law" in an extended
discussion that includes a recognition of the tensions among the paradigms represented by republican, liberal, and systems theories of law
he had introduced earlier (1992:468–537; Ingram 2010:193–220).
More of essence for us, however, is his argument that the bourgeois
paradigm of liberal law experiments a dissolution and is overcome
by the social-welfare paradigm. Since these constitutional approaches
have been exhausted, there is a search for something new, and the
"proceduralist paradigm" is the answer (Ingram 2010:221f.). Relying
on his previous discussion of Parsons, Habermas now understands
paradigms as the "background norms" that support a legal system and
determine how basic rights and constitutional principles are applied.
His aim is to articulate private and public autonomy, human rights,
and popular sovereignty. Consequently, he connects basic rights
with the liberal paradigm, relates popular sovereignty to republicanism (Habermas 1992:349–350), and postulates that the assumptions
behind the proceduralist paradigm are better revealed and justified
by Discourse Theory. The proceduralist paradigm criticizes the other
two models and proposes a system of rights that is not simply based
on private autonomy, but includes the public dimension of communicative and participatory rights that require the active role of civil
society and the public sphere (1992:399–400).

Why is this relevant to our discussion? The paradigm shift to a discursive approach can be clearly applied to human rights and help us
address the questions about the "human rights paradigm" raised earlier by An-Na'im. I want to use this term and follow William Talbott

in defining and differentiating worldviews in terms of human rights paradigms (Talbott 2005:19–35). The promulgation of the *Universal Declaration on Human Rights* definitely represents a paradigm shift as An-Na'im mentioned, but while the concept of paradigm has an "evolutionary" dimension, it is important to acknowledge the plurality of paradigms that can be found simultaneously today. Therefore, we can also affirm the possibility of moving from one to another. For example, metaphysics is still alive in religious worldviews, scientific (epistemic) thinking is central to our everyday life in a modern society, and communication is an essential component of every human endeavor. We can adopt this plural perspective as a way of classifying the different philosophical conceptions of "human"—and by extension, the conceptions of "human rights"—in contrast and complementarity with the mere positivity of law, objectivity of rights, and the binding force of contractual models.

Taking all this into consideration, we can already draw a few initial conclusions. First, there is not only one *human rights paradigm* but also a plurality of views in a historical transition process that goes from ancient metaphysical positions through epistemic views on positive law to a more contemporary move toward discourses. Second, in this historical evolution many came to disregard metaphysical positions and give more weight to a positivist account of rights, but this does not mean we got rid of metaphysical assumptions. Recently, another perspective has emerged, which focuses on humanity and its capability to express normative issues in discursive ways. Third, paradigm shifts are neither necessarily historically sequential nor purely linear because metaphysical, epistemic, and discursive approaches remain available to a culture and allow an individual or a society to move from one paradigm to another. Of course, this is not a simple matter and requires much discussion and justification. Moreover, we need account for the plurality of social conditions, locations, and cultural markers that influence individuals and groups in order to understand the movement toward an intercultural understanding of human rights. Finally, I turn my attention to multifarious practices based on definitions of human rights, seeing them not simply as a list of entitlements spelled out in terms of rules, laws, and formal procedures, but also as a set of values ascribed to different subjects, groups, and identities. Because a purely legal description of the *human rights paradigm* tends to overemphasize *rights* and downplay the meaning of *human*, I argue that both the concept of *rights* and the *human* dimension have to be seen through the lenses of a plurality of paradigms. Relying on the discursive paradigm, I therefore propose a discussion on how different paradigms yield different conceptions of human rights.

PHILOSOPHICAL PARADIGMS AND WORLDVIEWS ON HUMANITY AND RIGHTS

As I stated at the beginning of this chapter, contemporary views on human rights are built upon deep foundations that can be traced back in centuries and millennia. Having reviewed the perspective of Discourse Philosophy on this issue, I can now refer to three comprehensive worldviews on rights and humanity as paradigms that can be found across cultures: metaphysical traditions, epistemic views on constitutional rights often understood in terms of legal positivism, and contemporary discourses that account for cultural variables and propose both legal and cultural pluralism. Ancient traditions and religious views on humanity and ethics are controversial but still influential, civil rights claim their origin in revolutionary political theories of the Enlightenment, and contemporary documents, practices, and institutions reflect these previous views but advance a more discursive approach to human rights. By acknowledging these variables, I can also apply the model of the multidimensional discourse community.

Metaphysical Dualism

According to the metaphysical paradigm, there are ontological understandings of humanity and rights. Although most of these views are ancient, they still influence contemporary life, as seen in civil religion in the United States, the Confucian assumptions of the Chinese government, conceptions of person by the Catholic Church, international campaigns by Islamic organizations, and other groups. My aim is to show different cultural views on humanity and rights or duties, which now influence contemporary conceptions of human rights in different regional contexts and are in dialogue with these traditions. One of the oldest references to rights is the Hammurabi Code (1996) that determined the conduct of people based on a radical view of reciprocity that would be unacceptable today (Driver and Miles 1956; Ishay 2004). We have a glimpse of an analogous legal tradition through documents found at the village of Deir el-Medina and the Wisdom Literature (VerSteeg 2001; 2004:91–94). The interest in Egypt was revived after Napoleon Bonaparte's invasion of Egypt in 1798, the discovery of Tell el-Amarna in 1887, and the more recent "Arab Spring" in 2011. At each of these moments, there is a specific conception of law and humanity influencing daily affairs. In ancient times, full humanity was ascribed to the Pharaoh, whose attributes were derived from his supposed proximity to a deity, while others could never aspire to this stature (Wendell 1972; Assmann 1990; Hooker 1996). The role and rights of immigrants, women, and children were defined accordingly. How does this relate to our discussion? Interestingly enough, the democratic and revolutionary movements that emerged in Egypt and Tunisia in 2011, characterized as the "Arab Spring," represented a rights revolution that made use of information technology while making clear references to the millennial Egyptian cultural tradition as an additional source for their movement (al-Rahim 2011).

Another tradition in the understanding of rights and humanity stems from Asia. While criticizing universal human rights as Western values in disguise and questioning the imposition of such rights on their cultures, many countries have also attempted to reconsider their religious and cultural views. The millennial culture that has experienced a revival and received most attention in relation to human rights is Confucianism (Bell 2010). Confucianism defines social relationships holistically and with reference to the virtue of propriety [*li*], which demands the recognition of hierarchical structures and respect for the established social order. As registered in Confucius's *Analects*, a student ought to listen to his master, a son respect his father, a husband honor his wife, the youth give priority to elders and, similarly, a servant obey the lord and the subjects follow their ruler. The Confucian demand for "a profound vision of the qualities and modes of conduct necessary to be a full and worthy human being," surely indicates what counts as human (Confucius 1998). There is a highly abstract and demanding desideratum that provides less room for individual rights and puts more emphasis on duties. As we read in the *Analects* 4:5, "A superior man never abandons humanity, even for the lapse of a single meal." In contrast with this line of thought, we find the Indian philosophy and religion. Hindu texts and Jainism present a rich cosmology and metaphysics that certainly affects contemporary understandings of human rights. Although there have been arguments that Hinduism defines "caste rights" instead of human rights, there are Hindu elements reinterpreted by Mahatma Gandhi, which are being reassessed today (Sharma 2004). Still, these traditions do not seem to provide enough references to address women's rights, so the Indian Supreme Court has adopted current international human rights law to fill in this gap. Buddhism, however, insists on individuality and seems compatible with modern individual rights, despite its metaphysical tone (Siderits 2007; Edelglass and Garfield 2009). It presents a quest for individual liberation that starts with the recognition of human suffering, continues through the eightfold path, and aims at the *nirvana*, the ultimate enlightenment and liberation. This position is related to human rights, as affirmed by the Dalai Lama when he says that "it is the inherent nature of all human beings to yearn for freedom, equality and dignity, and they have an equal right to achieve that" (Dalai Lama 1998:xvii–xxi). Controversial as it may be, this view has received wider attention in North America and Europe. Within Asia, there are a number of differing positions on human rights that are based on the specific cultural traditions of each group. Contemporary approaches to human rights are inspired by ancient religious doctrines and philosophical assumptions that found their way into recent international documents.

If we turn our attention to Europe, the crisis of the European Union has brought renewed attention upon Greece and questions of economic rights, including discussions on the role of Greece as the foundation of the European culture. In this context, we can retrieve the relevance of ancient Greek philosophy for the discussion on human rights. In his "dialogues," Plato invariably has Socrates asking questions about piety, virtue, and justice in the life of the Athenian city [*polis*]. However, only selected persons were considered citizens of the *polis* and could take part in political dialogue. Although the ancient experiences in Athens became a model for modern democratic societies because it included different public spaces or participatory fora such as the public assembly [ekklesia], the city council [boulē], the court [dikasterion] as well as other public institutions in which the citizens of Athens exercised their rights, citizenship excluded women, children, slaves, and foreigners (Farrar 1988; Hansen 2006). This democratic shortfall can be traced back also to Aristotle, who provided a hierarchical view of humanity and society, based on a typology of rationality (*Nichomachean Ethics* 1095a, 1095b, 1103–1111, 1139b–1147b, 1216b). For him, humans (excluding women, children slaves, and foreigners) are both rational animals [*zoon logikon*] and "political animals" [*zoon politikon*] capable of acquiring language, communicating, and participating in social life. As stated in his *Politics*, there is also the assumption that humans give up their individuality to form a community as means to pursue happiness and the *common good*. These considerations indicate what kind of people were seen as fully humans, citizens, bearer of rights and, consequently, capable of participating in a political community. Recent discussions invariably return to these foundational models.

In relation to Africa, it is important to bear in mind that dictatorial regimes attempt to undermine the contemporary transition from situations of conflict to democracy and human rights by claiming that violations of rights are necessary steps of a developmental process. The violence described in the cases of Ethiopia, South Africa, Rwanda, and Sudan has been justified in these terms. However, there are old sources, myths, rituals, and practices in the African context to which many cultures appeal in order to promote human rights. For example, the Akan culture in West Africa differentiates among traditional principles such as *okra*, *mogya*, and *sunsum*, which yield rights to political participation and include procedures for consensus building, rights to trial, right to land, and right to religious freedom that invest people with humanity (Wiredu 1996:113–135). Similarly, the Yoruba culture of *orishas* related to the Oyo Empire, developed certain core values that are compatible with contemporary human rights discourses—especially the value of plurality expressed in the tolerance to polytheistic beliefs (Apter 1992). Yet another example is the Zulu conception of *ubuntu*, which has been popularized by Bishop Desmond Tutu during his leadership of the Truth and Conciliation Commission in South Africa (Prinsloo 1998; Murithi 2006).

These are a few brief examples of specific cultural justifications for human rights in various regions of the world. They show how religious and metaphysical assumptions are still employed to transition to more contemporary rights-based discourses. Some of the recalcitrant aspects limiting transitions in many contexts are often related to fundamentalist religious views, as Habermas has warned, so we need to include a brief review of the connection between religiosity and human rights, even if we restrict ourselves to Abrahamic religions (Witte and Vyver 1996; Kretzmer and Klein 2002). The Jewish tradition refers to Mosaic law and a lineage of many legal interpreters, such as those in the Rabbinic tradition. Although historically, the Hebrews considered themselves the "chosen people"—which is often understood today as ethnocentric, xenophobic, and belligerent—some prophets criticized these assumptions (Lorberbaum 2002). These prophets are often cited by contemporary civil rights and pacifist movements. For instance, Michael Walzer has shown the role of the prophet Amos in questioning the ethnocentric view from within the Jewish tradition (Walzer 1987:69–94; Brumlik 1999; Walzer, Lorberbaum, and Zohar 2000). The same is true of the messianic vision of Micah, Isaiah, and other prophets who were critics of Babylonian, Assyrian, and Jewish imperialism. The famous passage "And they shall beat their swords into plowshares" has become a motto for human rights activists and pacifists (Konvitz 1972). Analogous developments can be found in Christianity. Thomas Aquinas's theology is relevant to contemporary views on human rights due to his concept of natural law. For him, natural law is the underlying structure that orients both the providential acts of a deity and the possible prudential actions of humans. Natural law is above and beyond human law. To emphasize this difference, Aquinas uses two terms he inherited from the Roman tradition: "*lex*" and "*jus*" (Aquinas 1957; Lutz-Bachmann, Fidora, and Wagner 2010). The first denotes *law* while the second refers to what is *right* or *just*. Since Christian theology sees humans as created in the image of God, humans have been endowed with a natural rational capability and should be able to differentiate what is right or wrong as well as what is just or not (Finnis 1980, 1998). This formulation of natural rights continues to influence contemporary views on human rights. Finally, the Islamic tradition claims to better articulate the Hebrew, Greek, and Christian inheritance in a legal framework that evolves out of the Qur'an, brings different groups together, creates a jurisprudence [*fiqh*], and establishes schools [*madahib*] in which rules for daily life are developed. These rules go from matters of diet and hygiene through personal conduct and social relationships to religious rituals. Islamic law reached a high level of sophistication as it established a detailed set of rules to specify any course of action, thus serving as a strong guideline not only in religious matters, but also in the social, legal, and international arenas (Khan 2003). Recently, however, many questions have been raised regarding the relationship between *Shari'a* law and human rights, especially women's rights. For An-Na'im, it is nevertheless possible to reinterpret this tradition in a modern context and reassess the general principle ruling the situation of women in the Qur'an, *qawama* (3:34), without necessarily contradicting the Muslim precepts (An-Na'im 1987, 2008). Obviously, these main religious traditions related to the Abrahamic tradition have their divergences, but also provide rich resources that can be interpreted in different ways. My goal here is rather descriptive and, therefore, I will refrain from discussing their doctrines.

I have to limit myself to these cursory references that show a variety of metaphysical conceptions related to different contexts and traditions that correspond to contemporary geopolitical markers. They provide specific understandings of law, rights, and humanity, which are progressively established in writing, as we have seen in the *Hammurabi Code* and later in the *Torah*, *Bible*, and *Qur'an*. They also define a series of duties and rights around which individuals and communities define their identities. For sure, these traditions affirm particular understandings of humanity and rights that are often in conflict with contemporary human rights discourses. However, because they are still open to interpretation, there are possibilities of relating them or at least putting them in dialogue with epistemic understandings of human rights.

Epistemic Views and the Positivity of Law

We can define as epistemic those conceptions of human rights that prompt a shift from the metaphysical "natural law tradition" to modern positive law enshrined in constitutional frameworks. This is definitely a modern achievement. The juridical articulation of rights and humanity in early modern Europe occurs in light of the *canon* established after Thomas Aquinas appropriated Aristotelian categories. Juridical concepts such as law [*lex, jus*], power [*potestas, dominium*], and especially "law of peoples" [*jus gentium*] provided the norm guiding the political and commercial relationships Europeans were establishing with different cultures and worldviews in various geographic regions (Aquinas 1957; Tierney 1997; Lutz-Bachmann, Fidora, and Wagner 2010). As Europeans were exposed to the intercultural plurality of Arabs, Indians, Chinese, and Native Americans, they were prompted to ask questions central to any paradigmatic understanding of human rights: Are these people humans? Do they have rights?

Francisco de Vitoria was the first to attempt an answer to this question in relation to the rights of the American Indians (Vitoria 1934, 1943; Hanke 1949; Tierney 1997:22–23, 256–259; Cavallar 2002:94–95). Later on, Bartolomé de Las Casas wrote his *Brief Account of the Devastation of the Indies*, originally published in 1552 (1998), describing how the natives of the Americas were being mistreated and exploited by the Spaniards. He used Vitoria's arguments in order to defend the "humanity" and the "rights" of Indians in his debates with Ginés de Sepúlveda in 1555 (Hanke 1974). Similarly, the Scot George Buchanan was the first to criticize Portuguese colonialism in Brazil (Williamson 1996). These thinkers associated with the University of Salamanca left an important mark on an incipient modern international law and are being reassessed today, for traces of their thinking can be found in Grotius, Hobbes, Rousseau, and Kant, among many others who developed new epistemic conceptions of rights (Scott 1934). Their ideas correspond to a transition that leads to the European Enlightenment, a period that marks the moment in which nation-states emerge after the Treaty of Westphalia (1648), new political theories appear, and revolutions occur to declare independence from old regimes and establish new rights based on democratic constitutional frameworks. It is in this turn to modernity that we see the consolidation of both a culture of individual rights and the emphasis on positive law that influence current debates on human rights. Also here, there is a plurality of views to be considered as we move between Europe and the Americas. Before I proceed, it is important to realize that this movement occurs hand in hand with the development of modern imperialism and colonialism, in a contradictory process that becomes crystallized in international law (Koskenniemi 2001).

In Europe, we can observe a history of epistemic and individual arguments against imperialism and colonialism in Holland, England, France, Germany, and other countries that resented the Spanish domination during the sixteenth and seventeenth centuries. However, the repertoire of rights that emerged in this process had particular applications and supported other forms of European imperialism (Koskeniemmi 2001:130). In Holland, Hugo Grotius and his now classic book, *De iure belli ac pacis*, advances the natural rights tradition to indirectly criticize Spanish imperialism and argues for the independence of the seas, nature, and individuals from Spanish rule. He differentiates the Law of Nature from a human voluntary right, that is, a right derived from the civil power of the state [*lex*] as well as from an international convention understood as the right of peoples [*jus gentium*], a common distinction he takes from tradition (Lutz-Bachmann, Fidora, and Wagner 2010). He then concludes that these "three laws undoubtedly bind all men." However, this did not prevent Grotius's role in legally justifying Dutch colonialism and the actions of the West India Company (1625).

In England, the first important reference is Thomas Hobbes, who starts by defining human nature in *The Elements of Law* and then expands his views to discuss the political body in *De Corpore Politico* and *De Cive*. More importantly, however, is his differentiation between a "right of nature" [*jus naturale*] possessed by all humans and the "law of nature" [*lex naturalis*] in *Leviathan* (Martinich 1992, 1999). A complementary reference is John Locke. In his *Second Treatise of Government*, he affirms that "we must consider what estate all men are naturally in, and that is, a state of perfect freedom to order their actions, and dispose of their possessions and persons as they think fit, within the bounds of the law of Nature" (1988 IV:4). Based on this premise, he concludes that all humans have a natural right "to the advantages of Nature," which Locke defines as "right to dominion and sovereignty." However, this right is limited by the law of nature, which states that "no one ought to harm another in his life, health, liberty or possessions." Also here we find a clear contradiction, not between statements but between Locke's theory with its insistence on natural rights, private property, and liberty while accepting the exploitation of Native Americans and the slavery of Africans (Tully 1980:64–71; 1993:137–176). When we take these two aspects into account, it is undeniable that he ends up with at least two kinds of humans who may have rights or be deprived of them, depending on their nature. These developments are not only theoretical, but also they are crucial to the development of concrete political and social rights. It was in England that the "Glorious Revolution" overthrew the king in 1688 and established a Parliament that approved the *Bill of Rights* and the *Toleration Act* in 1689. The *Bill of Rights* is one of the first modern documents to forbid cruel punishments and excessive fines while granting several rights: freedom from interference from the government and freedom to speak, right to bear arms and to be Protestant, right to vote, and right not to be attacked by the army. The *Toleration Act* stopped the persecution of religious dissenters and nonconformists, established freedom of religion, reaffirmed the primacy of Protestantism, and stated the separation of church and state (Grell, Israel, and Tyacke 1991). Such events yielded a new series of reflections and the transition to modern conceptions of rights based on the use of reason, not necessarily on divine dispensations—even though the ghost of metaphysics continued to appear, especially in exclusionary conceptions of humanity.

What interests me here is to connect these developments of conceptions of rights and humanity to the revolutionary motivation that led to *The Declaration of Independence of the Thirteen Colonies* in North America on July 4, 1776. Unable to completely avoid metaphysics, the *Declaration* begins by affirming God's creation, the laws of nature, and human natural entitlements as "endowed by the Creator." Following the natural rights tradition, the *Declaration* adds "Life, Liberty and the pursuit of Happiness" as unalienable rights. Later, the Constitution of the United States affirms the principle of people's sovereignty, the differentiation of government branches, the definition of checks and balances for mutual control, and the granting of rights in the *Bill of Rights* in 1791. These are the philosophical premises from which an emerging constitutionalism is derived, yielding a transition from colonial to postcolonial state (Grimm 1991:31). Yet, although these rights were to apply to every person in the United States, a series of contradictions became evident. This can be seen in Thomas Paine and Thomas Jefferson. Paine was known for his strong advocacy for the independence of the American

166 BUILDING COSMOPOLITAN COMMUNITIES

colonies and for his defense of the "Rights of Man." In his view, rights
were given by nature from the beginning of creation and passed from
generation to generation because "all men are born equal." Jefferson
called the attention upon this fact and, in his *A Summary View of the
Rights of British America*, argued that those in the British colonies
inherited their rights from their ancestors in Britain. Through his role
in crafting the *Declaration of Independence*, the phrase "all men are
born equal" reappears (Engemann 2000; Larkin 2005). Although this
marks the inauguration of a new North American constitutional tradition, there is a problematic appeal to a metaphysical instance as the
justification of law, a focus on territorial sovereignty, and a restriction
of universal rights, so that women, children, slaves, and foreigners
were not counted as bearers of constitutional rights. The discrepancy
occasioned by these problems would lead to the continuing oppression of all those who were not considered fully "humans" (Jensen
1968; Ward 1972) and prompt reactions that go from the Civil War
and abolition of slavery in the 1860s to the universal suffrage in the
1920s and the civil rights movement in the 1960s. The transition
to civil rights in the United States presupposes this background and
continuously wrestles with it, as seen in Affirmative Action, the Civil
Rights Act, the Voting Rights Act, and the dismantling of the "Don't
Ask, Don't Tell" policy in the military. These cases exemplify transitions to a new generation of claims such as the right to work, right to
have credit, and the right to construct one's own narrative.

In France, the social-political views of Jean-Jacques Rousseau in his
Discours sur l'origine et les fondaments de l'inegalité parmi les hommes
relied on the view of a Native American "noble savage" [*le bon sau-
vage*] once alluded to by Michel de Montaigne to provide an alternative to Hobbes's notion of the natural state as "the war of all against
all" (Rousseau 1969 3:125–126, 146–147). He then proposed the
principle of popular sovereignty [*volonté générale, souverainété*] in *Le
Contrat social*, defining it as the legitimizing instance of the republican form of government. These ideas then functioned as philosophical
premises for revolutionary movements and the French *Declaration on
the Rights of Men* in 1789. In Germany, it is in Immanuel Kant that we
find a synthesis of these ideas and the modern foundation of human
rights. He starts with an emphasis on freedom and autonomy, then
expands them in terms of law and politics in his definition of "rights,"
and finally develops a conception of history, law, and citizenship based
on a "world citizenship" [*weltbürgerlich*] approach. It is in light of this
approach that he defines a "right of humanity" [*Recht der Menschheit*]
beyond the limits of the nation-state (Kant 1902 [*AA* 8]). Thus, in

Toward Perpetual Peace, published in 1795, he affirms that a new law of world citizenship should guarantee the individual rights to freedom, autonomy, and equality, based upon which other rights are derived. Kant not only argues that reason naturally mandates the end of all wars, but also presented further concrete reasons to justify the elimination of imperialism and colonialism (Bobbio 1969; Lutz-Bachmann and Bohman 1997; Cavallar 1999, 2002; Kleingeld 2011). These theories did not prevent, however, the violence of French colonialism in Africa and the geopolitics of German colonialism in Namibia or the dictatorship of National-Socialism in Europe (Douzinas 2000).

What should we make of these examples? The ideas and events inspired by these representative markers of the Enlightenment are considered to be the culmination of the transition from natural rights to civil and constitutional rights, as well as an anticipation of an international order later established through different steps, including the Geneva Convention, the League of Nations, the United Nations, and the *Universal Declaration on Human Rights*. As I have tried to indicate, despite the important progress made, there are many challenges to the epistemic idea of defining rational rules and legal procedures of an established civil constitution. As the colonial cases of exclusion of Native Americas, women, African Americans, children, and foreigners show, the defense of human rights could not be based only on a blind epistemic conception of rights. It always implicitly relied on assumptions about who counts as truly human. Modern constitutionalism relies on the assumption that "the people" grant legitimacy to a political order and its legal framework, but as I have indicated, many humans were arbitrarily left out because they were not considered humans.

Discursive Approaches

I now turn to positions that interpret human rights and the meaning of humanity in light of communicative and discursive approaches. The creation of the United Nations in 1945 and adoption of the *Universal Declaration on Human Rights* in 1948 mark a shift to a third paradigm that includes and supersedes previous traditions of rights, duties, and conceptions of humanity. We can now turn to some contemporary debates that emphasize the construction of discourses and the meaning of humanity. I want to show how they influence current debates on human rights and promote radical transitions.

The *Universal Declaration on Human Rights* sets out a list of 30 specific human rights that countries should respect and protect. These rights can be separated analytically to be studied and criticized: there are *basic rights* that guarantee freedom and autonomy; *security rights* that protect people from rape, torture, murder, and genocide; *processual rights* that forbid imprisonment without trial and control forms of punishment; *political rights* that promote democracy and participation through assembling, protesting, voting, and serving in public office; *equality rights* that denounce discrimination; *social rights* that provide for education, shelter, and nourishment; and *cultural rights* that allow for the expression of identities, languages, and cultural resources (Kymlicka 1995; Talbott 2005; Nickel 2007). Pogge, Nussbaum, Derrida, and others discuss the language of human rights, but focus less on the importance of *rights* and more on the meaning of *human*. Their perspectives bring us, then, back to my starting point.

Pogge tries to analyze human rights discourses by paying attention to terms such as "natural law," "natural rights," and "human rights." To him, this simple detail (the adding of "human" into the picture) is what makes a difference. Pursuing this point, he shows continuities and discontinuities in these terms. As he affirms, "By violating natural rights one wrongs the subject whose right it is. These subjects of natural rights are viewed as sources of moral claims and thereby recognized as having certain moral standing and value" (Pogge 2008:189). In talking about different languages or idioms for human rights, Pogge criticizes the natural law idiom for its references to God or to a harmonious order of the cosmos, and complements that "the adjective 'human'—unlike 'natural'—does not suggest an ontological status independent of any and all human efforts" (2008:191). Moreover, he adds "universality" beyond particularities, because all humans should have the same rights and participate in a collectivity that guarantees such rights. Once he settles this issue, Pogge is then in condition to propose an institutional understanding of human rights that involves two claims: (1) a social order is unjust if it denies or deprives some or all of its participants' rights; and (2) persons share a collective responsibility to promote the justice in this social order (2008:193). The subtle point here is that institutions shall serve all those implied in the adjective "human."

Nussbaum follows a similar strategy as she questions the limits of the languages emphasizing "rights" and insists on the need to highlight the human dimension at play in human rights (2004b). She starts with the assumption that humans are not necessarily equal, but have differences that need to be compensated for in certain situations, so that all humans have the right to pursue their full potential as humans. To say, for example, that women are de facto equal to men is to disregard centuries of oppression and to pretend that a simple nominal equalization would be able to repair this damage. Similarly, we cannot merely affirm that all humans are equal when we discriminate against people with disabilities. As Nussbaum explains, "the language of rights has a moral resonance that makes it hard to avoid in contemporary political discourse. But it is certainly not on account of its theoretical and conceptual clarity that it has been preferred. There are many different ways of thinking about what a right is, and many different definitions of 'human rights'" (2001a:212–213). Also here, the discursive attention to a simple adjective makes all the difference.

Along these lines, Nussbaum questions—in the same was as Pogge does—whether only individuals have rights. Other entities, families, ethnic, religious, and linguistic groups may claim rights as well. She also questions the correlation between duties and rights, and asks what rights entitle to. This answer may refer to goods, processes, goals, and other variables. For all these uncertainties and difficulties, she concludes that the language of rights is limited. As an alternative, she develops her "capabilities approach." Her proposal for *human* rights includes the rights to life, bodily health, senses and imagination, emotions and friendship, play, and control over one's environment (2001a:223–225). The capabilities approach deserves more attention, but my goal here is simply to introduce it. Undoubtedly, Nussbaum's point is directly related to the goals and purposes of being human: "Capability must be the goal because of the great importance the capabilities approach attaches to practical reason, as a good that both suffuses all the other functions, making them human rather than animal" (2001a:226). She does not deny the importance of rights, but insists on the need to make room for basic human capabilities.

These authors are obviously taking issue with the liberal concept of justice as "fairness" and its corresponding emphasis on rights. This corresponds to a new transition in the discussion of human rights and brings us closer to postmodern authors who insist on gestures, sentiment, emotions, and even silence as relevant in human rights discourses. Lyotard was the first to talk about a "postmodern condition" and use Wittgenstein to value the use of narratives in everyday life and advocate for the recognition of different cultures (Lyotard 1983). Derrida follows this same trajectory. Based on this enlargement of the communicative process, he also affirms that when we do not recognize the claims implicit in these narratives, we are being unjust to certain groups (Derrida 1982, 1994). Therefore, we have a moral obligation to keep the conversation going and add new interlocutors to our dialogue, so that their claims can be heard and their rights respected. In Derrida's article "Wears and Tears (Tableau of an Ageless World)," the play with words, the consideration of new technologies, the discussion of bodily and erotic interactions, the recognition of differences, and the inclusion of all these elements adds more complexity to the discussion of human rights discourses because "discourse" is not limited to language, but includes all kinds of expressions. Using his deconstructive method, he searches for gaps in our conceptions of rights and observes the ambiguity of human rights, especially in the talk about *humanitarian interventions.* He actually sees something positive in it: this discussion forces us to move beyond state-centered structures and design new projects worth pursuing: "Just as the concept of human rights has slowly been determined over the course of centuries through many socio-political upheavals (whether it be a matter of the right to work or economic rights, of the rights of women and children, and so forth), likewise international law should extend and diversify its field to include, if at least it is to be consistent with the idea of democracy and of human rights it proclaims, the *worldwide* economic and social field" (cited in Hayden 2001:265).

All this takes us back to Habermas and Apel, who identify this new wave of considerations as part of the discursive paradigm and confirm that discursive approaches are better suitable to contemporary times. They also help us to conclude this section. As discussed before, Habermas sees the possibility of adopting a discursive paradigm and considering both concepts of *rights* and *humanity* as co-originary [*gleich-ursprünglich*] in order to conceive of an indivisible conception of *human rights.* With this in mind, I will conclude this chapter by reflecting on how this paradigm can be related to the multidimensional perspective and orient us in defining human rights discourses.

THE UNIVERSALITY OF HUMAN RIGHTS AS AN ASPIRATIONAL DISCOURSE

The worldviews that I tried to review above indicate attempts to implement human rights based on metaphysical and religious views, and also the evolution to new legal, constitutional, and democratic frameworks. As I attempted to describe an incredible variety of positions involved in contemporary human rights discussions, theories, and practices, I also introduced various contexts, cultures, and peoples. Navigating this variety is definitely risky, but it has the advantage of providing a more dynamic and intercultural picture of the various issues at stake. Confronted with this complex scenario, I pursued three goals as a way of making sense of this wide plurality: to show that a legal understanding of human rights tends to emphasize the dimension of *rights* and downplay the meaning of *human*, thus disregarding important personal and cultural differences; to argue that the focus on *rights* often forgets the *human* dimension expressed differently in many cultures; and to propose a transition from *rights* to the *human* dimension in order to affirm the indivisibility of *human rights*.

Regarding the first goal, I recognized the different cultural traditions and worldviews that emerge out of specific paradigms and briefly identified some key conceptions of humanity and rights that have gone through transitions and shifts. Concerning the second objective, I showed that the roots of contemporary discourses on human rights are deep and go back to comprehensive views about humanity that can be traced to axial times. Finally, as I briefly went over the transition from an epistemic emphasis on positive law to a third paradigm I tried to show the cultural and historical underpinnings of this process and emphasize the need for a new focus on discourses about humanity and the ways of interacting with them. In this process, I referred to authors who have sought to link the discussion about human rights to questions concerning the meaning of humanity, human dignity, and human capabilities. This latter reference to humanity is not necessarily metaphysical, but it accounts for the contingencies of life, the plurality of views, and the possibility of reconstructing them discursively. Moreover, this discursive consideration of human rights is not necessarily limited to juridical terms.

How does this relate to the multidimensional conception of community? Although I recognized the evolutionary and linearity of paradigms, it is also important to acknowledge that older paradigms can survive and remain active as well as new paradigms can have regressive changes, simultaneously affecting different horizontal contexts that may correspond to different communities of communication with their respective discourses. Therefore, it is possible to move from one community to another when we make sense of intercultural perspectives and different types of discourse. It is relatively easy to describe and understand metaphysics as still applied in philosophy and religion, although scientific (epistemic) thinking is still central to many aspects of everyday life in a modern society. Similarly, it is also possible to understand how a person may go to a religious community on Sunday and claim her rights in the moral language of religious discourses but then participate in the activities of a scientific community on Monday and raise the same claims, but translated in epistemic terms. Consequently, what we need is an account of how we can shift our discourses from metaphysical through scientific or common pragmatic discourses, depending on both the intracultural institutions and the intercultural settings. I therefore adopt this perspective of various para-digms not simply as a way of classifying different philosophical concep-tions of rights, human, and, by extension, "human rights," but also to have a "key" for a dialogue amid this variety. Therefore, those who use cultural or religious categories to define "humanity" would fall into the ontological or metaphysical paradigm; those who rely somewhat exclusively on the specific constitutional framework of a given state would be related to the epistemic framework; while those who define humanity in wider discursive terms that account for this variety would be considered as following the communicative paradigm. The point in all this is to affirm diversity and plurality, while recognizing that it is possible to articulate this diversity by means of communication. By adding this proviso, I hope to open the possibility of understanding different frameworks, recognizing and comparing cultural and histori-cal differences, and seeing them in a porous relationship.

This leads to my conclusion of this chapter. Human rights are not only abstract international and national norms, laws, and rules but also concrete expressions of ontological, epistemic, and cultural assump-tions on what counts as humanity, which can be translated into dif-ferent discourses. Rights are embedded in cultures and paradigms that influence the way we develop and interpret legal frameworks, they are not immune from political and economic policies, and they are related to institutional structures in ways that can influence the effectiveness of a particular law or policy. Undoubtedly, social, economic, and cultural issues play a significant role in the implementation of rights and need to be taken into account when we consider a series of transitions prompted by the intrinsic ambiguity of the very term "human rights." The shift to the human dimension does not mean, however, a neglect of the legal framework. Rather, it challenges us to realize the complementary relation between strong national and institutional frameworks that pro-mote the juridification of human interactions and the equally strong assumptions underlying what we define as human. This double perspec-tive demands a fundamental reflection on the very meaning of *human rights* and the internal discursive and conceptual relationship between these two terms. Rights may be abstract and purposively general, but they are always related to concrete forms of being human. There is no uniformity in these concrete forms—which makes the task of account-ing for it more difficult—but applying the criteria of a multidimensional discourse community, we at least have a test to check if our understand-ings of human rights are open enough to claim universality.

6

Cosmopolitan Ideals and the
Norms of Universality

Cosmopolitanism is an old concept that has experienced a resurrection in contemporary political theory, law, international relations, and philosophy, especially in view of globalization. A changing global context has brought about challenges such as the weakening of nation-states, deregulating of economic sectors, volatility of financial markets, increased inequalities, growing poverty, political instability, ongoing military conflicts, transnational environmental problems, irreversible impacts of climate change, and many other pressing issues. As we become aware of the interconnected character of these global challenges as well as the difficulties associated with the task of guaranteeing human rights amid this complex state of affairs, we also realize the difficult task of finding comprehensive answers to complex global problems. Building new community structures, implementing human rights norms worldwide, and upholding ideals capable of wide acceptation could be an important part of the solution. Based on my previous arguments for a multidimensional discourse community, a plural account of changing communities, and recognition of overlapping paradigmatic views on the normativity of human rights, I will continue my dialogue with Discourse Philosophy in order to differentiate the plethora of proposals available and offer what I believe to be a more robust framework for a critical cosmopolitan outlook.

I want to locate cosmopolitan ideals in a field of tension between global plurality and global universality. How can we relate universality and globalization? Because some forms of globalization lack universal legitimacy but claim universalist acceptability, it is necessary to specify which type of global approach is compatible with a critical cosmopolitan ideal. I identify *universalism* with a negative sense of globalization that includes practices such as imperialism, economic domination, imposition of cultural values, and disrespect for differences. The subtle difference in reference to *universality* implies, on the contrary, a positive moral and aspirational dimension that serves as a normative guide amid the plethora of global problems. Based on which criteria? The test for multidimensionality shall help us verify whether the plural conditions involved in belonging to and participating in a community of communication are being fulfilled and if a discursive account of human rights can account for them. To these general criteria I now explicitly add the universality of cosmopolitan ideals by considering questions concerning the global protection of human rights, their relation to moral claims, and the reference to a realm of universal validity in relation to which these claims are raised.

COSMOPOLITANISM AND THE
CHALLENGES OF GLOBALIZATION

In their historic variations, cosmopolitan ideals have always claimed to foster universality by considering *all* humans as members of the same encompassing community. However, this assumption needs continuous scrutiny and justification, otherwise one could naively accept forms of universalism that impose or maintain arbitrary forms of exclusion. For example, as we have seen in our discussion of human rights, forms of exclusion have been justified by defining what is human, so that some people could be excluded as nonhumans: children were seen as not yet fully humans, women were considered deficient humans due to lack of rationality, and other groups were excluded from humanity due to the color of their skin, their gender, capabilities, or culture. These arguments affected corresponding definitions of cosmopolitanism, which, therefore, contradicted the very definition of cosmopolitan ideas. As a result, contemporary positions seek to define more precisely what is at stake in cosmopolitan views. These positions represent interdisciplinary attempts to come to terms with older metaphysical assumptions, limited or outdated epistemic categories, and more realist ways of securing individual freedom and equality, addressing social needs, promoting community interactions, and establishing the means necessary to navigate the complexity of globalization processes (Höffe 2004; Delanty 2012).

From a sociological perspective, Ulrich Beck criticizes the traditional sociological focus on nationalist frameworks and recognizes the particular challenges related to the European experience. He describes the challenges of a world risk society and proposes a more global outlook in a program that goes from a *Cosmopolitan Manifesto* (1998, reprinted in Brown and Held 2010) through a *Cosmopolitan*

Europe (Beck and Grande 2007) to a *Cosmopolitan Vision* (2006). In this process, he defines "cosmopolitanization" as a "reflective" attitude that promotes deterritorialized interactions. Such interactions create movements whose agents emerge "from within" and expand nonlinearly toward nonnational democratic institutions that deserve the label "cosmopolitan" (2006:81–86, 99f.). In my view, Beck is convincing in his critique of sociology. His critical conception of a "cosmopolitanization from below" involving movements of civil society, a "cosmopolitanization from outside" involving global politics, and "cosmopolitanization from above" involving supranational institutions is very helpful, for it describes dynamic social processes and infuses multidimensionality (Beck and Grande 2007:157–161). However, he seems less clear in providing a more compelling description of what is prescriptive in cosmopolitanization. He does mention the need to recognize the plurality of the external others, but it is not clear on what grounds this should rest. Similarly, Gerard Delanty concedes that "global forces have become more and more visible and take a huge variety of forms, from economic and technological to cultural and political," so that they need to be addressed by a critical normative perspective. For him, this is the task of a *critical cosmopolitanism* that does not simply rely on political philosophy, but includes the contributions of social sciences and moral theories in order to address four components of a "cosmopolitan imagination": cultural pluralism and heterogeneity, global-local relations, negotiation of territorial borders, and the reinvention of a political community around global ethics. A particular useful aspect for me is his conception of the interaction of plural values and an ethical ideal as a "site of tensions" because this obviously has a multidimensional interactive character (Delanty 2009:7, 15, 51–68, 79). Yet, individuality disappears from sight and this needs to be clearly integrated into the framework.

In the shadow of Rawls, there are many options within the tradition of "liberal cosmopolitanism" that merges political liberalism and moral egalitarianism while accounting for individuals. Interesting examples in this area are Kok-Chor Tan's *Justice without Borders* (2004) and Simon Caney's *Justice beyond Borders* (2005). Caney argues for a "humanity-centered" cosmopolitan political morality based on the premise that some of Rawls's principles of distributive justice are expandable at the global level and can be applied universally to *all* independently of morally arbitrary characteristics. This requires a global institutional framework that he defines as *cosmopolitan justice* (2005). Although debates around these topics are also defined by the concept of global justice—since some scholars such as Thomas Risse show little use for the term "cosmopolitanism" (2012:9, 82–84)—most salient positions use a variety of cosmopolitan categories. There is a talk of "moral and institutional" (Beitz 1999 and 2009; Tan 2004; Pierik and Werner 2010), "thick and thin" (Held 2010:75), and "weak and strong" forms of cosmopolitanism (Miller 2007:24–31). Scheffler uses the terminology of "extreme and moderate" cosmopolitanism to contrast the strong requirement to justify obligations and commitments in light of a global cosmopolitan principle with the more accommodating view that relaxes this demand and excludes certain special obligations from this requirement (Scheffler 1999:255–276). These are variations summarized by Pogge in terms of a tension between "moral and legal cosmopolitanism" (2008:175). I follow this distinction, but take issue with the institutional limitations drawn by Pogge. I agree that beyond its interactional fashion cosmopolitanism involves a duty to assist in the establishment of institutions that safeguard human rights and to become involved in eradicating poverty and promoting global health. However, Pogge limits global obligations to institutions in such a way that he explicitly says that an individual case of violence against *a* woman or other crimes would remain outside the scope of scrutiny (2008:57–58). Although his conception of human rights accounts for *individuals* as bearer of rights (2008:175), the individual dimension is weakened in the realm of cosmopolitan duties and responsibilities because it is tied mainly to how individuals participate in institution building.

A reference to global institutions surely requires a consideration of cosmopolitanism in relation to international political theory and normative international relations theory. On this front we see the echoes of the communitarian debate alluded to by Erskine (2008:8f.), which can be traced back to Mervyn Frost (1986), Andrew Linklater (1998), and Molly Cochran (1999), who defend a cosmopolitan approach from the charges coming from realism, Marxism, and pragmatism. What I find useful in this discussion is their consideration of poststructuralist and feminist antifoundationalist views, which are combined by Cochran in order to account for *contingencies* that both reveal who are the agents in cosmopolitan interactions and question the structures that domesticate them. It is on this basis that she questions the marginalization of women in international relations theory and cosmopolitanism. Ultimately, she sides with Richard Rorty's pragmatist views on contingency and solidarity, hoping that its combination with feminism can be useful and help to integrate gender issues in the cosmopolitan agenda (Cochran 1999:146–167, 220–230). Another attempt to integrate postmodern and poststructural theories into a conception of cosmopolitanism in international relations can be seen in Beardsworth, who describes the wide spectrum of cosmopolitanism and contrasts it with realism, Marxism, and postmodernism, but then concludes that political liberalism can better address the respective political, economic, and cultural challenges presented by these positions. Interestingly, Beardsworth proposes a *differentiated universalism* that, in his view, is true to "the more general fact that the practical implementation of cosmopolitan ideas is necessarily layered" (2011:231). This appears compatible with the multidimensional approach I defend because it includes a plural dimension, but I do not particularize universality in this way. Rather, I see the need for universality to emerge from a recognition of plurality. Beardsworth's intention is to distinguish between national, regional, and global institutional levels to offer the possibility of articulating them with a universal approach while maintaining that social agents can be embedded in various contexts (2011:159). However, he neither accounts for the identity of the agents in these contexts nor defines what would count as universality in relation to an interactive human dimension. His differentiated universalism appears to weaken universality.

So far, we can see that the multidimensional model helps us to detect the individual dimension missing in institutional approaches, the lack of institutional accounts in purely interactive models of cosmopolitanism, and the weak definition of universalism in positions that consider the importance of plurality. We can now refer to a critical political approach to global governance proposed by David Held in partnership with Daniele Archibugi. Held attempts, first, to identify, describe, and analyze the challenges of globalization (Held and McGrew 2003); second, to develop a whole program to address global challenges to both the nation-state and the interstate system (1995b; Archibugi, Held, and Köhler 1998); and third, to link these initiatives to the normative guidance of democratic practices at the global level (2010). Upon realizing the limits of national frameworks, he embraces the cosmopolitan alternative wholeheartedly. In Held's view, these challenges are to be addressed by means of a program that rethinks democracy and establishes new structures beyond the nation-state (1995a; see also Held in Lutz-Bachmann and Bohman 1997:235–251). This yields what Held sees as a "thick" form of cosmopolitanism defined as "the ethical and political space which sets out the terms of reference for the recognition of people's equal moral worth, their active agency and what is required for their autonomy and development" (2010:49). Out of this definition he derives autonomy and impartiality as two metaprinciples, which are complemented by eight principles: equal worth and dignity, active agency or self-determination, personal responsibility and accountability, consent or participation in noncoercive political processes, collective decision making through voting, inclusiveness of people affected by establishing more democratic decision making and subsidiarity of decisions, refraining from harming other, and promotion of sustainable development. Many critics note that Held arrives somewhat too readily to a list of prescriptions about the constitution of a new global order, so contradicting the participatory measures he proposes. For instance, he provides lists of issues related to politics, finance, security, the environment, and, above all, democratic representation. What is attractive for me in Held and Archibugi is the role of civil society as part of a multilayered institutional structure, but they seem to reduce cosmopolitanism to the idea of a multilevel self-governance without paying attention to individual and collective processes that occur at these various levels (Archibugi 2008:85f.). Held and Archibugi have been criticized also for their views on global governance. After realizing that they rely too heavily on institutional frameworks such as the United Nations without accounting for the agents involved in various global processes, they began to redefine the project of cosmopolitan democracy in order to make it open-ended and more sensitive to collective agency (Archibugi and Held 2011).

Parallel to these proposals, there remains a tension between liberal and communitarian approaches to global challenges. Toni Erskine contrasts between a communitarian "embedded cosmopolitanism" and a liberal "impartialist cosmopolitanism" based on Rawls's views (2008:39–42, 51f.). In her defense of the embedded perspective, she adopts Walzer's communitarianism and Gilligan's feminist ethics to conclude that community is a structure more flexible than liberal and realist theories assume (2008:170–175). I agree with Erskine that community should not be identified with the state but be open to individuality, even in the extreme case of combatant enemies who should be treated as members of "overlapping communities" (2008:2009). This concept is very helpful, but the dimension of universality is clearly missing in her account because she affirms that "moral commitments cannot be derived from our 'common humanity'" (2008:176). Gillian Brock criticizes Rawls as well, but she upholds impartiality and, based on a thought experiment, adapts Rawls's account of the "original position" and proposes a needs-based minimum floor principle to guarantee equality from the outset (2009:45f.; see also Gould 2004). I find this strategy very useful. She then expands this model by applying it globally to issues of poverty, humanitarian intervention, and working conditions (2009:45f., 232). Interestingly, she considers a needs account more basic than a human rights or a capabilities approach because, in her view, it addresses material needs more directly and early enough—both as concrete conditions to equality and as quasi-institutional instances to promote global justice. However, in being impartial she does not provide an account of who is involved in this process and thus she repeats the same problem Allen Buchanan identifies in Rawls's *Law of Peoples* (1999; Martin and Reidy 2006:150–151): the agents to be involved in real and just global interactions remain as abstract as the individuals in her fictional point of departure. In my opinion, this project lacks a concrete human component as the agent and subject of global justice.

Due to limits I identify in these positions, I need to move beyond these examples and take into consideration other approaches that offer a wider historical or cultural perspective and at the same time specify the agents and processes involved in cosmopolitan interactions. One example might be Pauline Kleingeld, who actually centers her attention on Kant's cosmopolitanism and the German context, but arrives to a variety of cosmopolitan theories that deal with peace, law, trade, and education as well as issues on culture, race, and colonialism that emerge in the eighteenth century and are somewhat reflected in contemporary debates (Kleingeld 2011:177–178). I say "somewhat" because racism, sexism, and colonialism continue below the radar in cosmopolitan theories that simply upgrade Kant's views without dealing with his shortcomings in these areas. Nevertheless, new critical perspectives arise that take a courageous look at such controversial issues and tell us who are affected by them (Breckenridge et al. 2002; Vertotec and Cohen 2002; Appiah 2003; Cheah 2003; van Hooft and Vandekerckhove 2011). In accounting for this variety, Eduardo Mendieta differentiates between civic, critical, and dialogic forms of cosmopolitanism, which radicalize the dimension of diversity and take subalternity into account (2007, 2009). He therefore defends a cosmopolitanism from below as "a version of cosmopolitanism that is grounded, enlightened, and reflexive, which corrects and supersedes Kant's own Eurocentric cosmopolitanism" (2009:241). I will return to these positions later on.

For now, all I need to say is that this initial overview tells us what to avoid and what to take from contemporary cosmopolitan theories. While reviewing them, I made use of the multidimensional approach and accepted some aspects in them that can enrich my own proposal. In the following considerations, I would like to connect this discussion to the perspectives on human rights I presented in the previous

chapter, then step back and take a global point of departure, so that cosmopolitan ideals can be related to the three main philosophical paradigms discussed before. By showing a historical transition and contemporary availability of metaphysical positions, epistemic conceptions of positive law, and the more contemporary move toward discourses, I believe I can come up with a more robust framework based on the multidimensional discourse community. In my view, the radical discontinuities we see in the understanding and definition of cosmopolitanism as well as the tension between Habermas and Apel can be understood as different moments in a transition toward a fully communicative understanding of cosmopolitanism that can account for plurality and claim universality.

FROM THE PLURALITY OF COSMOPOLITAN VIEWS TO GLOBAL UNIVERSALITY

Similar to the way I previously exemplified the conceptual and practical transitions in the definition of human rights, I will now take a look at cosmopolitanism according to a plurality of paradigms. Recognizing this plurality can help us shift our attention to the often-neglected human dimension in contemporary discussions and prepare our move toward an understanding of what a critical cosmopolitanism could be. I propose to step further back and—despite the risk of using traditional historical markers—refer to larger cultural frameworks that correspond to metaphysical, epistemic, and discursive perspectives on cosmopolitanism.

A Dualist Cosmopolitan Metaphysics

The first category I would like to use is that of a *dualist metaphysical cosmopolitanism*. Cosmopolitanism is an ancient theme whose echoes still resound. Obviously, this term is the combination of two important Greek words, *cosmos* and *polis*, which have deep roots in pre-Socratic philosophy. It is in this context that an encompassing definition of *cosmos* as a metaphysical unity emerges, which was supposed to make sense of reality and find the adequate place of humans in the world. We thus have a series of views on *cosmos* in Thales of Mileto, Pythagoras, Heraclitus, and many other ancient Greeks. It is with Heraclitus, however, that we find a first move toward a definition of *cosmopolis* and *cosmopolites*. *Cosmos* has been generally translated as "universe," surely influenced by a Pythagorean view of the *cosmos* as "harmony," which anticipates the idea of integrating several parts into a consistent whole—for example, humans as part of the universe. However, it is a fragment by Heraclitus that provides a crucial view that will be constitutive to later discussions on this theme. As he states, "This *cosmos*, the same for all, no god nor man has made, but it ever was and is and will be: fire ever living, kindled in measures and in measures going out" (Heraclitus 1903: Frag. B4).

According to Ruin, this is the oldest known preserved example of the very word *cosmos* being used not only to designate the wholeness of being but also to describe a special metaphysical realm in which all humans should participate. It is not too much of a stretch to claim that this statement is, in nuce, a possible anticipation of a declaration of universal rights (Ruin 2008). Yet, a more obvious step in this direction can be seen in Plato and Aristotle. In Plato's *Timaeus*, the *cosmos* becomes a realm of ideas, the source based upon which the world is created in its most essential ways. It is in this sense that he speaks of a metaphysical cosmology that will orient his political project. Aristotle's views are more empirically oriented, but he shares with Plato the goal of designing a project for the Athenian *polis*, in which the citizen [*polites*] is sharply distinguished from the isolated person, stranger, or noncitizen [*idiotes*] who did not participate actively in public affairs. In his *Politics*, Aristotle defined the citizen as "the one who participates in the decisions and rulings [*kriseos kai arches*] of the state," while the person who did not belong to a state was defined as noncitizen [*apolis*] (*Pol.* 1275a; Ruin 2008:40). The connection between *cosmos* and *polis* and the divergence between active civic leaders and those who did not belong to the polity is only implicit and needs to be revealed (Farrar 1988; Rubinstein 1998; Collins 2006; Hansen 2006, 2010).

As Nussbaum has reminded us, one of the earliest and most important references to *cosmopolis* is found in the Greek cynic, Diogenes of Sinope, who lived around 400–325 BCE and is now acknowledged as being one of the first to express the idea of being a citizen of the cosmos (Nussbaum 1997; Ruin 2008:40; E. Brown 2010). Asked by the Athenian citizens about his origin, belonging, and allegiance [*pothen eie*], Diogenes simply answered that he was a cosmopolitan—*cosmopolites*. Although this statement was probably registered by Diogenes Laertius in the third century of the Common Era (around 200 CE), long after Diogenes of Sinope allegedly affirmed it (Diogenes Laertius [1925] *Lives* II:65, 365), this expression is generally considered the birth certificate of cosmopolitanism (Moles 1996:105–120). This provocative answer was not only a radical way to affirm individual identity in view of the communitarian pressures that expected complete commitment and loyalty to the *polis*, the city-state, but also a form of affirming the possibility of being a citizen of the world, of being at home anywhere, of demanding the ancient right to hospitality and respect. In fact, this is an early example of anticonventionalism, for Diogenes systematically questioned and disobeyed the established community rules.

The most elaborated conception of ancient cosmopolitan metaphysics, which expands on this political meaning, is found in the Stoic tradition. This tradition initiated with the teaching and writings of Zeno of Citium (around 334–262 BCE), who studied with Diogenes and defined *cosmopolites* as a way of living in the world while at the same time being connected to a higher sphere beyond the contingencies of a particular *polis* (Schofield 1999:93–101). The Stoics were less concerned about constituting a particular state and focused their attention on defining a "community of all beings." For the early Stoic philosophy, this would require a communal law [*koinos nomos*] applicable to all (Vogt 2008:1–5, 161–164). However, one needed to meet a series of qualifications and fulfill many conditions in order to have rights, participate in the *polis*, and aspire to becoming a cosmopolitan. Despite Heraclitus's earlier formulation, not "all" could aspire to such goal. Only the philosopher or wise man was cosmopolitan par excellence and, therefore, occupied an ideal place in general Stoic cosmology. In the end, there is an elitist tone to this metaphysical cosmopolitanism because only those capable of the Stoic discipline and aware of its philosophical subtleties could aspire to participate in the *community of sages* that was equated to *cosmopolites*. The Stoic view of *cosmopolites* did not mean to include the *idiotes* (Vogt 2008:73, 76–86).

My insistence on the transliteration of the Greek word is intentional. I want to mark this particular metaphysical understanding and somewhat freeze it in time, so that we can better appreciate what is involved and avoid the projection of our modern "cosmopolitan" sensitivities to an old metaphysical concept. By simply highlighting a few aspects, I hope to have shown that this form of cosmopolitanism did not integrate "all." So far, I have only mentioned the metaphysical conditions to be a citizen of the world. But there are also more empirical conditions to be a *polites*, which function as impediments as well. It is well known that in order to be a citizen of the Athenian *polis* one had to be a recognized male member of the community, who in virtue of possessions could be a maker and subject of democratic laws, and based on the fulfillment of duties and responsibilities, such as paying taxes and helping in the defense of the *polis*, would have the right to vote, protection from violence, and special access to public spaces.

A similar structure guided the definition of the Roman *civitas*. Indeed, an important step in the metaphysical definition of cosmopolitanism can be found in the transition from Roman Stoicism to Christianity, as observed in the works of Cicero (Gill 1988; Cancik 2002). As Nussbaum explores the passage from Cynicism to Stoicism and provides a detailed reading of the tradition that goes from Zeno through Seneca to Cicero, she reminds us of the Stoic conception of humans as citizens of two communities: "The local community of our birth and the community of human argument and aspiration" (Nussbaum 1997:29). In the words of Plutarch, however, there should be only one way of life. Even though this single way is generally interpreted by Nussbaum in moral and ideal terms, the Stoics had an opportunity to develop institutions and contribute to the establishment of a real single world-state in their epoch: the Roman Empire. A citizen was then a *cives*, not only a member of a city [*civitas*], but also recognized as bearer of rights and owner of private property within the whole imperial jurisdiction. Moreover, Stoics held important political positions in the context of the Roman Empire: Cicero was a leader in the Roman *republica*, Seneca was a regent under Nero, Marcus Aurelius was emperor, and many other Stoics were accomplished politicians (Nussbaum 1997:30; 2004a:214–249). As argued by Eric Brown, the Stoics applied their ideas to real local politics and then identified *cosmopolis* with the Roman *patria*, which was enlarged to include a variety of members and other cultures (E. Brown 2010:16–18). The Roman Empire was a unifying cosmopolitan force in Europe and as exchange for the allegiance of different tribes and communities it conquered, it offered a valuable compensation, at least to those who had served in Roman legions and showed their commitment for a considerable amount of time. As it can be seen in the case of the Roman conquest of Israel or later in Germania, these individuals could become Roman citizens after finishing decades of military duty (Rüger 2000:502).

With Christianity, some elements of the earlier cosmological views were rescued, especially the idea that humanity is not limited to belonging to a particular community or simply bound to an allegiance to the Emperor: "Render therefore unto Caesar the things which are Caesar's; and unto God the things that are God's" (Matthews 22:21). In later theological interpretations, this yielded at least two outcomes. On the one hand, to be human is to be created in the image of God [*imago Dei*] and to belong to a wider spiritual community (Danielou 1976). This certainly appears as a more democratic condition. On the other hand, however, there are important demands and repressive elements that conditioned participation in the institutional version of the "community of saints." A brief reconstruction of the metaphysical paradigm in terms of the Christian theology radicalizes the assumption of ontological totality that we find in previous accounts.

Augustine is certainly the best reference here because he defined an alternative conception of *civitas* and, to a certain extent, democratized the Stoic elitist conception of cosmopolitan metaphysics. *Cosmos,* now translated as *universus,* was identified with the Catholic faith and connected to eternity, which was initially understood by Augustine as a matter of time. We cannot forget, however, that Catholicism was the official religion in Rome after 383 CE, which imposed a new imperial unity. It is not surprising, therefore, that in comparison with the plurality of conceptions of time in ancient Greek philosophy—which can be roughly transladed as sequential time [*chromos*], day [*hêmera*], present day [*semeron*], opportunity [*kairós*], epoch [*aíon*], and others—Augustine saw Christianity as the inaugurator of a *tempus modernus* that not only disregards but also literally represses the diversity of cultures characterized as *pagani* (*Conf.* XI.xiv.17). This ambiguity yields a new view of cosmopolitan citizenship, based on a dualism between the *civitas terrena* and the *civitas dei.* In order to strictly separate between historical contingences and cosmic or theological hope, Augustine differentiates between Babylon as the "city on Earth," with its Babelian confusion of languages and misunderstandings and Jerusalem as the "city of God." One is the diabolic city while the other is the spiritual community (*Civ. Dei* XVII.16). From this same perspective, Augustine interprets the internal tensions between the Roman culture and the church (Orbán 1980). The Roman Empire was about to collapse and Augustine proposed a view of a new polity oriented by Christian values. Thus, he adds that humans are citizens of two worlds: not only the rights granted by the Roman Empire, but most importantly, the membership in the Kingdom of God. As Kleingeld and Brown affirm in their overview of ancient Greek and Roman cosmopolitanism, "while Augustine can stress that this allows citizens in the city of God to obey local laws concerning 'the necessaries for the maintenance of life,' he must also acknowledge that it sets up a potential conflict over the laws of religion and the concerns of righteousness and justice" (*Civ. Dei* XIX.17; Kleingeld and Brown 2006).

Many other details could be presented about the continuing influence of Stoic cosmopolitanism and the different understandings of an implicit cosmopolitanism in Christianity. Yet, we have enough material to lead us to a conclusion. Cosmopolitanism has a metaphysical origin, but it is also applied *in concreto* in terms of rights to citizenship.

On the one hand, the metaphysical aspect implies a view of humanity as part of the universe and, therefore, as free to move beyond a particular and contingent community with its idiosyncrasies. On the other hand, this understanding is applied to reality, to local cities, and to questions of private property, military service, and political organization, which bring about not only the affirmation of the totality of a communal law, but also impose important arbitrary limitations that led to elitism and repression. This form of religious and metaphysical understanding of cosmopolitanism is definitively *dualistic* in a vertical sense and survives to this day in the very word "cosmopolitan." A profound metaphysical ambiguity is constitutive to this term. It is advisable, therefore, to qualify and differentiate it from the kinds of cosmopolitanism we find in modernity.

The Epistemology of World Citizenship

Now I want to mark the transition to the idea of modern individual rights within a nation-state by focusing on the epistemic concept of *world citizenship*. As we enter modernity, the term "cosmopolitan" reappears as part of the Enlightenment, when different cultures turned to ancient paganism and the Greek culture in order to question Catholic universalism (Gay 1967 2). There is, however, a subtle change that is often disregarded in contemporary discussions. Here we find a variety of terms in the European languages—"world citizen," "*Weltbürger*," "*citoyen du monde*," "*världsmedborgare*," and many others—which do not refer to the metaphysical and cosmic baggage we find in antiquity. Works such as the Abbé de Saint Pierre's *Projet pour rendre la paix perpetuelle en Europe*, Christian Wolff's *Jus gentium method scientific pertractatum*, and Émerich de Vattel's *Le droit de gens* (1758) stress the political, rational, and legal meaning of the term (Remec 1960; Cheneval 2010).

Kleingeld has provided a good overview of the varieties of cosmopolitanism in eighteenth-century Europe, especially Germany, and the different projects that used the designation "citizens of the world" (Kleingeld 1999:505; 2011:1–12). Going beyond the differentiation between moral and political forms of cosmopolitanism found in the philosophical tradition, she provides details about discussions on nationhood and patriotism in Germany in order to show six different types of projects on world citizenship: moral, political, legal, cultural—focusing on pluralism; economic—aiming at establishing an international free market; and romantic—that is, the ideal of humanity united by faith and love. She also indicates several other meanings of the word, which range from "traveler" and "traitor" to "freemason" and "francophile" (1999:506; 2011:18, 128, 179f., 197–199). The authors she discusses include Wieland, Kant, Fichte, Foster, Hegewisch, and Schlegel, but she then focuses on Kant's view on world citizenship as a tag [*welt-bürgerlich*] identifying forms of cosmopolitanism expressed in cultural, historical, political, economic, legal, and moral terms (2011:26–34, 44–49, 72–91, 120–123, 136–148, 161–176). Kant certainly constitutes the most important reference on this theme in modern times, so I will dedicate some attention to details in his philosophy.

Kant's position on this topic is presented in several ways in different texts and notes. In his short essay of 1784, "Idea for a Universal History from a Cosmopolitan Point of View," he talks about a "condition of world citizenship," [*weltbürgerliche Lage*]. In lectures given in 1793–1794—later published as the *Metaphysics of Morals Vigilantius*—he speaks of "world patriotism and local patriotism" [*Vaterlandsliebe*], adding that "both are required of the world citizen"(*AA* XVII 2.1:673–674; Kleingeld 2003, 2011; G. Brown 2009). In the essay "On the Common Saying: 'This May be True in Theory but It Does not Apply in Practice,'" he advocates for a federative world-republic that is justified in ethico-political terms also in *Religion Within the Limits of Reason Alone* (*AA* VI:94; Lutz-Bachmann 2005). All this culminates in his tract of 1795, *Toward Perpetual Peace*, where world citizenship is presented as a cluster of different legal aspects that go from the individual to the global level. Based on his ethical theory, Kant defends a right of humanity [*das Recht der Menschheit*] and insists that individual autonomy, equality, and republicanism beyond the limits of the modern nation-state would constitute the core of a right of world citizenship [*Weltbügerrecht*]. He not only recognized that individuals move between states, traders visit different countries, and persons have cultural interests about different regions, but also states in the third definitive article of *Perpetual Peace* that "world citizenship rights should be limited to the conditions of general hospitality" [*Hospitalität*]. With this criterion he writes that individuals should be free to move as global citizens in different parts of the world—thus affirming a value that is compatible with liberal individual rights—and defines a norm to assess situations of oppression. Kant's internal differentiation finally leads to a view of world citizenship as membership in an extensive community, guaranteed by world citizenship rights. He uses the concept of world citizenship rights to demarcate a new area beyond the limits of the nation-state. This resulted in the design of a legal system with different levels that would correspond to national law [*Staatsrecht*], international or comparative law [*Völkerrecht*] that, in turn, would correspond to the tradition "law of peoples" [*jus gentium*], and a law of world citizens [*Weltbürgerrecht*] (Lutz-Bachmann and Bohamn 1996).

Toward Perpetual Peace also presents arguments for a global order, cites circumstances of conflict between states using military forces, and asks whether it is possible to establish a foundation for peace (*AA* VIII:343). Kant begins his argument considering the demands of moral-practical reason, which mandates the end of all wars. In addition, he lists further concrete reasons that justify the elimination of war and colonialism. To develop his point, Kant goes from the case of the war between individuals in the state of nature to the situation of the war between states, which are conceived analogously to the reciprocal relations among individuals (*AA* VIII:349). This analogy is admittedly problematic, not only because nations are more complex structures than individuals—at least because a nation would include several individuals—but also because there are other kinds of relations between them. Kant partially acknowledges this problem when he notes that individuals may move between states, traders visit different countries, and persons may have cultural interests about different peoples (*AA* VIII:357–360). However, he does not address the problem. Despite the residual metaphysics that limits his views and the particular cultural limitations of the eighteenth century, there are some aspects that may be useful today. Among them, one could emphasize the principle of hospitality, which affirms that individuals should be free to move as world citizens in different parts of the world—provided that an individual behaves peacefully in another country and subsumes his or her individual legal person under categories of international law (*AA* VIII:357–358). With this, Kant provides a model for the guarantee of individual autonomy amid global processes (*AA* VIII:366), recognizes the participation of individuals in a community, and also defines a global framework within which persons can move freely. In my view, his proposal includes a dialectical relation between individual and community that can be applied at the global level.

Yet, Kant's position has had its polemic applications and its critics. Napoleon's abdication and the Congress of Vienna in 1814 would mark a new moment in which cosmopolitan ideals of peace and unity within Europe would reemerge in terms of very concrete projects for a "pan-European union of states" that established a compromise between Kantian universalism and Fichtean patriotism (Meinecke 1962:139; Cheah 2003:116–141). This revision of Kant can be seen, for instance, in Hegel's view of cosmopolitanism. On the one hand, he rejected Kantian abstract views and stressed the reality of war, colonialism, and

national contingencies; on the other, he affirmed the particularity of the
human being and the primacy of freedom over and above these contingencies. As he states, "It is part of education, of thinking as consciousness of the individual in the form of universality, that I am apprehended
as a universal person, in which all are identical. *A human being counts
as such because he is a human being,* not because he is a Jew, Catholic,
Protestant, German, Italian, etc." (Hegel 1970, *Rechtsphilosophie* [W 8]
§ 209, emphasis in original). It is possible, therefore, to see Hegel as
defending some form of cosmopolitanism interpreted as the "Spirit of
the World" [*Weltgeist*] (Douzinas 2007; Fine 2007). However, Hegel
continues, "this consciousness, which is the aim of thought, is of infi-
nite importance—and inadequate only if it is taken as a kind of *cosmopolitanism* fixed in opposing the concrete life of the state [*Staatsleben*]"
(*Rechtsphilosophie* [W 8] § 209). In the end, Hegel sides with the objective reality and the progressive implementation of rights in world history [*Weltgeschichte*] by means of existing political institutions (Hegel
1970; *Rechtsphilosophie* [W 8] § 340, §§ 341–344).

Though brief, this interpretation allows us to see the complex constitutional issues raised by new cosmopolitan political actors in history.
Hegel maintains a bourgeois view of historical events and downplays
the cosmopolitanism of the workers's movement, which was progressively emerging as an international leading force promoting revolutionary causes. Karl Marx and Friedrich Engels turned their attention
to this issue and their position can be interpreted as another form of
an ambiguous cosmopolitanism because they combined universal and
communitarian elements in a revolutionary project. This can be read
explicitly in the *Communist Manifesto* (Cornu 1948:31–35, 59–70;
Marx and Engels 1958 [*MEW* 4]:459–493; Rodolsky 1986). In the
Manifesto, the proletarian class is identified as having a universal character that justifies its claim to collective human rights [*Menschenrechte,
droits de l'homme*] beyond the mere individual rights of citizens within
a bourgeois society [*Rechte des Mitglieds der bürgerlichen Gesellschaft,
droits du citoyen*] (Achcar 2010:1892–1926). In his critique of bourgeois individualism, Engels indeed recognized that "cosmopolitan
liberalism" was important insofar as it questioned the *ancient régime*,
negated national differences, and strived toward a wider community
of freedom and solidarity. He added, however, that cosmopolitan liberalism would never actually lead to a greater goal because it was interested only on free trade as means to economic monopoly and political
domination of the bourgeois class. In fact, Marx and Engels propose
to substitute the "cosmopolitan free trade" [*der privategoistischen
Kosmopolitismus der Handelsfreiheit*] for the internationalism of the

proletarian class (Achcar 2010:1896, 1900). All this is summarized in the *Communist Manifesto*. If, on the one hand, the *Manifesto* affirms that "the bourgeoisie has through its exploitation of the world-market given a cosmopolitan character to production and consumption in every country" (Marx and Engels 1958 [*MEW* 4]:466), on the other it states that "workers have no fatherland" or nationality (Rodolsky 1965:330–337; Cheah 2003:180; Achcar 2010:1900). Therefore, when Marx and Engels conclude the *Manifesto* with the statement, "*Working Men of All Countries, Unite!*" (1958 [*MEW* 4]:466, emphasis in original), they are operating with some form of cosmopolitan idea that is radically opposed to what Hegel stood for. Only later, around 1859, in a more explicit critique of the Hegelian philosophy of right, they begin to explore the negative impact of cosmopolitan capitalism around the world and propose a proletarian form of cosmopolitanism expressed in terms of "the world community of productive laborers" (Cheah 2003:181; 2006:25–28, 54–55).

This leads us back to Kant. Today, there are many reasons to criticize, reassess, and transform Kantian philosophy in light of the criticisms presented by Hegel and Marx as well as in light of contemporary critiques of colonialism, imperialism, racism, and gender inequality. In his *Metaphysics of Morals*, Kant sees women as excluded from the right to be active citizens (*AA* VI:3, 14–15). Moreover, his position on race is very controversial. He often expresses chauvinistic views about the superiority of the German culture (Shell 1996; Bernasconi 2001:11–36; 2003:13–22; 2011). Also, as recent research shows, his understanding of physical geography reveals a series of other limitations in his views about world citizenship (Mendieta and Elden 2011). Still, the aspects he mentions to illustrate the movement of people beyond the limits of the nation-state have been radicalized in contemporary society and from the present-day perspective as well as with the distance of more than two hundred years, we can update and transform Kant's philosophy as a tool to address the challenges of globalization (Habermas 1996:192). We need to be mindful, however, that Kant actually spoke of "world citizenship," which should not be confused with metaphysical cosmopolitanism. He operated with the modern mindset and emphasized the epistemic dimension of "rights." This leads us to a third moment, related to contemporary views on cosmopolitanism.

Global Human Rights Discourses

I use the term "global human rights discourses" to characterize new conceptions that inherit traditional themes of cosmopolitan metaphysics and integrate epistemic views of world citizenship but adapt and upgrade them to the contemporary conditions of globalization. This, and the fact that I have argued for global plurality, explains why I need to keep the term "global" in evidence. In light of what I have discussed thus far, globality is a "truly inclusive" quality. Moreover, "human rights" are the equivalent to the *polites* and the world citizenship in global times, but cleansed from the problems we saw above because new positions are attentive to issues of inclusion and exclusion. Finally, these terms are interpreted in relation to discursive practices, for global human rights are to be understood as claims raised by individuals and groups in several contexts. These contexts are not defined in terms of nation-states and, therefore, global human rights discourses are not the same as international human rights. In sum, each of the terms above complements each other. Based on these explanations, I will now turn to the discursive paradigm and refer to positions that provide a communicative interpretation of the human component of human rights as related to cosmopolitan ideals.

I start by referring to a postmodern position related to the work of authors such as Lyotard and Derrida. Lyotard refers to cosmopolitanism indirectly in his review of Kant's philosophy of history. For him, cosmopolitanism is a negative term when it is affirmed as one of the metanarratives of modernity, as universal history or as a form of metaphysical determinism that is no longer credible and, therefore, has no legitimacy (1983, 1986). However, this same idea may have a positive meaning in aesthetics, if one recognizes the heterogeneity of narratives and language games repressed by metanarratives and brings them to the surface (Lyotard and Thébaud 1985). This is possible, according to Lyotard, if we turn to Kant's *Critique of Judgment* and rescue his notion of "transitions" [*Übergänge*] from one territory to another. However, the recognition of difference, respect for cultural boundaries, and movement on a case-by-case basis is only tenable if we avoid the temptation to affirm one particular form of politics, give it a universal status, and impose it upon others or claim to represent others (Lyotard 1991:25–30). As Lyotard states, "There is first a multiplicity of justices, each one of them defined in relation to the rules specific to each game" (Lyotard and Thébaud 1985:100). Based on this model, there is a possibility of affirming global human rights as the process of allowing forgotten narratives to be part of a communication process. In his Oxford Amnesty Lectures, "The Other's Rights," Lyotard reminds us that the very name of Amnesty International refers to *amnestos*, which means "the one who is forgotten" (1993:135–147). Because humanity itself has been forgotten, we need to be witness to the small events through which humanity expresses itself and make sure that silenced voices are heard. This also implies resisting what is inhuman (1993:15; 1988).

For Derrida, there is a similar dual approach. It is possible to talk about cosmopolitanism, provided that we deconstruct it by putting more emphasis on particular meanings and contextual interpretations of norms (1992:3–67; 2001). First, to take cosmopolitanism into consideration, Derrida rescues the ancient exclusionary relationships with strangers and *idiotes*—thus revealing the importance of language and discourse in defining cosmopolitan ideals. Here his example is the refugee status of ancient Hebrews in Egypt and Babylon, which serves as an archetype for the contemporary situation of refugees (1996, 1997, 2001). Second, he retrieves Kant's views on hospitality to strangers and criticizes Kant for proposing a right to "hospitality" and then restricting it, thus creating the precedent for the special conditions imposed today on immigrants, asylum seekers, and refugees (Derrida 2001:12–18; Still 2010: 29, 34). In all these cases, there is a clear relationship between cosmopolitan ideals and human rights. However, human rights are ambiguous as well and can be instrumentalized, as in the case of *humanitarian interventions* or in the case of refugees and immigrants, who have duties, but no rights. As an alternative, Derrida explores the relationship between philosophy and law in the depiction of both hospitality law and the "laws of hospitality," that is, between the legality and the morality involved in such relationships. The concept has multifarious connections and Derrida plays with its ambiguity: for instance, in statements such as *Le sujet es un hôte* and *Le sujet est ôtage*, he defines the individual as possibly a "host," "guest," or "hostage" of cosmopolitan relationships (Still 2010:4). He also makes room for bodily interactions and insists on the recognition of differences. Despite the problems he identifies in forms of hospitality, Derrida actually sees something positive in cosmopolitan ideals and human rights. I cannot do justice to the rich elements Derrida illuminates in his discussion, but I hope to have indicated a few themes that point to a discursive view of cosmopolitanism that focuses on the humanity of those who are the subjects of hospitality (for more details, see Still 2010).

The postmodern position on cosmopolitanism certainly presents important challenges that deserve response. A few authors have attempted to interpret postmodern and communitarian readings and critiques of cosmopolitanism in contrast to a Kantian approach. For instance, Garret Brown has attempted to respond to Derrida's critique of Kantian hospitality (G. Brown 2010). Beardsworth dedicates a whole chapter to the postmodern critique of cosmopolitanism, including a section on Derrida, focusing especially on Derrida's analysis of the incompatibility between legality and singularity and the difficulty of holding singularities together in a cosmopolitan ideal. Nevertheless, he recognizes that Derrida complements the process of building international structures and implementing human rights with a call for more attention to singular contexts. Derrida's double strategy has been applied especially in the analysis of humanitarian law in the area of international relations theory (Beardsworth 2011:189–197, 218–221)

What can we derive from these interpretations? In *Global Fragments*, Mendieta states that the affirmation of difference, fragments, and multiplicity "cannot be read as condoning a frivolous and insouciant form of postmodernism," but at the same time he concludes that "postmodernity, when appropriately matched up, arranges in a constellation of related concepts and must yield insights into the geopolitics of contemporary societies" (Mendieta 2007:7, 64, 59–77). I agree with his point. What this means is that a critique of universalism and the radical affirmation of one's particularity has to be understood as a critique of the move of stepping outside a particular local context in order to impose universalism. A claim to universality without any mediation runs the risk of becoming particularism. Therefore, if an approach to cosmopolitan ideals beyond metaphysical and epistemic impositions is still possible at all, it will have to pay attention to the contextual, local, and personal dimensions. This claim surely appears contradictory. How can we be cosmopolitan and affirm the personal, local, communitarian, or heterogeneous dimension? Avoiding these aspects could be understood as an echo of the classical cosmopolitan metaphysics. Postmodern authors rightly point out to this discrepancy by denouncing and then correcting the problems of such views. Instead of a metaphysical authority, they claim, one has only the contingency of particular events. Communitarians would certainly enlarge the chorus of those who oppose this form of cosmopolitanism. Instead of a subjective and individualistic moral obligation based on legal responsibility and allegiance to a nation-state, they expand the spectrum to include particular or neglected collectivities—including women, ethnic minorities, the poor, and victims of gender discrimination. According to the particularistic challenge to cosmopolitanism, upholding a critical position is not a matter of rationality, right, or responsibility, but rather an exercise in sensitivity, sensibility, and solidarity toward humanity.

These ideas may seem controversial but they are progressively finding echo in contemporary debates on cosmopolitanism (Mendieta

2007:7–13; 2009:241–258; Mendieta and Elden 2011). A new kind of "cultural cosmopolitanism" can be related to the work of Nussbaum, Appiah, Benhabib, Mignolo, and Erskine who insist precisely on the point that cosmopolitanism always needs to have a human face that reflects and criticizes the contemporary plural reality of globalization. Moreover, they express the solidarity with *minorities* and the *stranger* who is displaced or dislocated beyond the borders of acceptability as well as beyond the limits of legally, politically, or economically institutionalized structures. Mendieta summarizes many of these positions, saying that "this grounded, placed, rooted, and patriotic cosmopolitanism acknowledges the contingency and fragility of the kinds of institutions that enable our enacting cosmopolitanism or cosmopolitan iterations" (2009:253). Let me briefly consider some of these authors and highlight why their proposals advance ideas that may be constitutive to a critical perspective that is compatible with the multidimensional proposal.

In his book, *Cosmopolitanism: Ethics in a World of Strangers*, Appiah addresses the question of a culturally rooted cosmopolitanism. He warns that "when we seek to embody our concern for strangers in human rights law and when we urge our government to enforce it, we are seeking to change the world of law in every nation on the planet" (Appiah 2003:81). However, imposing one singular and universalistic project across nations and cultures has many side effects. This applies even when we deal with the case of contemporary slavery. Appiah shows that "international treaties define slavery in ways that arguably include debt bondage; and debt bondage is a significant economic institution in parts of South Asia." Opposing this practice in terms of a universal law that is blind to cultural differences may offend "people whose income and whose style of life depend upon it" (Appiah 2003:82). He concludes that if cosmopolitanism is understood solely as the enforcement of international law and approached as an absolute, it could well lead to more harm than good. At this point one may ask, how is this possible? Appiah responds that cultures have been able to change from within and adapt their norms throughout the centuries. For example, *dignitas* was an honor bestowed upon the elites but then *human dignity* emerged as a transformative concept to include all humans, in a process that involved multiple factors, not simply external imposition. Cultures have internal resources that can be prompted to motivate these transformations. I agree, for it is possible to say the same about cannibalism or head-hunting, which were once acceptable in some cultures and were progressively banned by them. Nonetheless, I believe that this happens not in isolation but through intercultural interactions that expose traditional views to alternative values. Upon reflection or based on pragmatic reasons, changes may occur. This cannot be a metaphysical wish, so we need to engage in purposive intercultural communication for this to occur.

A similar point is made by Benhabib, who represents a position that can be defined as a feminist cosmopolitanism and comes close to Erskine's proposal for an "embedded cosmopolitanism" (Erskine 2008:39–42) as well as to Ulrike Vieten's views on gender and cosmopolitanism (2012:1–11). In *Situating the Self: Gender, Community, and Postmodernism in Contemporary Ethics* (Benhabib 1992), she turns to postmodernism to consider their critique of homogeneity and totalitarianism, but at the same time she criticizes postmodern views on rationality and normativity. She also questions communitarianism for similar problems, especially due to the danger of totalitarian exclusion of individuals (1992:71–82). Moreover, she critiques the "generalized other" depicted in liberal ethics and proposes a consideration of a "concrete other" based on Gilligan's feminist revision of Kohlberg's theory of moral development (1992:164–170; Erskine 2008:150–180). As she establishes a dialogue with Linda Nicholson, Nancy Fraser, Judith Butler, and other feminist thinkers, Benhabib concludes that feminism is part of the broader transformations that have questioned modernity and affirmed a "situated criticism" (1992:225–228). However, she distances herself from postmodernism because it appears as a "retreat from utopia" (1992:228–230). This does not impede Benhabib from espousing the recognition of differences and diversity (2002), a point that informs her conception of cosmopolitanism.

Although Benhabib offers a strong criticism of postmodernism, the emphasis on concreteness and situatedness owes much to postmodern positions and influences her views on her proposal for another kind of cosmopolitanism that rejects the metaphysical and epistemic problems I have identified. This can be seen in *The Rights of Others: Aliens, Residents, and Citizens* (2004) and *Another Cosmopolitanism: Hospitality, Sovereignty, and Democratic Iterations* (Benhabib et al. 2006). Although Benhabib sides with Habermas and Critical Theory, she does acknowledge that his views on cosmopolitanism fail to account for "bounded communities" or to enlarge the scope of what counts as human: "Because the discourse theory of ethics articulates a universalist moral standpoint, it cannot limit the scope of the *moral conversation* only to those who reside within nationally recognized boundaries; it views the moral conversation as potentially including all of *humanity*" (Benhabib et al. 2006:18, emphasis in original).

After discussing Kant's cosmopolitanism and the international human rights regime (Benhabib et al. 2006:20–30), she identifies a "disaggregation of citizenship" (Benhabib et al. 2006:45) as exemplified by concrete cases of tensions with immigrants in Europe, especially the question about a Muslim woman wearing a scarf in France. This brings us back to the point I made in relation to Appiah, for Benhabib borrows the term "iteration" from Derrida and shows that when discriminated individuals insist on affirming their identity, contingencies, and claims, they exercise democratic iterations that augment the *"meaning of rights claims"* and promote the *"growth of the political authorship by ordinary individuals"* (Benhabib et al. 2006:49, emphasis in original). This communicative practice complements what we have seen in Appiah and explains, therefore, how change occurs from within. It is a process of raising claims that need to be reiterated, made visible and audible, so that change may eventually happen.

In her writings, Benhabib has certainly made use of postmodern and feminist categories that question a limiting conception of cosmopolitan rights that blindly accept the power of nation-states and their imposition of very limiting citizenship conditions for the granting and exercise of rights (Benhabib et al. 2006:171–175). In her view, rights are not dispensations from statecentric structures, but rather a legitimate and inalienable aspect of individuality and agency. Individuals are bearers of cosmopolitan rights and have, therefore, the possibility of questioning the imposed limits of the nation-state and moving beyond such limits. This is a proposal for a rooted cosmopolitanism that ought to recognize the rights of immigrants and promote hospitality as a way to acknowledge "concrete others" at the local and global levels.

Walter Mignolo complements and radicalizes this approach because he stresses the situation of coloniality and those who suffer under this situation. In his essay, "The Many Faces of Cosmopolis: Border Thinking and Critical Cosmopolitanism" (Cheah and Robbins 1998; Mignolo 2001:721–748), his point of departure is the implicit Eurocentrism of cosmopolitan projects and the need to call attention to differences that are left aside by classic authors such as Vitoria, Kant, Marx, and other defenders of modern forms of cosmopolitanism. Accordingly, he differentiates between three kinds of cosmopolitan projects related to modern colonialism: "The first of these designs corresponds to the sixteenth and seventeenth centuries, to Spanish and Portuguese colonialism, and to the Christian mission. The second corresponds to the eighteenth and nineteenth centuries, to French and English colonialism, and to the civilizing mission. The third corresponds to the second half of the twentieth century, to U.S.

and transnational (global) colonialism, and to the modernizing mission" (Mignolo 2001:725). The metaphysical cosmopolitanism of the Christian mission can be traced back to Augustine, but Mignolo highlights its theologico-political upgrade in Vitoria's concept of a universal (planetary) circle [*orbis universalis*]. The civilizing mission [*mission civilisatrice*] was promoted by the French and British empires as well as the colonial projects carried out by Holland, Belgium, and Germany. Here Mignolo shows how the cosmopolitan right [*ius cosmopoliticum*] became international law and culminates in Kant's world citizen law. Following Dussel and Eze, Mignolo reads Kant from the perspective of coloniality and reminds us of Kant's prejudices and racism regarding Amerindians, Africans, and South Europeans (1993; 2001:733–735). In a move akin to the deconstructionist and postmodern approaches, Mignolo attempts to demarcate the *locus enuntiationis* of these overarching discourses and propose a form of critical cosmopolitanism that recognizes differences, acknowledges the fatal outcomes of the missionary and civilizing or modernizing global designs, and reveals the silenced voices and forgotten histories that were victims of these processes (1995; 1999).

Mignolo connects postmodernism, cosmopolitanism, and human rights, very much in consonance with what we have seen so far, but he gives names and locates those affected by cosmopolitan projects. As he states, "Vitoria and Kant anchored cosmopolitan projects and conceptualizations of rights that responded to specific needs: for Vitoria, the inclusion of the Amerindians; for Kant, the redefinitions of person and citizen in the consolidation of the Europe of nations and the emergence of new forms of colonialism. The *United Nations Declaration of Human Rights* ([1948] 1997) that followed World War II also responded to the changing faces of the coloniality of power in the modern/ colonial world" (2001:736). This roughly corresponds to the paradigm shifts I identified. However, the condition of coloniality and sensitivity to differences allow Mignolo to identify a series of contradictions and oppressive structures that resulted in the violent repression of initiatives by indigenous peoples, provoked the Zapatista movement in Mexico, and other social movements that implicitly reveal limitations in contemporary human rights discourses. His proposed alternative is critical and dialogic, emerging from the various spatial and historical locations of the colonial difference: "Critical and dialogic cosmopolitanism as a regulative principle demands yielding generously ('convivially' said Vitoria; 'friendly' said Kant) toward diversity as a universal and cosmopolitan project in which everyone participates instead of 'being participated'" (2001:743; Mendieta

2007:10–12). Mignolo coins the term "diversality" to characterize this diversity as a universal or cosmopolitan project. I defined global plurality at the outset as the transition from multicultural and intercultural plurality to global universality, two necessary dimensions of the multidimensional discourse community.

Nussbaum shares similar concerns but focuses on in the inclusion of women and peoples with disability. Some authors have identified her with liberal theories on individual rights, but she has proposed important corrections and additions to these theories. Beyond her reconstruction of cosmopolitanism in Stoic and Kantian philosophy (Nussbaum 1996, 1997), she questions the limits of the liberal discourses emphasizing "rights." Rather, she insists on the need to highlight the human dimension at play in global human rights, including the role of emotions, the dimension of sexuality, and the acceptance of disabilities (Nussbaum 2004b). She starts with the assumption that humans are not necessarily equal, but have differences that need to be recognized and compensated in certain situations, so that all humans are able to pursue their full potential as humans. Consistent with her views on moral cosmopolitanism, she upholds universal values but avoids the language of rights. Instead, she lists capabilities that are not yet translated into established juridical language. In her view, this approach would serve to dismantle given structures that promote violence or discriminate against people with disabilities. As Nussbaum explains, focusing on discourses, "The idea of human rights is by no means a crystal-clear idea. Rights have been understood in many different ways, and difficult theoretical questions are frequently obscured by the use of rights language, which can give the illusion of agreement . . . the best way of thinking about rights is to see them as *combined capabilities*" (2001b:97–98).

Nussbaum's updating of Stoic cosmopolitanism is then related to her emphasis on human capabilities to offer a defense of universalist education and a proposal for a flexible global structure. In her view, the cosmopolitan quest for humanistic education is compatible with plurality because it allows the appreciation of differences: "citizens cultivating their humanity need, further, an ability to see themselves not simply as citizens of some local region or group but also, and above all, as human beings bound to other humans beings by ties of recognition and concern" (2003:10). Moreover, for this to be translatable into global actions that promote human capabilities, a "thin, decentralized, and yet forceful global public sphere" is necessary which upholds the value of humanity and allows for the expressions initiatives such as the international women's movement and organizations that care for victims of HIV/AIDS in various countries (2006:319).

As we can see in these contemporary authors, the discussion on cosmopolitanism is directly related to globalization processes and the need to affirm and respect human contingencies, particularities, and differences. In this process, these authors progressively address the question about individual rights, which are then expanded not as exclusive entitlements to citizens of particular nation-states but as human rights and universal human ideals. These views on cosmopolitanism, world citizenship, and global human rights discourses clearly question the emphasis on rights, the legal order, or international law under the aegis of globalization to give voice to those affected and excluded by the negative aspects of such processes. They downplay the epistemic dimension in order to highlight the complementarity of the human dimension. In so doing, they reveal and affirm the plurality of human perspectives required by the multidimensional conception of a community of communication.

THE CLAIM TO UNIVERSALITY IN CRITICAL COSMOPOLITAN IDEALS

I have now introduced the dimension of universality. This sends us back to Apel and Habermas. It is based on their contributions that I outline my own views on critical cosmopolitan ideals. Delanty clearly refers to the ethical universalism implicit in Habermas and Apel (Delanty 2009:55, 96–98). However, there are specific aspects that are presented by Apel and Habermas in different ways and need to be acknowledged. As I did in previous chapters, I will spell out these differences and read their contributions in detail. Apel's views essentially repeat his transcendental-pragmatic justification of ethics and are summarized in his essay on "Kant's 'Toward Perpetual Peace' as Historical Prognosis from the Point of View of Moral Duty" (1997). Habermas's initial systematic reading of Kant's cosmopolitanism can be traced back to *The Structural Transformation of the Public Sphere* but is reappraised in "Kant's Idea of Perpetual Peace, with the Benefit of Two Hundred Years' Insight" (1996), before being expanded in a series of publications, up to *The Crisis of the European Union: A Response* (2011). Although his takes on cosmopolitanism have been reviewed and criticized by several authors (Zolo 1999; De Greiff 2002; Fine 2007; Lafont 2008; Cronin 2011), I think my interpretation is a useful way to differentiate and integrate different lines that come together in his description of a cosmopolitan condition. I will briefly discuss Apel's position before turning to a detailed reading of Habermas.

In "Kant's 'Toward Perpetual Peace' as Historical Prognosis," Apel begins by indicating that Kant swings back and forth between metaphysical, juridical, ethical, and political arguments in order to postulate perpetual peace as the necessary course of history (1997:92–93; see Merkel and Wittmann 1996). *Perpetual Peace* is to be read in dialogue with Kant's whole critical endeavor, particularly his two main *Critiques* and his political writings. Apel also acknowledges that these Kantian texts have been questioned in almost every aspect in the two hundred years since they have been published, but among the many possible charges—including the postmodern critique—his main concern is the problem of historical determinism and its relationship to Kant's definition of a duty to pursue and bring about perpetual peace. It is possible to reconstruct Kant's cosmopolitanism as a critically and morally oriented "intent" [*weltbürgerliche Absicht*], provided that one questions his metaphysical dualism and his Augustinian postulate that humans are citizens of two worlds—a *mundus sensibilis* and a *mundus intelligibilis*. With this correction, one can reinterpret Kant as proposing an instance that enforces "legal duties" on citizens under the condition that "such an order presupposes the willingness of human beings to act morally and to be committed to justice" (Apel 1997:98). To argue for this point, Apel goes back to Kant's *Critique of Pure Reason* and his historical writings on cosmopolitanism to rescue the idea of "moral hope" (1997:111) and moral progress, concluding that the dialectics between the real and ideal community of communication can provide the justification for a theory of coresponsibility, which connects ethics or morality, law, and politics at the global level. When guided by a strong ethical principle, these elements prompt us to realize "the moral duty to bring about a legal system in both its national and cosmopolitan forms" (1997:123). Obviously, Apel repeats his previous points regarding the "ultimate justification" of ethics, which give the priority to Discourse Ethics as the basis upon which a Discourse Theory of Law and Politics is supposed to rest (2001).

In reacting to Apel's position, I make a few remarks. First, he complements deontology with a teleological aspect in his reassessment of Kant's endeavor as a whole, but he does not include the third *Critique* or the *Religionsschrift*, which are the loci that expand the concept of community as to include both systematic correlations among diverse elements and the motivating reasons for eschatological hope. Therefore, the elements of theoretical and practical plurality that Kant defines in terms of transitions [*Übergänge*] from one system to another are missing in Apel's account. Second, Apel's views on cosmopolitan ideals do not account for the plurality of communities because he goes directly from the real community to an ethical ideal, thus running the risk of hypostasizing a particular view as universal without specifically enabling a more plural participation in the construction of such a universal ideal. To be sure, Apel does say that the cosmopolitan project is a "regulative ideal," so that its institutional realization should be left to the practices of particular communities and social systems or institutions (2011:358–361). Notwithstanding, the postulate of coresponsibility should explicitly require the engagement of a plurality of individuals and communities in the realization of the projected ideal or in the concrete application of norms. Third, in a way similar to Pogge, Apel concludes that the moral right to participate in a communicative process and the moral obligation of others to allow this to happen ought to be defined as coresponsibility and serve as the foundation to human rights in a new cosmopolitan order. However, he does not clearly specify how this communicative process can occur in different ways in each system, giving the impression that it is limited to the strict reflection of a particular individual who recognizes a powerful logical argument. This reflection is necessary but not sufficient to prompt systemic action, for people could agree on a course of action and do nothing to implement it or have no conditions to apply it. Therefore, discursive practices are to be translated differently and internally in each social system. Finally, even though Apel shows the vertical relationship between ethical presuppositions and the many social systems that ought to be subordinated to moral norms—so that an appeal to morality remains as a last instance against injustices of legal systems—he still needs to provide a more horizontal clarification about the relationship among social systems—such as law, morality, politics, economics, and others. As we shall see, Habermas provides some answers to these questions.

In "Kant's Idea of Perpetual Peace," Habermas reviews and criticizes the historical premises of Kant's project for everlasting peace, analyzes his description of a federation of states as the best way to achieve this goal, and questions Kant's metaphysical conviction that this aim can be realized gradually. Habermas does not necessarily focus on Kant's starting point in practical reason, but rather highlights two aspects: his realistic description of war contrasted with an idealist proposal to "put an end to war forever" and his legal consideration of the right to go to war [*jus ad bellum*], which is to be superseded by a cosmopolitan right [*jus cosmopoliticum*], understood in moral terms. Clearly, Habermas finds a series of problems with Kant's suggestion of a *moral* or voluntary agreement as enough to guarantee a peaceful association, so he searches and finds passages in Kant's Doctrine of

Right where he states that a stable political union requires *legal* obligations based on a binding constitution (1996:196–197). However, Kant's reticence to accept a "constitutionally organized community" at the global level is based on his inability to surpass the traditional conception of sovereign nation-states bound to particular territories. In hindsight, Habermas identifies these problems but still sees many positive aspects to be rescued from Kant's project, provided that we adapt them dialectically to the contemporary global situation. Hence, after describing the changes in nation-states and a series of contemporary challenges such as new weapons of mass destruction, forms of transnational trade, changing political roles at a global level—such as the involvement of nongovernmental organizations—and the very existence of a new global framework for international relations represented by the United Nations, Habermas detects the "soft power" of subtle communicative structures at work in Kant's proposal. In effect, Kant recognizes that governments justify their policies publicly (even if only to pay lip service to them), fear public scrutiny (which explains the practice of censorship), and realize that philosophy has a key role in promoting a public debate about war and peace. Therefore, through the promotion of a public use of communicative freedom, Kant was able to "anticipate something so far in the future that is only now actually coming about: namely, his brilliant anticipation of a global public sphere" (Habermas 1996:205). Is this communicative space a reality or an ideal norm?

Habermas is much more interested in real and pragmatic aspects. In his interpretation of Kant, he clearly performs a discourse-theoretical reconstruction and makes three important revisions to make the Kantian project compatible with the contemporary situation: first, "the rights of the world citizen must be institutionalized in such a way that it actually binds individual governments. The community of peoples must at least be able to hold its members to legally appropriate behavior through the threat of sanctions [*Androhung von Sanktionen*]" (1996:208), and this requires a revision of the role of the United Nations; second, a cosmopolitan community needs to guarantee individual autonomy and human rights in the same way it prosecutes "crimes against humanity," a work done only partially by the United Nations; third, social and economic divisions need to be overcome as a condition to guarantee world peace (1996:210–216, 226–234). In the concluding part of this important programmatic article, Habermas does acknowledge that the goal of promoting a cosmopolitan project by improving the United Nations has had setbacks and faced skeptic charges. One example is Carl Schmitt's critique of a hypocritical "human rights rhetoric" that promotes wars in the name of cosmopolitanism with the argument that "crimes against humanity" were committed by Germany during World War II (1996:220–221). This is taken very seriously by Habermas, who identifies Schmitt's premises in the aesthetics of "the storm of steel" [*Stahlgewetter*] and argues that his views are largely based on a confusion between politics and morality. Yet, instead of giving up on a moral conception of human rights—as Schmitt does—Habermas proposes a democratic transition of morality into a positive system of law. As we shall see, Habermas sees this project as progressively becoming reality.

This essay brings in a nutshell several of Habermas's previous ideas, which have been later expanded in other texts (Zolo 1999:429f.). Within the constraints of this chapter, I limit myself to raise a few points. First, his reading of *Perpetual Peace* retrieves important aspects from *Structural Transformation of the Public Sphere* (1962:178–195), where he faults Kant for presenting two conflicting applications of the principle of "public use of reason" as a mediator between morality, law, and politics: on the one hand, there is the transition from a moral understanding of a "public of 'humans'" [*Publikum der "Menschen"*] to a political "public of citizens" supported by a republican constitution; on the other hand, the dimension of law is the instance that establishes a new cosmopolitan order, so prescinding of morality. Kant's contradictory conclusions are based on his dualistic metaphysics, but instead of siding with either one of these conceptions in *Structural Transformation of the Public Sphere*, Habermas maintains the tension and defers their mediation to the dialectics of Hegel and Marx. In "Kant's Idea of Perpetual Peace," he clearly takes the route of accentuating legality. Second, because his discussion of a "public sphere" relies largely on national contexts, Habermas is forced to review some of his assumptions in order to relate them to a cosmopolitan condition (Delanty 2009:107). Third, even though he had defended a co-originality thesis in *Between Facts and Norms* as a way to maintain the tension among morality, law, and politics, Habermas now seems to leave this co-originality thesis aside and affirms a certain centrality of legal discourses and a legal community, therefore limiting morality from interfering in the justification of legal principles (Forst 1994:395–400; 2007:117f., 157f.). In fact, his reconstruction of the "systems of law" does not seem to play an important role in "Kant's Idea of Perpetual Peace" because he is more interested in describing the global scenario and identifying theoretical obstacles to the implementation of a cosmopolitan condition, whereas *Between Facts and Norms* remains bound to the constitutional state at a national level.

Let me add other critical questions. Habermas maintains his acute sensitivity to conservative threats as he criticizes the anti-humanism implicit in the aesthetic conservatism of Schmitt, Jünger, and Heidegger, who uphold the particularist ideology of a *Volksgemeinschaft* or *Frontgemeinschat* in opposition to cosmopolitan ideas even after World War II; at the same time he seems to agree with the point that a moralizing discourse infects international law "in the name of humanity." To be sure, differently from Carl Schmitt, he is actually referring to the need to avoid metaphysics entering through the back door, so he concludes that "an *unmediated* moralization of law and politics would in fact serve to break down those protected spheres that we as legal persons have good reasons to want to secure" (1996:233, emphasis in original). Moreover, he is correct in affirming that in a cosmopolitan order the violations against human rights should not simply be condemned on moral grounds but prosecuted legally. However, this demand appears to depend on a moral claim that needs justification. Instead of pursuing this route, Habermas is rather interested in making sure that the Discourse Principle (D) has become neutral, the legal form [*Rechtsform*] takes the lead within a community of rights, and the claim to appropriateness substitutes correctness. As a result, all we have is a norm telling us that we *ought to be* both authors and addressees of laws granting rights and defining duties in a legal community. In my view, extra measures are needed to explain and justify why we ought to do so. For instance, in view of his discussion of Schmitt, one could ask, why are we justified to prosecute violators of human rights after World War II? A mere pragmatic and immanent answer is that violating human rights clearly goes against a legitimately established law. But as Schmitt states, human rights were not established as law before 1945 and the complex introduction of "crime against humanity" as well as a list of human rights was imposed in Germany retroactively by international powers, so it is fair to ask about the grounds of their legitimacy. Habermas has an answer to these questions: he says that a legal and political situation is an ongoing process grounded on the principle of publicity and on communicative freedom, which has some kind of normative superiority and allows for social transformations. But based on what? Transformations are not only progressive, but can be regressive as well and we need moral standards beyond specific constitutional frameworks to be able to judge them. Finally, in view of two possible readings of Kant—a focus on morality or on legality—Habermas accentuates the latter without giving up the former, but it is not clear to me from where legality and the obligation to follow the law is derived since he avoids any transcendental standpoint or basic hypothetical norm [*Grundnorm*] from which a constitutional framework is derived (Kelsen 1934:25, 77; Alexy 1986; Raz 1990:122; 2010). What Habermas does tell us is that moral arguments may influence legal reasoning by means of an intertwining process [*Verschränkung*], but for him this does not mean that morality is the source of the mandate to abide by just laws (Apel 1998:737; Forst 2007:171–172). Aware of these critical points, he updates his views on cosmopolitanism in subsequent texts according to five lines of arguments.

A first line is characterized by Habermas still operating within nation-state categories discussed in *Between Facts and Norms* but progressively making room for the inclusion of multicultural and intercultural plurality while avoiding conservative and communitarian particularities. This is done *internally* by reaffirming the neutrality of law and proposing *constitutional patriotism* as a way of moving nation-states away from ethnocentric homogeneity and bringing them closer to defining loyalty as an attachment to democratic constitutional frameworks (Müller 2007:21). Constitutional patriotism is initially used as a tool to criticize the German conservative historical revisionism represented by Ernst Nolte, who—like others involved in the so-called historians debate [*Historikerstreit*]—wanted to reaffirm the identity of the German *Volk*, depict the Holocaust as a harmless event, and propose a movement "back to normality" (Habermas 1985b; 1987:120–136; 1990:205; 1995:165; Apel 1988:370–374; Pensky 1995:67–77; Matuštík 2001:131). However, this same concept is used later to accept and accommodate the claims to inclusion raised by the feminist critique of Fraser and Benhabib and the communitarian proposal of Taylor (Habermas 1996:154, 237; Ingram 2010:221–234). Habermas agrees that a politics of recognition is necessary to correct the problems of male chauvinism, nationalism, racism, and colonialism, so he progressively includes multiculturalism in his analyses (1998:111–114; 1999), but adds that this recognition should not contradict individual freedoms guaranteed by a democratic constitution (1996:239f.), otherwise there would be an "ethical impregnation of the constitutional state" by particular values or conceptions of the good (1996:252). However, there is an opening to *external* worldviews as Habermas accepts Rawls's idea of an *overlapping consensus*. In this case he begins by saying that "the essential content of the moral principles embodied in international law is in conformity with the normative substance of the great prophetic doctrines and metaphysical interpretations affirmed in world history" (1990:30). However, he later distances himself from Rawls's metaphysical assumptions

(1996:85f., 97f.), and ultimately downplays this dimension in view of the challenges brought up by Southeast Asian communities and fundamentalist groups against the universality of human rights (1998). Also here, he identifies these challenges with the strategy of moralizing human rights, but now this charge is brought against metaphysical worldviews [*Weltbilder*]: if an overlapping consensus is possible at all, it can be justified only in light of an epistemic authority that is independent from these worldviews (1996:117). Obviously, the exposure to multicultural plurality prompts an opening of the nation-state and the categories of Habermas's Discourse Theory.

A second line searches for an antidote to both metaphysical totality and fuzzy morality, which implies a move toward *postnational constellation* and *postnational identity* while maintaining the requirement of *postmetaphysical thinking* in matters related to human rights (Matuštík 2001:209f.; Cronin 2011:198f.; Commissiong 2012:115f.). Both aspects point toward cosmopolitanism because they include changes in conceptions of territorial sovereignty and globalization processes (Habermas 1998:95–96). Habermas does not give up the previous point regarding the need for a neutral reference to a constitutional setting, but rather applies this requirement more explicitly to the case of a "transnational or global domestic policy" (1998:96, 135f.). His reasoning is straightforward: because our challenges are global, we now need a constitutional framework at both levels—national and supranational. However, a new challenge emerges: Is it possible to have a constitution beyond the level of the nation-state? This is answered by Dieter Grimm negatively (1991), as he states that a constitution necessarily refers to a nation and a *Volk*. I intentionally refer to this term in German to highlight its semantic field, views that range from a conservative longing for a homogeneous ethnic identity to a progressive view of popular sovereignty [*Volkssouveranität*], and the confusion between these two meanings (Maus 2011:18–19). Habermas's response and clear delimitation of national ethnic identity clarifies these meanings and points out to existing institutional processes within the European Union that allow for a postnational identity (1996:185–186). Still, Grimm replies that, technically speaking, the European Union is the result of intergovernmental treaties, not truly democratic processes with popular representation (Grimm 2011). Habermas seems to have accepted this: first, because he came to downplay the idea of postnational identity, although it is used by other authors who show the emergence of new identities or through the integration into the European Union (Matuštik 1993; Delanty 1995); second, because he later expressed more direct critiques to the democratic shortcomings in the European integration process. The result is a more careful and realist view on the future of a unified Europe as the basis for a future global domestic policy and a more direct dialogue with positions that point to coordinating problems, democratic deficit, and skepticism toward the European Union (Habermas 1998:135–156; 2001a:85–86). From this we can gather that the integration process in Europe has had so many obstacles that Habermas is prudent enough not to rely too heavily on its success as a condition for cosmopolitan order.

A third line, which follows immediately from the points above, can be identified in a series of writings that go deep into questions concerning the European Union and the proposal for a European Constitution, such as its multilevel system, principle of subsidiarity, and Comitology process. The central part of a collection titled *Times of Transition* focuses on transitions in Europe and includes a typology of four different positions—Euro-skeptics, Market-Europeans, Euro-Federalists, and Euro-Cosmopolitans—that attempt to address the simultaneous challenges of nationalism, regional integration, and globalization (Habermas 2001a:92, 98). The main target here is the skepticism represented by authors in the European media, against whom Habermas maintains his plea for European integration legitimized by a constitution built on the tradition of the *European Convention on Human Rights* (Habermas 2001a:106, 123–124). This constitutional proposal was ultimately rejected by European citizens in the Netherlands and France through national referenda, but independent of this outcome Habermas insists on the possibility of a regional community that keeps nation-states in their respective roles and at the same time subordinates them to a supranational structure that cannot be conceived as a form of world-state, but rather as a multilevel system [*Mehrebenensystem*] that keeps the three dimensions of nationalism, regional integration, and globalization in balance (2005:346). In view of the frustrated attempt to pass a European Constitution, there seem to be two options: to give up on this hope or try a different route. What is Habermas's way out? Despite many setbacks, the continuous skepticism toward a constitutional integration, and the several economic crises affecting its member states, he stays his course and upholds the hope for a robust European Union based on the constitutionality of international agreements and the promotion of human rights (2008:96). One could agree, as many have done, with Grimm's charge that Europe lacks sovereign collectivity and the collective rejection of a constitution would simply confirm this. However, after lamenting this outcome in *Europe: The Faltering Project* (2008), Habermas reassesses the whole situation in *The Crisis of the European Union: A Response* (2011), infusing new hopes in the debate as he optimistically shows that one of the innovations of the European Union is precisely the consideration of both European citizens and state citizens as constituting subjects (2011:62). On this basis, he suggests the possibility of upholding both the constitutional and the cosmopolitan project, provided that conceptual blockades [*Denkblockaden*] that negate the possibility of wider participation of citizens beyond the nation-state are removed (2011:48). The main blockade is clear: a conservative tradition bound to the nineteenth century that is represented mainly by Schmitt's disciples. All this seems to bring us back to internal polemics within Germany. Now the stakes are clearly higher, since the success of both the European Union and the United Nations is codependent on world citizenship ideals (2011:82). This leads to a few corrections in his multilevel proposal: beyond the European Union, members of an international community would elect their world citizen representatives, the United Nations would be limited to moral and legal issues related to the safeguard of human rights, and a global public sphere would educate all peoples about global issues to be decided at the level of the United Nations (2011:92–93). What grants a universal character to this arrangement? The complementarity of legal and moral norms. We are now back to a previous question: Which of these has the priority?

A fourth line responds to this question. Habermas clearly defends a *global domestic policy without global governance* [*Weltinnenpolitik ohne Weltregierung*] (1998:156, 167; 2001a:14) that requires the *juridification of international relations* [*Verrechtlichung der internationalen Beziehungen*] independently of the regionalization process (2004:113). This discussion is initiated in reference to the claim that the United Nations needs to have the quality of a "community of world citizens" [*Gemeinschaft von Weltbürgern*] and establish a more reliable structure for world governance as claimed by Held and Archibugi (1995; Archibugi et al. 1998; Habermas 1998:159). For Habermas, this goal can be pursued not necessarily through the implementation of world governance, but rather through a legal understanding of human rights: "It is not a simple coincidence that, therefore, only 'human rights,' i.e. legal norms with an exclusive moral content, constitute the normative framework in the cosmopolitan community" (1998:162). The expression "legal norms with an exclusive moral content" is a subtle improvement but does not provide a clear answer yet. The problem concerns the feasibility of a project that has proven to be so difficult even within the framework of the European Union, that the chances of successfully expanding it at the global level are really meager. However, Habermas sees the answer in a legally constituted cosmopolitan community that articulates different levels of cooperation but is neither a global organization based on transnational democracy nor a universal community of moral persons, but rather a public sphere that opens opportunities for wider participation in a global deliberative process (1998:166). This point brings us back to my initial considerations on the role of the public sphere, for it now seems that Habermas definitely expands and inserts it as an important condition for a critical cosmopolitanism. But again, what about the moral or ethical dimension? In *Time of Transitions* the answer to this question is introduced *via negationis*: in view of new wars in Kosovo and Iraq, the challenges of globalization that extrapolate the reach of constitutional rules within the nation-state, the fact that regional integration processes are being steered by economic policies and thus have a "democracy deficit," we need a juridification of cosmopolitanism (2001a:113–192). Global challenges make evident the underinstitutionalization of cosmopolitanism and, in view of this limitation, all that a politics of human rights has been able to do is to merely be an anticipation [*Vorgriff*] of a future cosmopolitan condition (2001a:35). In my view, this is not necessarily a problem. All that a moral position has to do is to point out this problem and delegate its solution to the political and juridical spheres. In other words, a strong moral or universal position such as Discourse Ethics or the Discourse Theory of Morality would have to guide the applications of discursive principles to a Discourse Theory of Law and a Discourse Theory of Politics as a condition for a critical cosmopolitan order. Would it be possible to accommodate this simple demand within the complex framework developed by Habermas?

Finally, Habermas develops his point about the juridification of international relations more systematically in *The Divided West* (2004). The first chapters of this book build on his analysis of transitional times but center their attention on a series of issues that emerged more clearly after both the terrorist attacks on September 11, 2001, and the invasion of Iraq in 2003. Habermas is more interested in the European reaction to both events, thus adding more elements to the third line of arguments mentioned above. More important for my goals is the chapter "Does the Constitutionalization of International Law Still Have a Chance?" He starts by stating that "a world dominated by nation-states is moving towards the postnational constellation of a world society," then questions the desirability of relying on the normative authority of a sole nation such as the United States— which was internationally demoralized after the invasion of Iraq but insists on a particularistic moralizing of world politics [*Ethisierung der Weltpolitik*]—and concludes that after two world wars the Charter of the United Nations and other similar initiatives have moved us in a direction toward the possibility of cosmopolitan law as proposed by Kant (Habermas 2004:113–114). In reassessing Kant's views on perpetual peace in light of a very concrete situation of contemporary war, Habermas now explicitly refers to a moral mandate of practical reason as point of departure, which yields two different outcomes.

On the one hand, Habermas contrasts Kant's project with the reality of power and war and finds enough statements in Kant's original texts to conceive of peace as a legal issue that requires a constitutionalization—not moralization—of international law. In a lapidary statement, he concludes that the Kantian cosmopolitan community is "a principle of law, not a commandment of morality" (2004:120). However, this position entails problems. According to Habermas, Kant analogously repeated the legal framework of the nation-state at the international level and this led to the assumption that cosmopolitan law would require the coercive power of a global republic [*Weltrepublik*] (Lutz-Bachmann and Bohman 2002; Habermas 2004:122; Cronin 2011:213). Contrary to this assumption, Habermas reaffirms that a law of world citizenship corresponds to the rights of individuals who retain their membership in a particular state but at the same time go beyond the state to become members of a wider community, which protects their human rights. This is not simply a dream, for the United Nations is already authorized to guarantee international security and promote human rights as well as implement human rights and intervene in nation-states when these rights are violated (Habermas 2004:135). Hence, the respect for human rights is already built-in as the source required for the legitimacy of a global constitutional process and can be applied at different levels, so that "there remains the conceptual possibility of a political system of several levels which has no state quality as a whole, but can guarantee peace and human rights at the supranational level without being a world government with a monopoly of power as well as work the problems of a global domestic policy at the transnational level" (Habermas 2004:146). Obviously, this is compatible with the proposal for a multidimensional community of communication or multidimensional discourse community that updates Kant's cosmopolitan project. To corroborate this point, Habermas dedicates the second part of this chapter to reconstruct the historical process between 1848 and 1948—from the rise of international law through the League of Nations to the United Nations and its *Universal Declaration on*

Human Rights—to show that, despite setbacks, there have been important transitions, innovations, and institutional renewals that support a postnational constellation. The ensuing changes since the end of the Cold War provide an opportunity to present an alternative agenda for the reform of the United Nations, provided that one keeps an eye on other conceptions of world order that need a continuous critique: the unilateralism of the neoconservative hawkish orientation of the United States during the administration of George W. Bush, the limitations of a hegemonic liberalism, the impersonal economics in neoliberal and postmarxist models, and—most importantly—the theoretical challenges presented by Schmitt. In reassessing his earlier diagnostics, Habermas concludes that Schmitt's views could be used to support the idea of a "clash of civilizations" and question the possibility of an "intercultural understanding of generally acceptable interpretations of human rights and democracy" (2004:192). Therefore, they need to be questioned. So far, the discussion reaffirms the priority of a legal approach, but there is another side to this discussion, which is closer to the idea of a global ethics or morality.

On the other hand, Habermas's detailed reading of Kant allows him to update his own position in a way that seems compatible with the multidimensional model. Although the tension between *rights* and *morality* remains, Habermas himself opens up a way to address this issue by recognizing that the world community is not a state, realizing that solidarity is not limited to the "context of a common political culture," and concluding that legal and political categories would apply differently to a community of world citizens (2011:88–90). In pursuing a cosmopolitan condition, we move away from the strict political character of a limited community to a more abstract global dimension in which human interests are "depoliticized" [*entpolitisiert*] and share a *moral point of view* (Habermas 2011:91). Here we are dealing with an equivalent to Kant's "kingdom of ends" that is inclusive. While the United Nations would still deal with issues of law and politics because ethics and morality do not suffice to address global issues, "*moral reasons are enough*" to justify its mandates to curb violence and promote human rights, which are then translated into juridical language. Here we find, finally, a new way of articulating the tension between law and morality. At this level of global universality, Habermas continues, any global citizen is in condition to form an intuitive moral judgment because any culture or religion already possesses a moral core that correlates to human rights discourses (2011:91–92). It is precisely in this context, where Habermas concludes that the participation in this universal discourse is based on the "supranational application of *presumptive shared* moral principles and norms," that he refers to the co-originality of *human dignity* and *human rights* (2011:37–38, emphasis in original). This important device maintains the tension and differentiation between *morality* and *law* within the discursive structure and at the same time affirms the possibility of an "overlapping discourse" relying on plural traditions (2011:17). Another point, which is not fully explored, refers to the possibility of avoiding the problems related to the interpretation of "peoples" as *Volk* by understanding them as *human*. Based on these developments that connect cosmopolitan ideals directly to global human rights discourses, I think that Habermas's conclusion serves to support my proposal for a critical multidimensional model.

All things considered, it seems to me that Habermas progressively arrives to a multidimensional model as he moves from the national through the postnational, then up to a regional transnational framework, before arriving to a global dimension that is not be centralized. He realizes that he cannot relinquish individuality or the plurality of multicultural and intercultural relationships to favor a conservative and ethnocentric nation-state. He does not want to get rid of the nation-state either, for this dimension possesses more democratic legitimacy than the regionally integrated structures of the European Union. As a result, he proposes a nonstate conception of supranational community that would hold a multilevel system together (Habermas 2005:346; 2008:96–97), clearly subordinating the European Union to a wider global structure of a cosmopolitan community that would lend it a complementary legitimacy and validity based on discursive procedures. Such procedures are to be understood in terms of a Discourse Ethics or Discourse Theory of Morality. Taking all this into consideration, we can draw a few conclusions. First, it is clear that a conception of *cosmopolitan ideals* is dependent on an understanding of *global human rights discourses* in which the legal focus on rights is complemented by a nonmetaphysical understanding of human dignity. Second, human rights clearly prompt us to account for plurality and accommodate multicultural and intercultural differences, but this plurality is not an end in itself. It needs to be scrutinized and justified in postmetaphysical terms. Third, as Habermas develops a constructive approach that progressively expands the framework in order to define a critical cosmopolitan approach in multidimensional terms, the ultimate global role is finally given to morality. Fourth, as he considers the multiple dimensions of a *multilevel* system without losing sight of individuality, collectivity, plurality, and global universality, there is a division of labor among the different types of discourses he had defined earlier, which correspond to different community realms. Simultaneously, he is aware of the negative challenges represented by *individualism, ethnocentrism* or *particularism, plural relativism,* and the *universalism* of a world government at each juncture. Finally, we can identify a subtle change that yields a different mediation between *morality, law,* and *politics.*

The discussion on what counts as a critical cosmopolitan project remains open, but it definitely points toward a global ethics or morality. Critical cosmopolitan ideals require the recognition of specific communitarian spheres within which individuals are inserted and certain discourses apply—a "legal person" as bearer of rights would raise legal claims in a respective legal context or community in which these claims are valid (Forst 1994:48–55; 2007:318–325). Moreover, because individuals are not necessarily members of a single community but can move in and out or belong to *multiple* particular communities—as in the case of dual citizenship or in the case of citizenship in a particular European state and in the European Union—we need to account for plurality (Erskine 2008:170–171, 254). This is what Habermas sees as the rights of individuals who retain their membership in a particular state but at the same time move beyond the state to become members of a wider community, which protects their human rights. Consequently, the dimensions of the public sphere need to be *expanded* as well. What is global or universal in all this? Global universality is not the empirical and real expansion of the communication community by acknowledging global plurality, but rather the aspirational element that gives us the mandate to engage in real processes and guides us in our movement in and out of political, legal, cultural, and even religious communities. Global ethics or morality have to remain an ideal. Many communities already have certain standards in place, which are generally capable of addressing and responding to the claims of its members. However, whenever these communities fail, we can still appeal to what Habermas defines as the presumptive shared moral principles and norms.

This brings me back to the beginning of this chapter. In his proposal for a cosmopolitan imagination, Delanty affirms that "cosmopolitanism is not a generalized version of multiculturalism" and borrows some elements from Habermas and Apel to suggest the wider inclusion of plural agents in the discursive process—even religious fundamentalists—as the normative dimension of critical cosmopolitanism (2009:109, 172–173). However, as I discussed Habermas and Apel in more detail, I concluded that this is not enough. Claims brought up to a global public sphere are to be assessed through political and legal discourses and measured against the existing repertoire of human rights. Meanwhile, Discourse Ethics or a Discourse Theory of Morality needs to remain skeptical and vigilant because the appeal to moral norms occurs whenever there is the exhaustion of these other means. One example is the case of a refugee or immigrant who is not considered as a citizen or bearer of rights in a particular community. Because legal or political communities are often closed to this person or this person is not familiar with the particular legal or political discourse, an ethical appeal is all that she has left and this should prompt us to address this case as a violation of human rights. Once this appeal is adequately addressed by juridification or institutionalization processes, our moral reason steps back, but remains vigilant.

THE IDEAL OF A MULTIDIMENSIONAL DISCOURSE COMMUNITY

I have attempted to review a series of discourses on cosmopolitanism and develop a typology that makes sense of them, so that I could better identify which forms are susceptible to a critique based on the perspective of Discourse Philosophy. As I stated at the beginning, there is a difference between what should be called *universalism*—that is, the imposition of one encompassing globalized model upon others without considering their situation—and *universality*—that is, the ethical demand to be more inclusive, as spelled out in norms such as (D).

In reviewing recent cosmopolitan conceptions, I maintained a critique of the universalism represented by positions that impose a metanarrative that occludes the fragmented, heterogeneous, and plural expressions of excluded individuals, groups, and cultures. This could be seen in Athens, among the Stoics, in medieval Christianity, and in modern conceptions based on the exclusivity of rights granted by the nation-state to selected persons. Simultaneously, I came to highlight an anthropological sensitivity to plurality and to a discursive recognition of a variety of language games that reveal several understandings of the human being. It is precisely this attempt to open up cosmopolitanism for the inclusion of new perspectives that deserves the characterization as *universality*. Although there are elements pointing in this direction in the three paradigms discussed, previous conceptions remained bound to metaphysical and epistemic restrictive categories. In observing these limits, I maintained my critique of universalism while affirming universality. Both cases require that a cosmopolitan project keeps the conversation going and adds new interlocutors to our dialogue, so that the claims of subaltern, forgotten, and oppressed peoples can be heard, their rights respected, and their humanity acknowledged. The problem with "universalist" projects is that they are not universal enough—in the ethical sense of the term—because they do not open possibilities for more inclusion. It is fair to conclude, therefore, that metaphysical and epistemic forms of cosmopolitanism are rather identified with universalism while the attempt to be more inclusive without falling into the traps of dualism and positivism represents a universal and critical form of upholding cosmopolitan ideals. Hence, I identify this new version of cosmopolitan ideals with global human rights discourses.

Surely, Apel and Habermas share an allegiance to the communicative paradigm. I also think that their positions are compatible with this newer perspective. According to Apel, any discussion on ethics, human rights, international law, and cosmopolitanism needs to take the global human situation as point of departure and have the unlimited participation in communicative processes as the normative criterion to judge their practices. For him, emphasis should be given to a communicative form of moral cosmopolitanism. In Habermas's view, it is possible to adopt a discursive paradigm and relate it to the upholding of human rights and constitutional guarantees. I have criticized what at times appear as a kind of positivistic emphasis on an epistemic conception of rights and institutions, but after discussing his views in detail, it became clear that he progressively comes to complement discourses on rights with discourses on humanity and state that both concepts of *rights* and *humanity* are co-originary, internally connected in the contemporary definition of *human rights*, and institutionalized at national and regional levels. Ultimately, however, they are expressed as shared moral principles at the global level. Therefore, Habermas provides a strong internal link, much more precise than external metaphysical generalities about the human being and much more open than the specific view of rights as individual entitlements. He helps us to understand the constitutive aspects of an indivisible conception of *global human rights discourses* that must serve as backbone to contemporary cosmopolitan ideals.

In concluding this chapter, I would like to highlight certain points in my analysis. First, there is not only one *paradigm* or one form of *cosmopolitanism* but also a plurality of views in a historical transition process that goes from ancient metaphysical positions through epistemic views on positive law to a more contemporary move toward cosmopolitan discourses. Second, in this historical evolution many came to disregard metaphysical positions and give more weight to a positivist account of citizenship and rights, which corresponds to what is often defined as a liberal cosmopolitanism that claims to be global. Recently, another perspective has emerged, which reflects on many issues regarding plurality, humanity, capabilities, and discourses. Third, these paradigms are not merely historic or indicative of linear evolution because metaphysical, epistemic, and discursive approaches remain available to a culture and allow a society to move from one paradigm to another; moreover, there can be regressive movements as well. Finally, as I described this multiplicity, I proposed to relate the paradigmatic forms of cosmopolitan ideals to their own terminology: metaphysical positions insist on the cosmological perspective, being adequately named *cosmopolites* while modern views based on the nation-state or international law adopt the language of rights and speak rather of a *world citizenship*. What would characterize a critical version of cosmopolitan ideals based on a multidimensional community of communication? The concept of *global human rights discourses*, which would apply to all and could be claimed by anyone.

This chapter also involves a coming to terms with different philosophical positions. On the one hand, guided by my discussion of Apel and Habermas, I mapped different philosophical currents from which we need to maintain a critical distance. There are liberal interpretations that oppose communitarianism but nevertheless accept a form of national liberalism as solution to particularism, thus stopping short of endorsing global or universal responses to contemporary issues. This subtle way of expressing particularity by affirming a form of nationalism has the disadvantage of coming close to conservative notions of *Volksgemeinschaft* and territorial sovereignty that we have questioned. On the other hand, some theories are prone to move away from individualism and nationalism and easily accept the trend of a "post-national constellation," but then face difficult choices concerning a feasible model that is operational at either regional or global level and does not lose what is gained at smaller scales. Moreover, whenever there is a strong claim to universal values as the normative antidote to particularism, there is the burden to show how this differs from an imperialist standpoint or from a unipolar global governance. In reaffirming my commitment to the critical tradition and to the multidimensional model I proposed, I reiterate my option for a position that aims to guarantee individual freedoms, show awareness of community contexts, recognize differences, affirm tolerance, and promote human rights as universal values in a process that promotes cosmopolitan ideals from below.

For sure, what I present as the virtual membership in a multidimensional discourse community is an ideal whose implementation is

a difficult task. It could be argued that such proposal runs the risk
of being highly abstract and hardly workable because we need to
be constantly aware of many concrete challenges that would render
such ideal inoperable. Keeping track of all these issues is surely difficult. However, I hope to have insisted sufficiently on the point that
my proposal has the advantage of easily putting these challenges in
perspective. The aspects I introduced before as constitutive to the
multidimensional conception of a community of communication
ultimately need to be considered together, in their inherent plurality and interdependence, so that *human rights* can be affirmed across
all levels: individuality, collectivity, plurality—both multiculturally and
interculturally—and universality, always based on the normativity of
participatory discursive practices. Only that which can be upheld amid
these various challenges can aspire to universal validity as a cosmopolitan ideal.

CONCLUSION

7

Cosmopolitanism Communities under Construction

Adapting what Kant once said regarding the Enlightenment, we can ask, do we live in a cosmopolitan time or condition? Definitely, we do not. Cosmopolitanism is an ideal rather than reality. However, we can have many experiences that anticipate or indicate aspects of what this cosmopolitan condition might be. We may also experience what cosmopolitanism is not. How would we know? In order to even identify what we are talking about, we need a cosmopolitan ideal. In the previous chapters, I argued that the concept of a multidimensional discourse community can help us in this regard if we account for its intricate aspects and relate them to questions concerning community, human rights, and universal norms. Possessed with these tools we are in a condition to identify and evaluate individual behavior, actions by nation-states, supranational projects such as the European Union, and point out what counts as a possible anticipation of a critical cosmopolitan ideal.

Expanding the Critical Project: A Multidimensional Discourse Community

The first chapter presented a specific *tradition of critique* in the German context, which goes from Immanuel Kant through Theodor Adorno to Jürgen Habermas and continues today in the work of a new generation of scholars who constitute a truly global school of thought. This tradition is in continuous transformation—and this also applies to Habermas and Apel, who have changed their views on several issues. I not only took this tradition of critique as my point of departure, but I also placed it in relation with other traditions while observing its internal transformations. In view of the transformations within the critical tradition and the shortcomings in previous approaches,

Discourse Philosophy seems to me the best articulated and most robust revision of critical theories available because it has expanded the traditional framework of critique to translate and update a series of important themes in terms of discourses. While concentrating on the work of Habermas and Apel, I also showed some limits in their answers to new challenges brought up by multicultural societies, intercultural interactions, and global processes. Therefore, it is necessary to take into account the differences between Habermas and Apel and consider both Apel's *Transcendental Pragmatics* and *Discourse Ethics* as well as Habermas's *Universal Pragmatics* and *Discourse Theory of Law, Politics, and Morality* in order to use their respective tools to address specific problems. My conclusion was that we make use of their different approaches by accounting for differences in the process of justification and application of norms. Therefore, it is possible and necessary to articulate all the tools available in a larger project I defined as *Critical Discourse Philosophy*.

The most important point taken from Discourse Philosophy is the emphasis on a *community of communication*, which is used and expanded in different ways by Apel and Habermas. While Apel takes this concept from Charles S. Peirce and applies it in a more theoretical way, he also connects it with ethics, morality, and other practical issues, proposing a dialectics between the *real and the ideal communities of communication*. Habermas, in turn, has the same concept as point of departure, but then expands and changes its usage by specifying the ways in which we communicate in particular settings. Thus, he offers a typology of *discourses* that can be applied horizontally to different kinds of questions; he also identifies communicative practices and redefines the roles of the *Discourse Principle* (D) and the *Universalization Principle* (U) without necessarily giving up the normative dimension implicit in them. He does adopt, however, a weaker reading of such principles, which brings new challenges to his position. In any case, his theory allows us to account for a *political community*, a *legal community*, or a *moral community*, which are to be understood as *plural communities of communication*—that is, as the application of communicative rationality and discourse procedures in different institutional settings. In each case, Habermas insists on the need to articulate and avoid reductions between the individual and a community, while Apel emphasizes the difference between the factual community in which we operate and the normative and ideal community we anticipate counterfactually as we engage in communication and reflect on the very meaning of our communicative actions. A tension between morality and legality has remained throughout our discussion as an evidence of the difference between Apel and Habermas and the difficulty of mediating these two issues.

While clearly relying on the contributions of Apel and Habermas, I identified pending issues in their approach to matters related to plurality and the global condition, so I developed a complementary scheme to articulate their differences and to cover these missing areas. With this, we arrive to my proposal for a *multidimensional discourse community* that includes the simultaneous consideration of *individuality, collectivity, plurality,* and *universality.* This is specified more clearly later on, when the difference and complementarity between two aspects under plurality is highlighted: *multicultural plurality*—which is internal to collectivity—and *intercultural plurality*—which corresponds to the external multiplicity of communities with their respective cultures and worldviews. Habermas has a particular concern with religious worldviews and the possibility of metaphysics infiltrating certain areas without proper mediation, but I left these dimensions relatively open, in order to allow for enough flexibility for them to be generally applicable. As a result, the structure of this multidimensional discourse community is depicted in figure 7.1.

With this structure, I attempt to define a model to guide my considerations and provide a test upon which anyone could evaluate different positions. Therefore, based on this multidimensional scheme, I am not simply interested in a dualistic tension between reality and ideality or between facts and norms, but on the simultaneity of various dimensions that we experience daily but neither separate analytically

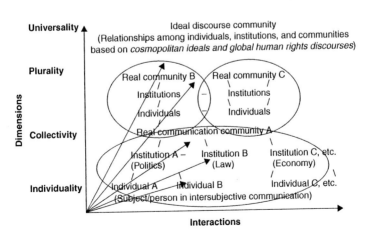

Figure 7.1 Flexible multidimensional discourse community.

nor bring together in a synthesis. Differently from Apel, the issue here is not simply to point out the gap and necessary mediation between real and ideal levels of *justification*. I want this and more, including an account of diversity and multicultural aspects that Apel does not spell out in his Discourse Ethics. Similarly, I followed Habermas in granting a clear place for individuality and its relation to collectivity while maintaining the tension between these dimensions to avoid the reduction of individuality to communitarian settings. In reference to both Habermas and Apel, universality is strongly emphasized, although what counts as universal seems contentious between them. Ultimately, I partially sided with the stronger emphasis on ethics and morality provided by Apel and partially agreed with Habermas regarding the need for institutional implementation and juridification processes, but I did not necessarily "weaken" the universal dimension. Rather, I corrected and complemented it by putting it in a more direct relation with individuality and collectivity. This led to the conclusion that in times of globalization, universality needs to be more directly related to what I define as *global plurality*. With this, I mean that universality cannot simply be a projection from an individual onto others based on logical criteria alone—such as requiring that a given norm be accepted without accounting for differences or imposing a global political structure. Rather, global universality requires that we be attentive to the next person, the missing possibility, the other culture, or even the exception to the rule. Global universality requires that we use the multidimensional model to open up the community of communication at the empirical level to all possible participation and questions. An immanent universality is expressed trough *global human rights discourses*.

This realization led me to add more vehemently the dimension of plurality. If universality needs to be a dynamic critical concept in times of globalization, it needs to be coupled with and corrected by plurality. Conversely, plurality alone could lead us to relativism if it were not related to the "control" of universality. Therefore, combining both requirements yields a more balanced approach that complements the reality and the concept of a community of communication. Still, an inner division is needed in order to better specify the internal plurality of local communities—which I defined as multicultural plurality that designs mechanisms to better address the internal multiplicity of contemporary societies—and the external variety beyond the communities with which we are familiarized. The internal plurality or multicultural plurality is purposively vague because my intention is not necessarily to define what counts as difference, but rather to indicate that individuals can freely question a particular community and move to another or also question a particular community with strong codes that bring about exclusion and compel an individual to look for alternatives, to construct or adapt a new identity. Beyond a particular society, there are other communities that represent radically different worldviews or paradigms that make the dynamic process of coming in and out of particular settings even more complex. I defined this process as intercultural plurality. Complementing this model, we have the empirical global conditions that are to be guided by ideal universality, but this dimension of global universality cannot be accepted if it does not mirror the previous dimensions and is plural enough to guarantee open participation. This means that global universality—whereby *universality* is always the critical ideal clause that questions whether globality is inclusive enough—is a way of bringing heaven to earth.

In summary, the model of a *multidimensional discourse community* attempts to make sure that individuality does not get lost in a community, but is put in relationship with several dimensions that go from the interpersonal or intersubjective relationship with other individuals to the level of communities in interaction, in search for the normativity of a truly universal ideal that, as such, cannot be realized—because if it does, it ceases to be an ideal—but compels us to keep moving forward with the process of building cosmopolitan communities.

APPLICATION AND JUSTIFICATION OF NORMS

Throughout this book I insist on revealing plural dimensions implicit in various issues. On the one hand, I uphold *individuality, collectivity, plurality,* and *universality* as complementary aspects that need to be taken into consideration in relation to each other. I use this approach to develop, amplify, and test a multidimensional model of discourse community capable of revealing "isms" that are incompatible with a critical perspective. On the other hand, I have indicated the very opposite of what constitutes the multidimensional community: *individualism, collectivism, pluralism,* and *universalism.* Within these categories, individualism can be expressed as solipsism or subjectivism, which have been criticized because they contradict the dimension of intersubjectivity implicit in discourses. Similarly, collectivism can be identified with ethnocentrism, particularism, and acritical forms of communitarianism. Although the philosophy of communitarianism is ambiguous and sophisticated enough to avoid any easy classification, I avoided the label as much as I could. This is difficult because I agree with some of its contributions to social and political philosophy. Habermas has a profound sensibility to the perils of a coercive collectivism, having identified and denounced the several forms and disguises used to affirm contingencies or prejudices, as exemplified by the association of ideas such as people and community—*Volk* and *Gemeinschaft*, then combined in the conservative conception of a *Volksgemeinschaft*—which have deep negative connotations in the German context. Beyond this, he progressively arrives to the proposal for a multilevel community of world citizens—*Weltbürgergemeinschaft*—as alternative. I identify this instance with a multidimensional community of communication. The same attention is needed regarding cultural relativism because it implies the acceptance of anything or the skeptical negation of everything. In opposition to this, I have sided with those who insist on norms and the possibility of submitting ideas and actions to scrutiny and evaluation. This does not mean, however, an acceptance of universalism and its various corollaries such as absolutism and fundamentalism.

Yet, as I tried to chart this complex terrain, several questions remained unanswered. For instance, how can we distinguish solipsism from personal individuality? The same person can act differently at different moments according to distinct circumstances and in relation to specific communities. I am not simply referring to a psychological issue, but to the fact that we have different language games and discourses that obey specific rules, so that individual cases need to be acknowledged instead of simply assuming generalities. Persons may be included or rejected as members of a community—broadly conceived to include groups or nation-states—through force or not and this needs to be recognized and qualified because belonging to a certain community could be a contingency or a choice. Another question may be, how can we separate cultural relativism from the recognition of cultural differences? We can affirm that we are different from others and at the same time recognize and respect this difference without necessarily concluding that all groups or cultures are on the same standing. Neither should we consider these issues by simply being indifferent to differences. We need some kind of universality to help us qualify what is culturally positive and ethically acceptable in the affirmation of otherness. These and other questions can be answered or at least sorted out, by applying the concept of multidimensional discourse community in its normative sense.

This leads to the difference between *justification* and *application*. In the attempt to consider discursive norms, I have insistently asked questions about justification. Such questions invariably led me to affirm cosmopolitanism as an *ideal*. However, individuality, collectivity, and plurality are to be seen as categories that must come together to complement ideal universality. These categories correspond to a subset of norms while terms referring to personal identity, intersubjective relations, multicultural societies, intercultural interactions, and global conditions indicate the concrete instances in which such norms are applied. Universality is a value while globalization is a fact. Therefore, an expression such as *global universality* means the attempt to realize or implement a universal ideal at a global level, even though this is surely a daunting task. Moreover, as we apply idealized categories to each level of the multidimensional model, we are guided not by metaphysical or epistemic impositions but rather by participatory discursive structures. Therefore, the (D), in a strong reading, is the normative element that backs this constructive process as the criterion overseeing that each of these levels is interpreted in communicative terms. This principle has a profound moral dimension, thus providing the fundamental norm based upon which we judge all the dimensions in the model I have proposed.

HUMAN RIGHTS AND COSMOPOLITAN IDEALS

The pursuit of global universality can be seen in the development of human rights discourses. However, in describing a plurality of positions involved in contemporary human rights discussions, theories, and practices, I showed that an utterly legal understanding of *human rights* tends to emphasize the dimension of *rights*, downplay the meaning of *human*, disregard cultural differences, and disdain the moral point of view. Based on this, my goal was to argue that human rights discourses cannot aspire to global universality if we forget the human dimension expressed differently in many cultures. Finally, I proposed a transition from the mere emphasis on rights to the human dimension in order to be able to affirm the internal *indivisibility of humanity and rights* made explicit in the very discursive reading of human rights.

In this process, I used another tool of Discourse Philosophy: the understanding of philosophical positions according to three *paradigms*. The first paradigm refers to *metaphysics*, the second to *epistemic* approaches, and the third to *discourse* or *communication*. This allowed me to identify shifts in conceptions of *humanity* and *rights* as well as the emergence of contemporary discourses on *human rights* that provide alternatives to the problems identified by the multidimensional perspective. Although I recognize the evolutionary and linear dimension of paradigms, I also acknowledge older paradigms and worldviews since they can survive and remain active, simultaneously affecting different horizontal contexts that may correspond to different *communities of communication* with their respective discourses. As individuals move from a community to another, there is a possibility of moving from one paradigm or worldview to another. Once we understand human rights as concrete expressions of ontological, epistemic, and cultural assumptions on what counts as humanity and rights, we can better define human rights. The shift to the human dimension does not mean, however, a neglect of the legal framework. Rather, it challenges us to realize the complementary relation between strong national and institutional frameworks that promote the juridification of human interactions and the equally strong cultural assumptions that define what counts as human. This double perspective demands a fundamental reflection on the very meaning of human rights and the internal relationship between these two terms. Habermas's conclusion that both concepts of human rights and human dignity are *co-originary* provides a formula that is internal to discourses.

Taking the different paradigms into consideration, it is fair to conclude that there is not only one form of cosmopolitanism but also a plurality of views in a historical transition process that goes from ancient metaphysical positions through epistemic views on positive law to a more contemporary move toward cosmopolitan discourses. Understanding this historical evolution is useful to identify problems with metaphysical assumptions and limits with epistemic reductions. To highlight these differences, I used the term "cosmopolites" in its ancient connotation as well as the idea of a *world citizenship*, thus identifying the contexts in which these concepts emerge. A more contemporary approach would have to be compatible with the multidimensional perspective. Upholding the criteria of a multidimensional discourse community is a daunting task, but, if human rights can be affirmed across all levels: individuality, collectivity, plurality (both multicultural and intercultural), and universality based on the normativity of a participatory discourse, then a community can aspire to universal validity. The goal of being a recognized participant in *global human rights discourses* by the sheer fact of being human corresponds to a *cosmopolitan ideal* based upon which we judge our communities. Obviously, this is yet another way of reading and applying the (D): only those projects that are truly inclusive and make room for the participation of an ever-growing number of individuals in a global discourse about their human rights deserve to be called cosmopolitan ideals. We have not reached this ideal yet, but there are many positive examples to say that this project is under construction. It is our duty to contribute to the building of such cosmopolitan communities.

BIBLIOGRAPHY

Abdel-Nour, F. (2004). "Farewell to Justification: Habermas, Human Rights, and Universalist Morality," *Philosophy and Social Criticism* 30/1 (2004): 73–96.

Achcar, G. (2010). "Kosmopolitismus, moderner," in W. F. Haug, F. Haug, and P. Jehle [Hrsg.], *Historisch-Kritisches Wörterbuch des Marxismus* (Hamburg: Argument Verlag), Band 7/11: 1892–1926.

Addison, J. (1711 [1961]). "The Pleasures of Imagination," in S. Elledge [Ed.], *Eighteenth Century Critical Essays* [Vol. 1] (Ithaca, NY: Cornell University Press), 41–76.

Adorno, T. (1997). *Gesammelte Schriften* (Frankfurt: Suhrkamp).

Adorno, T., and M. Horkheimer (2002). *Dialectic of the Enlightenment: Philosophical Fragments* (Stanford, CA: Stanford University Press).

Adorno, T., K. Popper et al. (1976). *The Positivist Dispute in German Sociology* (London: Heinemann).

Alexy, R. (1986). *Theorie der Grundrechte* (Frankfurt: Suhrkamp).

Allison, H. (1990). *Kant's Theory of Freedom* (Cambridge, UK: Cambridge University Press).

al-Rahim, A. (2011). "Whither Political Islam and the 'Arab Spring'?," *The Hedgehog Review* (Fall 2011): 8–22.

Anaya, J. (2004). *Indigenous Peoples in International Law* (Oxford, UK: Oxford University Press).

Anderson, B. (1983). *Imagined Communities: Reflections on the Origin and Spread of Nationalism* (London: New Left Books).

Anderson, J. (2000). "The 'Third Generation' of the Frankfurt School," *Intellectual History Newsletter* 22 (2000) at http://www.phil.uu.nl/~joel/research/publications/3rdGeneration.htm, accessed on July 18, 2011.

An-Na'im, A. (1987). "The Rights of Women and International Law in the Muslim Context," *Whittier Law Review* 9/3 (1987): 491–516.

——— (1990). "Human Rights in the Muslim World: Socio-Political Conditions and Scriptural Imperatives," *Harvard Human Rights Journal* 3 (1990): 13–52.

——— (1992). "Towards a Cross-Cultural Approach to Defining International Standards to Human Rights: The Meaning of Cruel, Inhuman, or Degrading Punishment," in A. An-Na'im [Ed.], *Human Rights in Cross-Cultural Perspective: A Quest for Consensus* (Philadelphia, PA: University of Pennsylvania Press), 19–43.

An-Na'im, A. (1995). "Toward an Islamic Hermeneutics for Human Rights," in Abdullahi A. An-Na'im et al. [Eds.], *Human Rights and Religious Values* (Grand Rapids, MI: Eerdmans), 229–242.

——(2000). "Human Rights and Islamic Identity in France and Uzbekistan: Mediation of the Local and Global," *Human Rights Quarterly* 22/4 (November 2000): 906–941.

—— (2001). "Human Rights in the Arab World: A Regional Perspective," *Human Rights Quarterly* 23/3 (2001): 701–732.

—— (2008). "Shari'a in the Secular State: A Paradox of Separation and Conflation," in P. Bearman, W. Heinrichs, and B. Weiss [Eds.], *The Law Applied: Contextualizing the Islamic Shari'a* (New York: I. B. Tauris, 2008), 321–341.

—— (2010). *Islam and Human Rights* [Collected Essays in Law Series] (Surrey: Ashgate).

Apel, K.-O. (1950). *Dasein und Erkennen. Eine erkenntnistheoretische Interpretation der Philosophie Martin Heideggers* (Bonn: Rheinische-Friedrich-Wilhelm Universität [Doctoral Diss.]).

—— (1963). *Die Idee der Sprache in der Tradition des Humanismus von Dante bis Vico* [*Archiv für Begriffgeschichte*, Bd. 8] (Bonn: Bouvier).

——(1967). *Analytic Philosophy of Language and the "Geisteswissenscahften"* (Dordrecht: Reidel).

—— (1973). *Transformation der Philosophie* [2 Vols.] (Frankfurt: Suhrkamp).

——(1975/1981). *Der Denkweg von C. S. Peirce. Eine Einführung in den amerikanischen Pragmatismus* (Frankfurt: Suhrkamp) [English translation (1981) *From Pragmatism to Pragmaticism* (Amherst, MA: University of Massaschusetts Press)].

—— (1976a). "Sprechakttheorie und transzendentale Sprachpragmatik zur Frage ethischer Normen," in K.-O. Apel [Hrsg.], *Sprachpragmatik und Philosophie* (Frankfurt: Suhrkamp), 10–173.

—— (1976b). "Das Problem der philosophischen Letztbegründung im Lichte einer transzendentalen Sprachpragmatik. Versuch einer Metakritik des 'kritischen Rationalismus,'" in B. Kanitscheider [Hrsg.], *Sprache und Erkenntnis. Festschrift für G. Frey* (Innsbruck: Innsbrucker Beiträge zur Kulturwissenschaft), 55–82.

——(1977). "Transcendental Semiotics as First Philosophy" [Ernst Cassirer Lectures—Typescript 1977] [English partial trans.], in K.-O. Apel (1994) *Selected Essays* [Vol. 1: Towards a Transcendental Semiotics] (Atlantic Highlands, NJ: Humanities Press), 112–131.

—— (1979). *Die "Erklären:Vestehen"—Kontroverse in transzendentalprag-matischer Sicht* (Frankfurt: Suhrkamp).

—— [Hrsg.] (1980). *Praktische Philosophie/Ethik I. Reader zum Funkkolleg* (Frankfurt: Fischer).

—— (1983). "Ist die Ethik der idealen Kommunikationsgemeinschaft eine Utopie? Zum Verhältnis von 'Ethik, Geschichtsphilosophie und Utopie'" in W. Voßkamp [Hrsg.], *Utopieforschung*, Bd. I (Stuttgart: Metzler), 325–355.

———— [with D. Böhler and G. Kadelbach] (1984a). *Praktische Philosophie/Ethik: Dialoge* [2 Volumes] (Frankfurt: Fischer).
———— [with D. Böhler and K.-H. Rebel] (1984b). *Praktische Philosophie/Ethik: Studientexte* [3 Volumes] (Frankfurt: Fischer).
———— (1988). *Diskurs und Verantwortung* (Frankfurt: Suhrkamp).
———— (1990). "Diskursethik als Verantwortungsethik. Eine postmetaphische Transformation der Ethik Kants," in R. Fornet-Betancourt [Hrsg.], *Ethik und Befreiung* (Aachen: Augustinus Buchhandlung).
———— (1992). "Diskursethik vor der Problematik von Recht und Politik: Können die Rationalitätsdifferenzen zwischen Moralität, Recht und Politik selbst noch die Diskursethik normativ-rational gerechtfertig werden?," in K.-O. Apel and M. Kettner [Hrsg.], *Zur Anwendung der Diskursethik in Politik, Recht und Wissenschaft* (Frankfurt: Suhrkamp), 29–62.
———— (1993). "Diskursethik vor der Herausforderung der Philosophier der Befreiung: Versuch einer Antwort an Enrique Dussel, I. Teil: Vorüberlegungen," in R. Fornet-Betancourt [Hrsg.], *Diskursethik oder Befreiungsethik?* (Aachen: Augustinus Buchhandlung).
———— (1994). *Selected Essays* [Vol. 1: Towards a Transcendental Semiotics] (Atlantic Highlands, NJ: Humanities Press).
———— (1996a). *Selected Essays* [Vol. 2: Ethics and the Theory of Rationality] (Atlantic Highlands, NJ: Humanities Press).
———— (1996b). "Plurality of the Good? The Problem of Affirmative Tolerance in a Multicultural Society from an Ethical Point of View," *Ratio Juris* (1996): 199–212.
———— (1997). "Kant's 'Toward Perpetual Peace' as Historical Prognosis from the Point of View of Moral Duty," in M. Lutz-Bachmann and J. Bohman [Eds.], *Perpetual Peace. Essays on Kant's Cosmopolitan Ideal* (Cambridge, MA: MIT Press), 79–110.
———— (1998). *Auseinandersetzungen in Erprobung des transzezndentalpragmatischen Ansatzes* (Frankfurt: Suhrkamp).
———— (1999). "Zum Verhältnis von Moral, Recht und Demokratie," in P. Siller and B. Keller [Hrsg.], *Rechtsphilosophische Kontroversen der Gegenwart* (Baden-Baden: Nomos), 27–40.
———— (2000). *The Response of Discourse Ethics* (Louvain: Peeters Publishers).
———— (2001). "On the Relationship between Ethics, International Law and Politico-Military Strategy in Our Time: A Philosophical Retrospective on the Kosovo Conflict," *European Journal of Social Theory* 4/1 (2001): 29–39.
———— (2011). *Paradigmen der Ersten Philosophie* (Frankfurt: Suhrkamp).
Appiah, K. A. (2003). *Cosmopolitanism: Ethics in a World of Strangers* (New York: W. W. Norton).
Apter, D. (1992). *Black Critics & Kings. The Hermeneutics of Power in Yoruba Society* (Chicago: The University of Chicago Press).
Archard, D. (2010). "Children's Rights," in E. Zalta [Ed.], *The Stanford Encyclopedia of Philosophy* (Winter 2003 Ed.), at http://plato.stanford.edu/entries/rights-children/, accessed on December 14, 2012.

Archibugi, D. (2008). *The Global Commonwealth of Citizens: Towards Cosmopolitan Democracy* (Princeton, NJ: Princeton University Press).

Archibugi, D., and D. Held (1995). *Cosmopolitan Democracy: An Agenda for a New World Order* (Cambridge, UK: Polity Press).

——— (2011). "Cosmopolitan Democracy: Paths and Agents," *Ethics and International Affairs* 25/4 (December 2011): 433–461.

Archibugi, D., D. Held, and M. Köhler [Eds.] (1998). Re-imagining Political Community (Cambridge, UK: Polity Press).

Arendt, H. (1959). *The Human Condition* (New York: Anchor).

——— (1977). *Eichmann in Jerusalem: A Report on the Banality of Evil* [revised and expanded from the 1963 original edition and including a postscript] (London: Faber & Faber).

Aslan, Ö., and Z. Gambetti (2011). "Provincializing Fraser's History: Feminism and Neoliberalism Revisited," *History of the Present: A Journal of Critical History* 1/1 (Summer 2011): 130–147.

Assmann, J. (1990). *Maat. Gerechtigkeit und Unsterblichkeit im Alten Ägypten* (München: Beck).

Augustine (1947). *Obras de San Agustín* (Madrid: BAC).

Austin, J. L. (1962). *How to Do Things with Words* (Oxford, UK: Clarendon Press).

Bassiouni, C. (1999). *Crimes against Humanity in International Criminal Law* (The Hague: Martinus Nijhoff).

Baxter, D. (2011). *Habermas: The Discourse Theory of Law and Democracy* (Stanford, CA: Stanford University Press).

Baynes, K. (1992). *The Normative Grounds of Social Criticism: Kant, Rawls, and Habermas* (Albany, NY: State University of New York Press).

Beardsworth, R. (2011). *Cosmopolitanism and International Relations Theory* (Cambridge, UK: Polity Press).

Beck, L. W. (1960). *A Commentary on Kant's "Critique of Practical Reason"* (Chicago: University of Chicago Press).

——— (1961). "Das Faktum der Vernunft," *Kant-Studien* 52 (1960/1961), 271–282.

Beck, U. (1998). *The Cosmopolitan Manifesto* (Cambridge, UK: Polity Press).

——— (2006). *The Cosmopolitan Vision* (Cambridge, UK: Polity Press).

Beck, U., and E. Grande (2007). *Cosmopolitan Europe* (Cambridge, UK: Polity Press).

Beitz, C. (1999). *Political Theory and International Relations* (Princeton, NJ: Princeton University Press).

——— (2009). *The Idea of Human Rights* (Oxford, UK: Oxford University Press).

Bell, D. (1976). *The Cultural Contradictions of Capitalism* (New York: Basic Books).

Bell, D. A. (1993). *Communitarianism and Its Critics* (Oxford, UK: Oxford University Press).

——— (2010). *China's New Confucianism: Politics and Everyday Life in a Changing Society* (Princeton, NJ: Princeton University Press).

Bell, D. A., and J. Bauer [Eds.] (1999). *The East Asian Challenge for Human Rights* (Cambridge, UK: Cambridge University Press).

Bellah, R. (1967). "Civil Religion in America," *Daedalus* 96 (1967): 1–21.

—— (1970). "Civil Religion in America," in R. Bellah [Ed.], *Beyond Belief* (New York: Harper & Row), 168–192.

—— (1975). *The Broken Covenant. American Civil Religion in Time of Trial* (New York: Seabury).

Bellah, R., and H. Joas [Ed.] (2012). *The Axial Age and Its Consequences* (Cambridge, MA: Harvard University Press).

Bellah, R., R. Madsen, W. Sullivan, A. Swidler, and S. Tipton (1985). *Habits of the Hearth. Individualism and Commitment in American Life* (Berkeley, CA: University of California Press).

Benhabib, S. (1986). *Critique, Norm, and Utopia: A Study of the Foundations of Critical Theory* (New York: Columbia University Press).

—— (1992). *Situating the Self: Gender, Community, and Postmodernism in Contemporary Ethics* (London: Routledge).

—— (2002). *The Claims of Culture: Equality and Diversity in the Global Era* (Princeton, NJ: Princeton University Press).

—— (2004). *The Rights of Others: Aliens, Residents, and Citizens* (Cambridge, UK: Cambridge University Press).

Benhabib, S., and D. Cornell [Eds.] (1987). *Feminism as Critique* (Ithaca, NY: Cornell University Press).

Benhabib, S., and F. Dallmayr [Eds.] (1990). *The Communicative Ethics Controversy* (Cambridge, MA: MIT Press).

Benhabib, S. [with J. Waldron, B. Honig, and W. Kymlicka] (2006). *Another Cosmopolitanism: Hospitality, Sovereignty, and Democratic Iterations* [Tanner Lectures, ed. R. Post] (Oxford, UK: Oxford University Press).

Benjamin, W. (1989). *Gesammelte Schriften* [Hrsg. von R. Tiedemann u. H. Schweppenhäuser] (Frankfurt: Suhrkamp).

Bernasconi, R. (2001). "Who Invented the Concept of Race? Kant's Role in the Enlightenment Construction of Race," in Robert Bernasconi [Ed.], *Race* (London: Blackwell), 11–36.

—— (2003). "Will the Real Kant Please Stand Up? The Challenge of Enlightenment Racism to the Study of the History of Philosophy," *Radical Philosophy* 117 (January/February 2003): 13–22.

—— (2006). "Kant and Blumenbach's Polyps: A Neglected Chapter in the History of the Concept of Race," in S. Eigen and M. Larrimore [Eds.], *The German Invention of Race* (Albany, NY: State University of New York), 13–22.

—— (2011). "Kant's Third Thoughts on Race," in E. Mendieta and S. Elden [Eds.], *Reading Kant's Geography* (Albany, NY: State University of New York), 291–318.

Bernstein, J. M. (1994). *The Frankfurt School: Critical Assessments* [6. Vols.] (London: Routledge).

Berry, D. (1992). *America's Utopian Experiments: Communal Havens from Longwave Crisis* (Hannover, NH: University Press of New England).

Bielefeldt, H. (1995). "Muslim Voices in the Human Rights Debate," *Human Rights Quarterly* 17/4 (1995): 587–617.

——— (1998). *Philosophie der Menschenrechte. Grundlagen eines weltweiten Freiheitsethos* (Darmstadt: Wissenschaftliche Buchgesellschaft).

Bobbio, N. (1969). *Diritto e stato nel pensiero di Emanuele Kant* (Turin: Giapichelli).

Boff, C. (1981). *Comunidade Eclesial. Comunidade Política* (Petrópolis: Vozes).

Boff, L. (1981). *Igreja, Carisma e Poder* (Petrópolis: Vozes).

Bohman, J. (2007). *Democracy across Borders: From Dêmos to Demoi* (Cambridge, MA: MIT Press).

Bottomore, T., and P. Goode (1978). *Austro-Marxism* (Oxford, UK: Clarendon Press).

Breckenridge, C., et al. [Eds.] (2002). *Cosmopolitanism* (Durham, NC: Duke University Press).

Brock, G. (2009). *Global Justice: A Cosmopolitan Account* (Oxford, UK: Oxford University Press).

Brown, E. (2010). "Die Erfindung des Kosmopolitanismus in der Stoa," in M. Lutz-Bachmann et al. [Eds.], *Kosmopolitanismus: Zur Geschichte und Zukunft eines umstrittenen Ideals* (Weilerswist: Velbrück), 9–24.

Brown, G. (2009). *Grounding Cosmopolitanism: From Kant to the Idea of a Cosmopolitan Constitution* (Edinburgh: Edinburgh University Press).

——— (2010). "The Laws of Hospitality, Asylum Seekers, and Cosmopolitan Right: A Kantian Response to Jacques Derrida," *European Journal of Political Theory* 9/3 (2010): 1–20.

Brown, G., and D. Held [Eds.] (2010). *The Cosmopolitan Reader* (Cambridge, UK: Polity Press).

Bruendel, S. (2004). "Die Geburt der 'Volksgemeinschaft' aus dem 'Geist von 1914'. Entstehung und Wandel eines 'sozialistischen' Gesellschaftsentwurfs," *Zeitgeschichte-online* [Thema: Fronterlebnis und Nachkriegsordnung. Wirkung und Wahrnehmung des Ersten Weltkriegs], (Mai 2004), at http://www.zeitgeschichte-online.de/md=EWK-Bruendel, accessed on December 17, 2012.

Brumlik, M. (1999). "Zur Begründung der Menschenrechte im Buch Amos," in H. Brunkhorst, W. Köhler, and M. Lutz-Bachmann [Eds.], *Recht auf Menschenrechte* (Frankfurt: Suhrkamp), 11–19.

Brunkhorst, H. (2002). *Solidarität: Von der Bürgerfreundschaft zur globalen Rechtsgenossenschaft* (Frankfurt: Suhrkamp).

Buchwalter, A. (1991). "Hegel, Marx, and the Concept of Immanent Critique," *Journal of History of Philosophy* 29/2 (April 1991): 253–279.

Bühler, K. (1934). *Sprachtheorie. Die Darstellungsfunktion der Sprache* (Jena: G. Fischer).

Burg, P. (1974). *Kant und die französische Revolution* (Berlin: Duncker & Humblot).

Bürger, P. (1974). *Theorie der Avantgarde* (Frankfurt: Suhrkamp).

——— (2000). *Ursprung ddes Postmodernen Denkens* (Weilerswist: Velbrück).

Calasanti, T., and A. Zajicek (1993). "Reweaving a Critical Theory: The Socialist-Feminist Contributions," *Rethinking Marxism—Journal of Economics, Culture & Society* 6/4 (1993): 87–103.

Cancik, H. (2002). "'Dignity of Man' and 'Persona' in Stoic Anthropology: Some Remarks on Cicero, *De Officiis* I, 105–107," in D. Kretzner and E. Klein [Eds.], *The Concept of Human Rights in Human Rights Discourse* (The Hague: Kluwer), 19–39.

Caney, S. (2005). *Justice beyond Borders: A Global Political Theory* (Oxford, UK: Oxford University Press).

Car, B., and S. Ellner (1993). *The Latin American Left: From the Fall of Allende to Perestroika* (Boulder, CO: Westview Press).

Castañeda, J. (1993). *Utopia Unarmed: The Latin American Left after the Cold War* (New York: Alfred Knopf).

Cavallar, G. (1999). *Kant and the Theory and Practice of International Right* (Cardiff: University of Wales Press).

——— (2002). *The Rights of Strangers* (Aldershot, UK: Ashgate).

Chandler, N. D. (2006). "The Possible Form of an Interlocution: W. E. B. DuBois and Max Weber in Correspondence, 1904–1905," *The New Centennial Review* 6/3 (Winter 2006): 193–239.

Chang, W., and L. Kalmanson [Eds.] (2010). *Confucianism in Context: Classic Philosophy and Contemporary Issues, East Asia and Beyond* (Albany, NY: State University of New York Press).

Chapman, J., and I. Shapiro [Eds.] (1993). *Democratic Community* [*NONOS XXXV*] (New York: New York University Press).

Cheah, P. (2003). *Spectral Nationality: Passages of Freedom from Kant to Postcolonial Literatures of Liberation* (New York: Columbia University Press).

——— (2006). *Inhuman Conditions: On Cosmopolitanism and Human Righs* (Cambridge, MA: Harvard University Press).

Cheah, P., and B. Robbins [Eds.] (1998). *Thinking and Feeling beyond the Nation* (Minneapolis, MN: University of Minnesotta Press).

Cheneval, F. (2010). "Die kosmopolitische Dimension des 'consensus praesumtus.' Von Christian Wolff zu John Rawls un darüber hinaus," in M. Lutz-Bachmann, A. Niederberger, and P. Schink [Hrsg.], *Kosmopolitanismus: Zur Geschichte und Zukunft eines umstrittenen Ideals* (Welerswist: Velbrück), 122–145.

Chwaszcza, C. (2010). "The Concept of Rights in Contemporary Human Rights Discourse," *Ratio Juris* 23/3 (September 2010): 333–364.

Cochran, M. (1999). *Normative Theory in International Relations: A Pragmatic Approach* (Cambridge, UK: Cambridge University Press).

Cohen, J., and A. Arato (1992). *Civil Society and Political Theory* (Cambridge, MA: MIT Press).

Collins, S. (2006). *Aristotle and the Rediscovery of Citizenship* (Cambridge, UK: Cambridge University Press).

Commissiong, A. (2012). *Cosmopolitanism in Modernity: Human Dignity in a Global Age* (Lanham, MD: Lexington Books).

Cone, J. (1972). *The Spirit and the Blues* (New York: Seabury Press).

Confucius (1998). *The Analects of Confucius* (New York: Ballantine Books).

Cooper, A. A., Third Earl of Shaftesbury (1711 [1999]). *Characteristics of Men, Manners, Opinions, Times* (Cambridge, UK: Cambridge University Press).

Cornu, A. (1948). *Karl Marx et la Révolution de 1848* (Paris: Presses Universitaires de France).

Cranston, M. (1967). "Human Rights: Real and Supposed," in D. D. Raphael [Ed.], *Political Theory and the Rights of Man* (Bloomington, IN: Indiana University Press), 43–51.

Crocker, D. (1983). *Praxis and Democratic Socialism: The Critical Social Theory of Markovic and Stojanovic* (Atlantic Highlands, NJ: Humanities Press).

Cronin, C. (2011). "Cosmopolitan Democracy," in B. Fultner [Ed.], *Jürgen Habermas: Key Concepts* (London: Acumen), 196–221.

The Dalai Lama (1998). "Human Rights and Universal Responsibility," in D. Keown, C. S. Prebish, and W. R. Husted [Eds.], *Buddhism and Human Rights* (Surrey: Ashgate), xvii–xxi.

Dallmayr, F. (2002). "'Asian Values' and Global Human Rights," *Philosophy East & West* 52/2 (April 2002): 173–189.

Danielou, J. (1976). *A History of Early Christian Doctrine* [The Gospel Message and Hellenistic Culture, Vol. II] (London: Darton, Longman & Todd), 7–99.

De Bary, W., and T. Weiming [Eds.] (1998). *Confucianism and Human Rights* (New York: Columbia University Press).

De Greiff, P. (2002). "Habermas on Nationalism and Cosmopolitanism," *Ratio Juris* 15/4 (December 2002): 418–438.

de Vattel, É. (1758). *Le droit de gens* [3 vols., with facsimile of French edition and English translation, ed. J. B. Scott] (Washington: Carnegie Institute).

Delanty, G. (1995). *Inventing Europe: Idea, Identity, Reality* (London: Palgrave MacMillan).

——— (2009). *The Cosmopolitan Imagination: The Renewal of Critical Social Theory* (Cambridge, UK: Cambridge University Press).

——— [Ed.] (2012). *Routledge International Handbook of Cosmopolitan Studies* (London: Routledge).

Derrida, J. (1982). *Margins of Philosophy* (Chicago: Chicago University Press).

——— (1992). "Force of Law: The Mystical Foundation of Authority," in D. Cornell, M. Rosenfeld, and D. G. Carlson [Eds.], *Deconstruction and the Possibility of Justice* (London: Routledge), 3–67.

——— (1994). *Specter of Marx: The State of the Debt, the Work of Mourning, and the New International* (New York and London: Routledge).

——— (1996). *Le monolinguisme de l'autre* (Paris: Galilée).

———(1997). *De l'hospitalité: Anne Dufourmantelle invite Jacques Derrida à répondre* (Paris: Calmann-Lévy).

——— (2001). *Cosmopolitanism and Forgiveness* (London: Routledge).

Di Federico, G. [Ed.] (2011). *The EU Charter of Fundamental Rights: From Declaration to Binding Instrument* (Dordrecht: Springer).

Diogenes Laertius (1925). *Lives of Eminent Philosophers* [Trans. R. D. Hicks, Vol. II] (Cambridge, MA: Harvard University Press).

Doder, D. (1993). "Belgrade Professor Who Fought Tito Now Scorned as Serb Leader," *Chronicle of Higher Education* (April 7, 1993): A37–A38.

Donnelly, J. (2003). *Universal Human Rights in Theory and Practice*, 2nd Edn. (Ithaca, NY, and London: Cornell University Press).

——— (2007). *International Human Rights* (Boulder, CO: Westview Press).

Douzinas, C. (2000). *The End of Human Rights: Critical Legal Thought at the Turn of the Century* (Oxford, UK: Hart Publishing Ltd).

——— (2007). *Human Rights and Empire: The Political Philosophy of Cosmopolitansm* (New York: Routledge).

Driver, G. R., and J. C. Miles (1956). *The Babylonian Laws* (Oxford, UK: Clarendon Press).

Dubiel, H. (1985). *Theory and Politics: Studies in the Development of Critical Theory* (Cambridge, MA: MIT Press).

DuBois, W. E. B. (1899). *The Philadelphia Negro: A Social Study* (Philadelphia, PA: University of Pennsylvania Press).

——— (1995 [1905]). *On Sociology and the Black Community* (Chicago: University of Chicago Press).

Dummett, M. (1973). *Frege: Philosophy of Language* (London: Duckworth & Co).

——— (1993). *Origins of Analytic Philosophy* (Cambridge, MA: Harvard University Press).

Dussel, E. (1986). *Ética Comunitaria. Liberta o Pobre!* (Petrópolis: Vozes).

——— (1988). *Hacia un Marx Desconocido: Un Comentario a los Manuscriptos del 61–63* (Tztapalapa: Siglo XXI).

——— (2000). *Ética da Libertação* (Petrópolis: Vozes).

——— (2009). *Política de la Liberación* (Madrid: Editorial Trotta).

Dworkin, R. (1981). *Taking Rights Seriously* (London: Duckworth).

Edelglass, W., and J. Garfield [Eds.] (2009). *Buddhist Philosophy: Essential Readings* (Oxford, UK: Oxford University Press).

Eisenstadt, S. [Ed.] (1986). *The Origins and Diversity of Axial Age Civilizations* (Albany, NY: State University of New York).

Engemann, T. [Ed.] (2000). *Thomas Jefferson and the Politics of Nature* (Notre Dame: University of Notre Dame Press).

Erman, E. (2005). *Human Rights and Democracy: Discourse Theory and Human Rights Institutions* (Aldershot: Ashgate).

Erskine, T. (2008). *Embedded Cosmopolitanism: Duties to Strangers and Enemies in a World of Dislocated Communities* (Cambridge, UK: Cambridge University Press).

Farr, A. (2009). *Critical Theory and Democratic Vision: Herbert Marcuse and Recent Liberation Philosophies* (Lanham, MD: Lexington Books).

Farrar, C. (1988). *The Origins of Democratic Thinking: The Invention of Politics in Classical Athens* (Cambridge, UK: Cambridge University Press).

Ferry, J.-M. (1987). *Habermas : l'éthique de la communication* (Paris: Presses Universitaires de France).

Ferry, J.-M (1994). *Philosophie de la communication* [Vol. 1, *De l'antinomie de la vérité à la fondation ultime de la raison*; Vol. 2, *Justice politique et démocratie procédurale*] (Paris: Éditions du Cerf).

Fidora, A., M. Lutz-Bachmann, and A. Wagner [Eds.] (2010). *Lex und Jus. Beiträge zur Begründung des Rechts in der Philosophie des Mittelalters und der Frühen Neuzeit* (Stuttgart: frommann-holzboog).

Fine, R. (2007). *Cosmopolitanism* (London: Routledge).

Finlayson, J., and F. Freyenhagen (2011). *Habermas and Rawls: Disputing the Political* (New York: Routledge).

Finnis, J. (1980). *Natural Law and Natural Rights* (Oxford, UK: Oxford University Press).

——— (1998). *Aquinas: Moral, Political, and Legal Theory* (Oxford, UK: Oxford University Press).

Flynn, J. (2003). "Habermas on Human Rights: Law, Morality, & Intercultural Dialogue," *Social Theory & Practice: An International and Interdisciplinary Journal of Social Philosophy* 29/3 (2003): 431–457.

Forman, M. (1998). *Nationalism and the International Labor Movement: The Idea of the Nations in Socialist and Anarchist Theory* (University Park, PA: Pennsylvania State University Press).

Forst, R. (1994). *Kontexte der gerechtigkeit* (Frankfurt: Suhrkamp).

——— (2003). *Toleranz in Konflikt: Geschichte, Gehalt und Gegenwart eines umstrittenen Begriffs* (Frankfurt: Suhrkamp).

———(2007). *Das Recht auf Rechtfertigung* (Frankfurt: Suhrkamp).

———(2011). *Kritik der Rechtfertigungsverhältnisse: Perspektiven einer kritischen Theorie der Politik* (Berlin: Frankfurt).

Fraser, N. (1989). *Unruly Practices: Power, Discourse, and Gender in Contemporary Social Theory* (Cambridge, UK: Polity Press).

——— (1997). *Justice Interruptus: Critical Reflections on the Postsocialist Condition* (London: Routledge).

———[with Axel Honneth] (2003). *Redistribution or Recognition? A Philosophical Exchange* (London: Verso).

Frege, G. (1884). *Grundlagen der Arithmetik: Eine logisch-mathematische Untersuchung über den Begriff der Zahl* (Breslau: W. Koebner).

Freire, P. (1970). *Pedagogia do Oprimido* (Rio de Janeiro: Paz e Terra).

Freitag, B. (1987). *Teoria Crítica: Ontem e Hoje* (São Paulo, SP: Brasiliense).

Fromm, E. (1999). *Gesammelteausgabe* (München: Deutsche Verlags-Anstalt).

Frost, M. (1986). *Towards a Normative Theory of International Relations* (Cambridge, UK: Cambridge University Press).

Gabus, J.-P. (1998). "Paul Tillich et l'École de Francfort: Bilan d'une recherche," *Revue d'Histoire et de Philosophie Religieuses* 78 (1998): 313–331.

Gandler, S. (1999). *Peripherer Marxismus. Kritische Theorie in Mexiko* (Hamburg: Argument Verlag).

Gay, P. (1967). *The Enlightenment* (New York: Norton).

Genovese, E. (1995). "Martin Luther King Jr.: Theology, Politics, Scholarship" [Review of *The Papers of M. L. King Jr.* Vol. 2], *Reviews in American History* 23/1 (March 1995): 1–12.

Gill, C. (1988). "Personhood and Personality: The Four-Personal Theory in Cicero, *De Officiis* 1," *Oxford Studies in Ancient Philosophy* 6 (1988): 169–199.

Gilroy, P. (1993). *The Black Atlantic: Modernity and Double Consciousness* (Cambridge, MA: Harvard University Press).

Gómez, V. (1996). "La Teoría Crítica en España: Aspectos de una recepción," *Logos. Anales del Seminario de Metafísica* 30 (1996): 11–41.

Gottfried, P. (1988). *The Conservative Movement* (Boston: Twayne Publ).

Gould, C. (2004). *Globalizing Democracy and Human Rights* (Cambridge, UK: Cambridge University Press).

Gregory, E. (2007). "Before the Original Position: The Neo-Orthodox Theology of the Young John Rawls," *Journal of Religious Ethics* 35/2 (2007): 179–206.

Grell, O. P., J. Israel, and N. Tyacke [Eds.] (1991). *From Persecution to Toleration: The Glorious Revolution and Religion in England* (Oxford, UK: Oxford University Press).

Grice, P. (1981). "Presupposition and Conversational Implicature," in P. Cole [Ed.], *Radical Pragmatics* (New York: Academic Press), 183–197.

Grimm, D. (1991). *Die Zukunft der Verfassung* (Frankfurt: Suhrkamp).

——— (2011). *Die Zukunft der Verfassung II: Auswirkungen von Europäisierung und Globalisierung* (Berlin: Suhrkamp).

Grotius, H. (1625). *The Law of War and Peace* [*De jure belli ac pacis*] (Roslyn, NY: Walter Black).

Günther, K. (1988). *Der Sinn für Angemessenheit. Anwendungsdiskurse in Moral und Recht* (Frankfurt: Suhrkamp).

——— (1994). "Diskurstheorie des Rechts oder Naturrecht in diskurstheoretischem Gewande?," Kritische Justiz 4 (1994): 470–487.

——— (2005). *Schuld und kommunikative Freiheit* (Frankfurt: Vittorio Klostermann).

Gutiérrez, G. (1971). *Teología de la Liberación* (Lima: CEP).

Gutman, A. (1985). "Communitarian Critics of Liberalism," *Philosophy and Public Affairs* 14 (Summer): 308–322.

Habermas, J. (1962). *Strukturwandel der Öffentlichkeit* (Frankfurt: Suhrkamp).

——— (1963). *Theorie und Praxis* (Frankfurt: Suhrkamp).

———(1967). *Zur Logik der Sozialwissenschaften* (Frankfurt: Suhrkamp).

——— (1968a). *Erkenntnis und Interesse* (Frankfurt: Suhrkamp).

——— (1968b). *Wissenschaft und Technologie als Ideologie* (Frankfurt: Suhrkamp).

——— (1971a). *Philosophisch-politische Profile* (Frankfurt: Suhrkamp).

——— [with Niklas Luhmann] (1971b/1982). *Theorie der Gesellschaft oder Sozialtechnologie? Was leistet die Systemforschung?* [expanded edition in 1982] (Frankfurt: Suhrkamp).

——— (1973). *Legitimationskrise im Spätkapitalismus* (Frankfurt: Suhrkamp).

Habermas, J. (1976a). *Zur Rekonstruktion des historischen Materialismus* (Frankfurt: Suhrkamp).

——— (1976b). "Was heißt Universalpragmatik?," in K.-O. Apel [Hrsg.], *Sprachpragmatik und Philosophie* (Frankfurt: Suhrkamp), 174–272.

Habermas, J. (1981a). *Theorie des kommunikativen Handelns* (Frankfurt: Suhrkamp).

——— (1981b). *Kleine politische Schriften I–IV* (Frankfurt: Suhrkamp).

——— (1983). *Moralbewußtsein und kommunikatives Handeln* (Frankfurt: Suhrkamp).

——— (1984). *Vorstudien und Ergänzungen zur Theorie des kommunikativen Handelns* (Frankfurt: Suhrkamp).

——— (1985a). *Der philosophische Diskurs der Moderne* (Frankfurt: Suhrkamp).

——— (1985b). *Die Neue Unübersichtlichkeit* [*Kleine politische Schriften V*] (Frankfurt: Suhrkamp).

———(1986). *The Tanner Lectures on Human Values VIII*, [Ed. S. McMurrin] (Salt Lake City, UT: University of Utah Press).

——— (1987). *Eine Art Schadensabwicklung* [Kleine politische Schriften VI] (Frankfurt: Suhrkamp).

——— (1988). *Nachmetaphysisches Denken* (Frankfurt: Suhrkamp).

——— (1990). *Die nachholende Revolution* [*Kleine politische Schriften VII*] (Frankfurt: Suhrkamp).

——— (1991a). *Texte und Kontexte* (Frankfurt: Suhrkamp).

——— (1991b). *Erläuterung zur Diskursethik* (Frankfurt: Suhrkamp).

——— (1992). *Faktizität und Geltung. Beiträge zur Diskurstheorie des Rechts und des demokratischen Rechtsstaats* (Frankfurt: Suhrkamp).

——— (1995). *Die Normalität einer Berliner Republik* [*Kleine Politischen Schriften VIII*] (Frankfurt: Suhrkamp).

———(1996). *Die Einbeziehung des Anderen* (Frankfurt: Suhrkamp).

———(1998). *Die postnationale Konstellation* (Frankfurt: Suhrkamp).

———(1999). *Wahrheit und Rechtfertigung. Philosophische Aufsätze* (Frankfurt: Suhrkamp).

———(2001a). *Zeit der Übergänge* [*Kleine Politischen Schriften IX*] (Frankfurt: Suhrkamp).

———(2001b). *Glauben und Wissen* (Frankfurt: Suhrkamp).

——— (2001c). *Kommunikatives Handeln und detranszendentalisierte Vernunft* (Stuttgart: Reclam).

——— (2001d). *Die Zukunft der menschlichen Natur: Auf dem Weg zu einer liberalen Eugenik?* (Frankfurt: Suhrkamp).

——— (2004). *Der gespaltene Westen* [*Kleine Politischen Schriften X*] (Frankfurt: Suhrkamp).

——— (2005). *Zwischen Naturalismus und Religion: Philosophische Aufsätze* (Frankfurt: Suhrkamp).

———(2008). *Ach Europa* [*Kleine Politischen Schriften XI*] (Berlin: Suhrkamp).

——— (2009). *Philosophische Texte* [Studienausgabe, 4 Bd.] (Frankfurt: Suhrkamp).

———(2011). *Zur Verfassung Europas: Ein Essay* (Berlin: Suhrkamp).

———(2012). *Nachmetaphysisches Denken II* (Berlin: Suhrkamp).

Hammurabi (1996). "The Code of Hammurabi," in R. Hooker [Ed.], *World Civilizations*. Webpage of Washington State University, at http://www.wsu.edu/~dee/MESO/CODE.HTM, accessed on March 6, 2011.

Hanke, L. (1949). *The Spanish Struggle for Justice in the Conquest of America* (Philadelphia, PA: University of Pennsylvania Press).

———— (1974). *All Mankind Is One: A Study of the Disputation between Bartolomé de Las Casas and Juan Ginés de Sepúlveda in 1550 on the Intellectual and Religious Capacity of the American Indians* (DeKalb, IL: Northern Illinois University Press).

Hansen, M. H. [Ed.] (1993). *The Ancient City-State* (Copenhagen: The Royal Danish Academy of Sciences and Letters).

———— (2006). *Polis: An Introduction to the Ancient Greek City-State* (Oxford, UK: Oxford University Press).

———— (2010). "The Concepts of *Demos, Ekklesia,* and *Dikasterion* in Classic Athens," *Greek, Roman, and Byzantine Studies* 50 (2010): 499–536.

Hart, H. L. A. (1962). *The Concept of Law* (Oxford, UK: Clarendon Press).

Haug, W. F. (1973). *Bestimmte Negation* (Frankfurt: Surhkamp).

Hayden, P. (2001). *Philosophy of Human Rights.* (St. Paul, MN: Paragon House).

Hegel, G. W. F. (1970). *Werke* (Frankfurt: Suhrkamp).

Heidegger, M. (1927). *Sein und Zeit* (Tübingen: Max Niemeyer).

Held, D. (1980). *Introduction to Critical Theory. From Horkheimer to Habermas* (London: Hutchinson).

———— (1995a). *Cosmopolitan Democracy. An Agenda for a New World Order* (Cambridge, UK: Polity Press).

———— (1995b). *Democracy and the Global Order: From the Modern State to Cosmopolitan Governance* (Stanford, CA: Stanford University Press).

———— (2010). *Cosmopolitanism: Ideals and Realities* (Cambridge, UK: Polity Press).

Held, D., and A. McGrew [Eds.] (2003). *The Global Transformations Reader: An Introduction to the Globalization Debate* (Cambridge, UK: Polity Press).

Henrich, D. (1963). "Das Problem der Grundlegung der Ethik bei Kant und in spekulativen Idealismus," in P. Engelhardt [Hrsg.], *Sein und Ethos* (Mainz: Matthias-Grünewald), 350–386.

———— (1973). "Der Begriff der sittlichen Einsicht und Kants Lehre vom Faktum der Vernunft," in G. Prauss [Hrsg.], *Kant: Zur Deutung seiner Theorie von Erkennen und Handeln* (Köln: Kiepenheuer & Witsch), 90–105.

———— (1975). "Die Deduktion des Sittengesetzes," in A. Schwan [Hrsg.], *Denken im Schatten des Nihilismus* (Darmstadt: Wissenschaftliche Buchgesellschaft), 52–112.

————[Hrsg.] (1983). *Kant oder Hegel?: Uber Formen der Begrundung in der Philosophie* [*Veroffentlichungen der Internationalen Hegel-Vereinigung*] (Stuttgart: KlettCotta).

Heraclitus (1903). "Fragmente," in H. Diels and W. Kranz [Eds.], *Die Fragmente der Vorsokratiker* [Vol. 1] (Berlin: Weidmannsche Buchhandlung), 58–88.

Herman, B. (1993). *The Practice of Moral Judgment* (Cambridge, MA: Harvard University Press).

Herstein, G. (2009). "The Roycean Roots of the Beloved Community," *The Pluralist* 4/2 (Summer 2009): 91–107.

Hine, R. (1953). *California's Utopian Communities* (New York: Norton).

Hobbes, T. (1640). *The Elements of Law* (Cambridge, UK: Cambridge University Press).

―――― (1651 [1993]). *Leviathan* (Cambridge, UK: Cambridge University Press).

Hoff, J., A. Petrioli, I. Stuetzle and F. O. Wolf [Hrsg.] (2006). *Das Kapital neu lesen—Beitraege zur radikalen Philosophie* (Muenster: Westfaellisches Dampfboot).

Höffe, O. (1996). "Eine Weltrepublik als Minimalstaat. Zur Theorie internationaler politischer Gerechtigkeit," in R. Merkel and R. Wittmann [Hrsg.], *"Zum ewigen Frieden"*. *Grundlagen, Aktualität und Aussichten einer Idee von Immanuel Kant* (Frankfurt: Suhrkamp), 154–171.

―――― (2004). *Wirtschaftsbürger—Staatsbürger—Weltbürger. Politische Ethik im Zeitalter der Globalisierung* (München: C. H. Beck).

Höhn, G., and G. Raulet (1978). "L'École de Francfort en France: Bibliographie critique," *Esprit* 5 (1978): 135–147.

Home, H. [Lord Kames] (1762). *Elements of Criticism* (Edinburgh: Walker & Greig).

Honneth, A. (1992). *Kampf um Anerkennung* (Frankfurt: Suhrkamp).

―――― (2001). *Leiden an Unbestimmtheit. Eine Reaktualisierung der Hegelschen Rechtsphilosophie* (Stuttgart: Reclam).

―――― (2007). *Pathologien der Vernunft. Geschichte und Gegenwart der Kritischen Theorie* (Frankfurt: Suhrkamp).

Honneth, A., and A. Wellmer [Hrsg.] (1986). *Die Frankfurt Schule und die Folgen* (Berlin: W. de Gruyter).

Honneth, A., and C. Mencke [Hrsg.] (2006). *Theodor W. Adorno. Negative Dialektik* (Berlin: Akademie Verlag).

Hooker, R. (1996). "Law and Order in Ancient Egypt," in R. Hooker [Ed.], *World Civilizations*. Webpage of Washington State University at http://reshafim.org .il/ad/egypt/ law_and_order/index.html, accessed on March 6, 2011.

Horkheimer, M. (1989). *Gesammelte Schriften* (Frankfurt: Fischer).

Hudson, J. B. (2002). "Diversity, Inequality, and Community: African Americans and People of Color in the United States," in P. Alderson [Ed.], *Diversity and Community: An Interdisciplinary Reader* (Oxford, UK: Blackwell), 141–166.

Huntington, S. (1996). *The Clash of Civilizations and the Remaking of World Order* (New York: Simon & Schuster).

Ilting, K.-H. (1971). "The Structure of Hegel's Philosophy of Right," in Z. Pelczynski [Ed.], *Hegel's Political Philosophy: Problems and Perspectives* (Cambridge, UK: Cambridge University Press), 90–110.

―――― (1972). "Der naturalistische Fehlschluß bei Kant," in Beck (1972) and in M. Riedel [Hrsg.], *Rehabilitierung der praktischen Philosophie*, Bd. I (Freiburg: Rombach), 113–130.

Ingram, D. (2009). "Of Sweatshops and Subsistence: Habermas and Human Rights," *Ethics & Global Politics* 2/3 (2009): 193–217.

—— (2010). *Habermas: Introduction and Analysis* (Ithaca, NY: Cornell University Press).

Ishay, M. (2004). *The History of Human Rights: From Ancient Times to the Globalization Era* (Berkeley, CA: University of California Press).

Jaspers, K. (1949). *Urprung und Ziel der Geschichte* (München: Piper).

Jay, M. (1973). *The Dialectical Imagination: A History of the Frankfurt School and the Institute of Social Research, 1923–1950* (Boston: Little, Brown).

Jensen, M. (1968). *The Founding of a Nation: A History of the American Revolution, 1763–1776* (Oxford, UK: Oxford University Press).

Joas, H. (1980). *Praktische Intersubjektivität. Die Entwicklung des Werkes von G. H. Mead* (Frankfurt: Suhrkamp).

Kant, I. (1902). *Gesammelte Schriften* [Hrsg. von der Königlichen Preussischen Akademie der Wissenschaften—*Akademieausgabe* (*AA*)] (Berlin: W. de Gruyter).

—— (1960). *Werke* [Hrsg. W. Weischedel] (Darmstadt: Wissenschaftliche Buchgesellschaft).

Kaulbach, F. (1982). *Immanuel Kant* (Berlin: W. de Gruyter).

Kellner, D. (1989). *Critical Theory, Marxism, and Modernity* (Cambridge, UK: Polity Press).

Kelsen, H. (1934). *Reine Rechtslehre* [2008 Studienausgabe] (Tübingen: Mohr Siebeck).

Kettler, D. (1975). "Herbert Marcuse. Alienation and Negativity," in A. Crispigny and K. Minogue [Eds.], *Contemporary Political Philosophers* (New York: Dodd, Mead & Co.), 1–48.

Khan, M. (2003). *Human Rights in the Muslim World* (Durham, NC: Carolina Academic Press).

Kirk, R. (1953). *The Conservative Mind: From Burke to Elliot* (Chicago: Regnery).

Kleingeld, P. (1993). "The Problematic Status of Gender-Neutral Language in the History of Philosophy: The Case of Kant," *Philosophical Forum* 25 (1993): 134–150.

—— (1999). "Six Varieties of Cosmopolitanism in Late 18th Century Germany," *Journal of the History of Ideas* 60/3 (1999): 505–524.

—— (2003). "Kant's Cosmopolitan Patriotism," *Kant-Studien* 94 (2003): 299–316.

—— (2007). "Kant's Second Thoughts on Race," *The Philosophical Quarterly* 57/229 (October 2007): 573–592.

—— (2010). "Moral Consciousness and the 'Fact of Reason,'" in A. Reath and J. Timmermann [Eds.], *Kant's Critique of Practical Reason: A Guide* (Cambridge, UK: Cambridge University Press), 55–72.

—— (2011). *Kant and Cosmopolitanism: The Philosophical Ideal of World Citizenship* (Cambridge, UK: Cambridge University Press).

Kleingeld, P., and E. Brown (2006). "Cosmopolitanism," in E. N. Zalta [Ed.], *The Stanford Encyclopedia of Philosophy*, at: http://plato.stanford.edu/entries/cosmopolitanism, accessed on December 11, 2012.

Kohlberg, L. (1981). *Essays on Moral Development* [Vol. I: *The Philosophy of Moral Development*] (San Francisco: Harper & Row).

242   BIBLIOGRAPHY

Kolakowski, L. (1978). *Main Current of Marxism* (Oxford, UK: Oxford University Press).

Konvitz, M. (1972). *Judaism and Human Rights* (New York: Norton).

Korsgaard, C. (1996). *The Sources of Normativity* (Cambridge, UK: Cambridge University Press).

Koselleck, R. (1977). *Kritik und Krise: Eine Studie zur Pathogenese der bürgerlichen Welt* (Frankfurt: Suhrkamp).

Koskenniemi, M. (2001). *The Gentle Civilizer of Nations: The Rise and Fall of International Law: 1870–1960* (Cambridge, UK: Cambridge University Press).

Kreimendahl, L. (1990). *Kant. Der Durchbrich von 1769* (Köln: Dinter).

Kretzmer, D., and E. Klein [Eds.] (2002). *The Concept of Human Rights in Human Rights Discourse* (The Hague: Kluwer).

Kuehn, M. (1987). *Scottisch Common Sense in Germany (1768–1800)* (Kingston: McGill-Queen's University Press).

——— (2002). *Kant: A Biography* (Cambridge, UK: Cambridge University Press).

Kuhn, T. (1970). *The Structure of Scientific Revolutions* (Chicago: University of Chicago Press).

Kymlicka, W. (1989). *Liberalism, Community and Culture* (Oxford, UK: Clarendon Press).

——— (1995). *Multicultural Citizenship. A Liberal Theory of Minority Rights* (Oxford, UK: Clarendon Press).

——— (2001). *Politics in Vernacular: Nationalism, Multiculturalism and Citizenship* (Oxford, UK: Oxford University Press).

——— (2002). *Contemporary Political Philosophy: An Introduction* (Oxford, UK: Oxford University Press).

Lafont, C. (1999). *The Linguistic Turn in Hermeneutic Philosophy* (Cambridge, MA: MIT Press).

——— (2008). "Alternative Visions of a New Global Order: What Should Cosmopolitans Hope for?," *Ethics & Global Politics* 1/1–2 (2008): 1–20.

——— (2010). "Accountability and Global Governance: Challenging the State-Centric Conception of Human Rights," *Ethics & Global Politics* 3/3 (2010): 193–215.

Langlois, A. (2001). *The Politics of Justice and Human Rights* (Cambridge, UK: Cambridge University Press).

Larkin, E. (2005). *Thomas Paine and the Literature of Revolution* (Cambridge, UK: Cambridge University Press).

Las Casas, B. (1998). *Obras Completas* (Madrid: Alianza Editorial).

Libânio, J. (1976). *Comunidade Eclesial de Base* (Rio de Janeiro: PUC).

Linklater, A. (1998). *Transformation of Political Community* (Cambridge, UK: Polity Press).

——— (2007). *Critical Theory and World Politics: Citizenship, Sovereignty, and Humanity* (London: Routledge).

Locke, J. (1689 [1975]). *An Essay Concerning Human Understanding* [ed. P. Nidditch] (Oxford, UK: Clarendon Press).

———— (1690 [1988]). *Two Treatises of Government* [ed. P. Laslett] (Cambridge, UK: Cambridge University Press).

Longuenesse, B. (2005). *Kant on the Human Standpoint* (Cambridge, UK: Cambridge University Press).

Lopes, A., and R. Gary (1993). "Marxism's Feminism: Bebel and Zetkin in Opposition," *Rethinking Marxism—Journal of Economics, Culture & Society* 6/3 (1993): 66–78.

Lorberbaum, Y. (2002). "Blood and the Image of God: On the Sanctity of Life in Biblical and Early Rabbinic Law, Myth, and Ritual," in D. Kretzmer and E. Klein [Eds.], *The Concept of Human Rights in Human Rights Discourse* (The Hague: Kluwer), 55–86.

Luban, D. (2004). "A Theory of Crimes against Humanity," *Yale Journal of International Law* 29 (2004): 85–167.

Luckhardt, C. G. (1978). "Beyond Knowledge: Paradigms in Wittgenstein's Later Philosophy," *Philosophy and Phenomenological Research* 39/2 (December 1978): 240–252.

Lukow, P. (1993). "The Fact of Reason: Kant's Passage to Ordinary Moral Knowledge," *Kant-Studien* 84/2 (1993): 204–221.

Lutz-Bachmann, M. (2005). "Das 'ethische geimeine Wesen' und die Idee einer Weltrepunlik. Der Beitrag der *Religionsschrift* Kants zur politischen Philosophie internationaler Beziehungen," in M. Städler [Hrsg.], *Kants "Ethisches Geimeinwesen": Die Religionsschrift zwischen Vernunftkritik und praktischer Philosophie* (Berlin: Akademieverlag), 207–219.

Lutz-Bachmann, M., A. Fidora, and A. Wagner [Eds.] (2010). *Lex and Ius* (Stuttgart: forman-holzboog).

Lutz-Bachmann, M., A. Niederberger, and P. Schink [Hrsg.] (2010). *Kosmopolitanismus: Zur Geschichte und Zukunft enes umstrittenen Ideals* (Weilerswist: Velbrück).

Lutz-Bachmann, M., and J. Bohman [Hrsg.] (1996). *Frieden durch Recht. Kants Friedensidee und das Problem einer neuen Weltordnung* (Frankfurt am Main: Suhrkamp).

———— [Eds.] (1997). *Perpetual Peace* (Cambridge, MA: MIT Press).

———— [Hrsg.] (2002). *Weltstaat oder Staatenwelt?* (Frankfurt: Suhrkamp).

Lutz-Bachmann, M., W. Köhler, and H. Brunkhorst [Hrsg.] (1999). *Recht auf Menschenrechte. Menschenrechte, Demokratie und internationale Politik* (Frankfurt: Suhrkamp).

Lyotard, J.-F. (1983). *Le Différend* (Paris: Minuit).

———— (1986). *Le enthousiasme. La critique kantienne de l'historie* (Paris: Galilée).

———— (1988). *L'inhumain: Causeries sur le temps* (Paris: Galilée).

———— (1991). *Leçons sur l'"Lanalytique du sublime": Kant, Critique de la faculté de juger* (Paris: Galilée).

———— (1993). "The Other's Rights," in S. Shute and S. Hurley [Eds.], *On Human Rights* (New York: Basic Books), 135–147.

Lyotard, J. F., and J. L. Théb aud (1985). *Au juste* (Paris: Christian Bourgeois).

Macedo, S. (1995). "Liberal Civic Education and Religious Fundamentalism: The Case of God v. John Rawls?," *Ethics* 105/3 (April 1993): 468–496.

MacIntyre, A. (1967). *Secularization and Moral Change* (London: Oxford University Press).

——— (1981). *After Virtue* (Notre Dame: University of Notre Dame Press).

——— (1988). *Whose Justice? Which Rationality?* (Notre Dame: University of Notre Dame Press).

Mansilla, F. H. C. (1970). *Introducción a la teoría crítica de la sociedad* (Barcelona: Seix Barral).

Marcuse, H. (1955). *Reason and Revolution: Hegel and the Rise of Social Theory* (Boston, MA: Beacon Press).

——— (1962). *Eros and Civilization: A Philosophical Inquiry into Freud* (Boston, MA: Beacon Press).

——— (1964). *One-Dimensional Man: Studies in Ideology of Advanced Industrial Society* (London: Routledge).

——— (1972). *Counterrevolution and Revolt* (Boston, MA: Beacon Press).

Mardones, J. M. (1990). "La recepción de la Teoría Crítica en España," *Isegoría* 1 (1990): 131–138.

Maritain, J. (1947). *La personne et le bien commun* (Paris: Desclée de Brower).

Martin, R., and D. Reidy [Eds.] (2006). *Rawls' Law of Peoples: A Realistic Utopia?* (Malden, MA: Blackwell).

Martinich, A. P. (1992). *The Two Gods of Leviathan: Thomas Hobbes on Religion and Politics* (Cambridge, UK: Cambridge University Press).

——— (1999). *Hobbes: A Biography* (Cambridge, UK: Cambridge University Press).

Marx, K., and F. Engels (1958). *Werke* [*MEW*] (Berlin: Dietz Verlag).

——— (1960). *Gesammelte Schrfiten* [*GS*] (Berlin: Dietz Verlag).

Matuštík, M. (1993). *Postnational Identity: Critical Theory and Existential Philosophy in Habermas, Kierkegaard, and Havel* (New York: Guilford Press).

———(2001). *Jürgen Habermas: A Philosophical-Political Profile* (Lanham, MD: Rowman & Littlefield).

Maus, I. (1992). *Aufklärung der Demokratie. Rechts- und demokratischtheoretischen Überlegungen im Anschluss an Kant* (Frankfurt: Suhrkamp).

——— (2011). *Über Volkssouveranität. Elemente einer Demokratietheorie* (Berling: Suhrkamp).

May, L. (2005). *Crimes against Humanity: A Normative Account* (Cambridge, UK: Cambridge University Press).

Mead, G. H. (1934). *Mind, Self, and Society* [Ed. Ch. Morris] (Chicago, IL: The University of Chicago Press).

Meinecke, F. (1962). *Cosmopolitanism and the National State* (Princeton, NJ: Princeton University Press).

Menand, L. (2001). *The Metaphysical Club: A Story of Ideas in America* (New York: Farrar, Straus & Giroux).

Mendieta, E. (2003). *The Adventures of Transcendental Philosophy: Karl-Otto Apel's Semiotics and Discourse Ethics* (Lanham, MD: Rowman & Littlefield Publishers).

────── (2007). *Global Fragments: Globalizations, Latinamericanisms, and Critical Theory* (Albany, NY: State University of New York Press).

────── (2009). "From Imperial Do Dialogical Imperialism," *Ethics & Global Politics* 2/3 (2009): 241–258.

Mendieta, E., and C. Kautzer [Eds.] (2009). *Pragmatism, Nation, and Race: Community in the Age of Empire* (Bloomington, IN: Indiana University Press).

Mendieta, E., and S. Elden [Eds.] (2011). *Reading Kant's Geography* (Albany, NY: State University of New York Press).

Merkel, R., and R. Wittmann [Hrsg.] (1996). *"Zum ewigen Frieden". Grundlagen, Aktualistät und Aussichten einer Idee von Immanuel Kant* (Frankfurt: Suhrkamp).

Michelni, D., R. Maliandi, and J. de Zan [Eds.] (2007). *La ética del discurso. Recepción y crítica desde América Latina* (Río Cuarto: Ediciones del ICALA).

Mignolo, W. (1993). "Colonial and Postcolonial Discourses: Cultural Critique or Academic Colonialism?," *Latin American Research Review* 28/3 (1993): 120–134.

────── (1995). *The Darker Side of Renaissance. Literacy, Territoriality and Colonization* (Ann Arbor, MI: Michigan University Press).

──────(1999). *Local Histories. Global Designs. Coloniality, Subaltern Knowledges, and Border Thinking* (Princeton, NJ: Princeton University Press).

────── (2001). "The Many Faces of Cosmo-polis: Border Thinking and Critical Cosmopolitanism," *Public Culture* 12/3 (2001): 721–748.

Moles, J. L. (1996). "Cynic Cosmopolitanism," in R. B. Branham and Goulet-Cazé [Eds.], *The Cynics: The Cynic Movement in Antiquity and Its Legacy* (Berkeley, CA: University of California Press, 1996), 105–120.

Morris, C. (1938). *Foundations of the Theory of Signs* (Chicago: The University of Chicago Press).

Morsink, J. (2009). *Inherent Human Rights: Philosophical Roots of the Universal Declaration* (Philadelphia, PA: University of Pennsylvania Press).

Mounier, E. (1950). *Oeuvres* (Paris: Editions du Seuil).

Moyn, S. (2010). *The Last Utopia: Human Rights in History* (Cambridge, MA: Harvard University Press).

Mulhall, S., and A. Swift (1992). *Liberals & Communitarians* (Oxford, UK: Blackwell).

Müller, J.-W. (2007). *Constitutional Patriotism* (Princeton, NJ: Princeton University Press).

Murithi, T. (2006). "Practical Peacemaking Wisdom in Africa: Reflections on Ubuntu," *The Journal of Pan African Studies* 1/4 (June 2006): 25–34.

Nascimento, A. (1995). "De Volta para a Comunidade: Considerando a Moral da Ética Comunitarista," *Simpósio* 38 (1995): 131–144.

────── (1996). "Vom 'Leibapriori' zur Dialektik der realen und idealen 'Kommunikationsgemeinschaft': Die Antwort Apels an Descartes und Leibniz," in *Akten des deutschen Kongresses für Philosophie* (Leipzig: Deutsche Gesellschaft für Philosophie), 870–878.

Nascimento, A. (1997a). "Die vielfältigen Dimensionen der Rationalität," in A. Nascimento and K. Witte [Eds.], *Grenzen der Moderne*. *Europa & Lateinamerika* (Frankfurt: IKO Verlag), 21–33.

——— [with J. Sathler] (1997b). "Black Masks on White Faces: Liberation Theology and the Quest for Syncretism in the Brazilian Context," in E. Mendieta, L. Lorentzen, D. Batstone, and D. Hopkins [Eds.], *Liberation Theology and Postmodernity in the Americas* (New York: Routledge), 95–124.

——— (1998a). "The Fact of Pluralism and the Multicultural Quest for Community," in A. Nascimento [Ed.], *A Matter of Discourse: Community and Communication in Contemporary Philosophies* (Aldershot: Ashgate), 3–26.

———[Ed.] (1998b). *A Matter of Discourse: Community and Communication in Contemporary Philosophies* (Aldershot: Ashgate).

——— (2003a). "Teoría Crítica, Globalización y Derechos Humanos: Un contrapunto entre Kant y Habermas," in J. Lima Torrado [Ed.], *Globalización y Pensamiento Crítico* (Madrid: DILEX/Universidad Complutense), 428–453.

———(2003b). "Habermas: Introdução a um Debate Filosófico" [Guerra, terrorismo e as relações internacionais], *Impulso* 35/15 (2003): 109–111.

——— (2006). "Karl-Otto Apel's Philosophy of Communication," in C. MacIwain [Ed.], *Global Communication and Culture* (Cresskill, NJ: Hampton Press), 61–74.

———(2007a). "Derechos Humanos y el MERCOSUR," in J. Lima Torrado [Ed.], *Derecho, stado, Mercado: Europa y Latinoamérica* (Madrid: DILEX/Universidad Complutense), 595–612.

——— (2007b). "Two Conflicting Interpretations of Immanuel Kant's Views on Community: Kommunikationsgemeinschaft or communauté de sentiments?," in *Proceedings of the 10th International Kant Congress* (Berlin: De Gruyter), 709–719.

——— (2012). "Syncretism as a Form of Multicultural Politics?," *Latin American and Caribbean Ethnic Studies* 7/2 (July 2012): 115–136.

Nash, G. (1976). *The Conservative Intellectual Movement in America since 1945* (New York: Basic Books).

Negt, O. (2003). *Kant und Marx. Ein Epochengespräch* (Göttingen: Steidl Gerhard Verlag).

Nevin, T. (2003). *Ernst Jünger and Germany: Into de Abyss, 1914–1945* (Durham, NC: Duke University Press).

Nickel, J. (2007). *Making Sense of Human Rights* (Malden, MA: Blackwell).

Niebuhr, K. W. (2004). "Biblisch-theologische Grundlagen des Communio-Begriffs im Zusammenhang der Ekklesiologie mit besonderem Bezug auf 'Communio Sanctorum,'" *Kerygma und Dogma* 50 (2004): 90–125.

Niederberger, A., and P. Schink [Hrsg.] (2001). *Globalisierung: Ein Interdisziplinäres Handbuch* (Stuttgart: J. B. Metzler).

Nisbet, R. (1953). *The Quest for Community* (Oxford, UK: Oxford University Press).

——— (1976). *The Social Philosophers* (Forgmore: Paladin).

Nmehielle, V. (2001). *The African Human Rights System: Its Laws, Practices and Institutions* (The Hague: M. Nijhoff).

Noerr, G. S. (2000). "Zwischen Sozialpsychologie und Ethik—Erich Fromm und die 'Frankfurt Schule,'" *Mitteilungen des Instituts für Sozialforschung* [Johann Wolfgang Goethe-Universität Frankfurt am Main] Heft 11 (September 2000): 7–40.

Nussbaum, M. (1996). "For love of Country," in J. Cohen and M. Nussbaum [Eds.], *For Love of Country? A Debate on Patriotism and Cosmopolitanism* (Boston, MA: Beacon Press), 3–21.

——— (1997). "Kant and Cosmopolitanism," in M. Lutz-Bachmann and J. Bohman [Eds.], *Perpetual Peace* (Cambridge, MA: MIT Press), 25–57.

——— (2001a). *The Fragility of Goodness* (Cambridge, UK: Cambridge University Press).

——— (2001b). *Women and Human Development: The Capabilities Approach* (Cambridge, UK: Cambridge University Press).

——— (2003). *Cultivating Humanity: A Classical Defense of Reform in Liberal Education* (Cambridge, MA: Harvard University Press).

——— (2004a). "Duties of Justice, Duties of Material Aid: Cicero's Problematic Legacy," in S. Strange and J. Zupko [Eds.], *Stoicism: Traditions and Transformations* (Cambridge, UK: Cambridge University Press), 214–249.

——— (2004b). *Hiding from Humanity: Disgust, Shame, and the Law* (Princeton, NJ: Princeton University Press).

——— (2006). *Frontiers of Justice: Disability, Nationality, Species Membership* (Cambridge, MA: Harvard University Press).

O'Neill, O. (1989). *Constructions of Reason. Exploration of Kant's Practical Philosophy* (Cambridge, UK: Cambridge University Press).

——— (1992). "Vindicating Reason," in P. Guyer [Ed.], *A Cambridge Companion to Kant* (Cambridge, UK: Cambridge University Press), 280–308.

Okin, S. M. (1989). "Reason and Feeling in Thinking about Justice," *Ethics* 99/2 (1989): 229–249.

——— (1991). "Justice as Fairness—for Whom?," in I. Shanely and C. Pateman [Eds.], *Feminist Interpretations and Political Theory* (University Park, PA: Pennsylvania State University Press), 181–198.

Olasky, M. (2000). "Compassionate Conservatism," *Veritas. A Quarterly Journal for Public Policy in Texas* (Fall 2000): 6–11.

Oliveira, M. A. (2003). *Reviravolta Lingüístico-pragmática na Filosofia Contemporânea* (São Paulo, SP: Edições Loyola).

Orbán, A. P. (1980). "Ursprung und Inhalt der Zwei-Staaten-Lehre in Augustinus *De Civitate Dei*," *Archiv für Begriffsgeschichte* 24 (1980): 171–194.

Parsons, T. (1978). *Action Theory and the Human Condition* (New York: Free Press).

Patomäki, H. (2003). "Problems of Democratising Global Governance: Time, Space and the Emancipatory Process," *European Journal of International Relations* 9 (2003): 358–369.

Patomäki, H. (2011). "Towards Global Political Parties," *Ethics & Global Politics* 4/2 (2011): 81–102.

Patomäki, H., and D. Held (2006). "Problems of Global Democracy: A Dialogue," *Theory, Culture & Society* 23 (2006): 115–133.

Peirce, C. S. (1931). *Collected Papers [CP]* [Vol. I–VI, ed. C. Harthorne and P. Weiss; Vols. VII–VIII ed. A. Burks, 1931–1958] (Cambridge, MA: Harvard University Press).

Pensky, M. [Ed.] (1995). "Universalism and the Situated Critic," in S. K. White [Ed.], *The Cambridge Companion to Habermas* (Cambridge, UK: Cambridge University Press), 67–94.

——— (2005). *Globalizing Critical Theory* (Lanham, MD: Rowman & Littlefield).

Pierik, R., and W. Werner [Eds.] (2010). *Cosmopolitanism in Context: Perspectives from International Law and Political Theory* (Cambridge, UK: Cambridge University Press).

Pippin, R. (1989). *Hegel's Idealism: The Satisfactions of Self-Consciousness* (Cambridge, UK: Cambridge University Press).

Pogge, T. (1989). *Realizing Rawls* (Ithaca, NY: Cornell University Press).

——— (2008). *World Poverty and Human Rights: Cosmopolitan Responsibilities and Reforms* (Cambridge, UK: Polity Press).

Pompa, L. (1990). *Vico: A Study of the New Science* (Cambridge, UK: Cambridge University Press).

Prinsloo, E. (1998). "Ubuntu Culture and Participatory Management," in P. Coetzee and A. Roux [Eds.], *The African Philosophy Reader* (London: Routledge), 41–51.

Proops, I. (2003). "Kant's Legal Metaphor and the Nature of a Deduction," *Journal of the History of Philosophy* 41 (2003): 209–229.

Quint, H. (1964). *The Forging of American Socialism: Origins of the Modern Movement* (New York: Bobbs-Merrill).

Rahner, J. (2010). "Communio—Communio ecclesiarum—Communio hierarchica: Anmerkungen zu einer notwendigen theologischen Differenzierung des Communio-Begriffs," *IKZ "Communio"* 39 (2010): 665–679.

Rancière, J. (1967). "Le concept de critique et la critique de l'économie politique des 'manuscrits' de 1844 au 'Capital,'" in L. Althusser, E. Balibar, R. Establet, P. Macherey, and J. Rancière [Eds.], *Lire le Capital* (Paris: Maspero), 81–199.

Rasmussen, D. [Ed.] (1996). *The Handbook of Critical Theory* (Oxford, UK: Blackwell).

——— [Ed.] (1990). *Universalism vs. Communitarianism* (Cambridge, MA: MIT Press).

Rawls, J. (1971). *A Theory of Justice* (Cambridge, MA: Harvard University Press).

——— (1980). "Kantian Constructivism in Moral Theory," *Journal of Philosophy* 77/9 (1980): 515–572.

——— (1985). "Justice as Fairness: Political not Metaphysical," *Philosophy and Public Affairs* 14/3 (Summer 1985): 223–251.

——— (1987). "The Idea of an Overlapping Consensus," *Oxford Journal of Legal Studies* 7/1 (1987): 1–25.

——— (1993). *Political Liberalism* (New York: Columbia University Press).

——— (1995). "Reply to Habermas," *The Journal of Philosophy* 92/3 (March 1995): 132–180.

——— (1999). *The Law of Peoples* (Cambridge, MA: Harvard University Press).

——— (2009). *A Brief Inquiry into the Meaning of Sin and Faith: An Interpretation Based on the Concept of Community* (Cambridge, MA: Harvard University Press).

Raz, J. (1990). *Practical Reason and Norms* (Oxford, UK: Clarendon Press).

——— (2010). "Human Rights without Foundations," in S. Besson and J. Tasioulas [Eds.], *The Philosophy of International Law* (Oxford, UK: Oxford University Press), 321–338.

Rehg, W. (1994). *Insight and Solidarity: The Discourse Ethics of Jürgen Habermas* (Cambridge, MA: MIT Press).

Remec, P. (1960). *The Position of the Individual in International Law according to Grotius and Vattel* (The Hague: Nijhoff).

Riedel, M. [Hrsg.] (1975). *Materialien zu Hegels Rechtsphilosophie* (Frankfurt: Suhrkamp).

Risse, M. (2012). *On Global Justice* (Princeton, NJ: Princeton University Press).

Ritter, J. (1965). *Hegel und die Französische Revolution* (Frankfurt: Suhrkamp).

Rockwell, R. (2004). "Hegel and Critical Social Theory: New Perspectives from the Marcuse Archives," *The Sociological Quarterly* 45/1 (2004): 141–159.

Rodolsky, R. (1965). "Worker and Fatherland: A Note on a Passage in the *Communist Manifesto*," *Science and Society* 29/3 (Summer 1965): 330–337.

——— (1986). *Engels and the "Non-Historic" Peoples: The National Question in the Revolution of 1848* (Glasgow: Critique Books).

Rorty, R. [Ed.] (1967). *The Linguistic Turn; Recent Essays in Philosophical Method* (Chicago: University of Chicago Press).

Rouanet, S. P. (1991). *As Razões do Iluminismo* (São Paulo, SP: Companhia das Letras).

Rousseau, J.-J. (1975). *Œuvres complètes* (Paris: Gallimard).

Royce, J. (1913). *The Problem of Christianity* [reedition in 2001] (Washington, DC: Catholic University of America Press).

Rubinstein, L. (1998). "The Athenian Political Perception of the *Idiotes*," in P. Cartledge, P. Millett, and S. von Reden [Eds.], *Kosmos. Essays in Order, Conflict, and Community in Classical Athens* (Cambridge, UK: Cambridge University Press), 125–143.

Rüger, C. (2000). "Roman Germany," in A. K. Bowman, P. Gamsey, and D. Rathbone [Eds.], *The Cambridge Ancient History: The High Empire, A.D. 70–192* (Cambridge, UK: Cambridge University Press), 496–513.

Ruin, H. (2008). "Belonging to the Whole: Critical and 'Heraclitical' Notes on the Ideal of Cosmopolitanism," in R. Lettevall and M. K. Linder [Eds.], *The Idea of Kosmopolis: History, Philosophy and Politics of World Citizenship* (Huddinge: Södertörns högskola), 31–50.

Rush, F. [Ed.] (2004). *The Cambridge Companion to Critical Theory* (Cambridge, UK: Cambridge University Press).

Salter, M. [Ed.] (2003). *Hegel and Law* (Aldershot: Ashgate).

Salter, M., and J. Shaw (1994). "Towards a Critical Theory of Constitutional Law: Hegel's Contribution," *Journal of Law & Society* 21/4 (December 1994): 464–486.

Sandel, M. (1982). *Liberalism and the Limits of Justice* (New York: New York University Press).

Saner, H. (1983). *Kant's Political Thought: Its Origins and Development* (Chicago: Chicago Univ. Press).

Sassoon, D. (1996). *One Hundred Years of Socialism* (New York: Free Press).

Schäfer, A. (2001). "W. E. B. DuBois, German Social Throught, and the Racial Divide in American Progressivism: 1982–1909," *The Journal of American History* (December 2001): 925–949.

Scheffler, S. (1999). "Conceptions of Cosmopolitanism," *Utilitas* 11/3 (November 1999): 255–276.

Schmidt, A. (1962). *Der Begriff von Natur in der Lehre von Karl Marx* (Frankfurt: Europäische Verlagsanstalt).

Schnädelbach, H. (1987). *Vernunft und Geschichte. Vorträge und Abhandlungen* 1 (Frankfurt: Suhrkamp).

——— (1992). *Zur Rehabilitierung des "animal rationale." Vorträge und Abhandlungen* 2 (Frankfurt: Suhrkamp).

Schofield, M. (1999). *The Stoic Idea of the City* (Chicago: University of Chicago Press)

Schottroff, W. (1987). "Nur ein Lehrauftrag. Zur Geschichte der jüdischen Religionswissenschaft an der deutschen Universität," *Berliner Theologische Zeitschrift* (1987): 197–214.

——— (1990). "Martin Buber an der Universität Frankfurt am Main (1923–1933)," in D. Stoodt [Ed.], *Martin Buber, Erich Foerster, Paul Tillich. Evangelische Theologie und Religionsphilosophie an der Universität Frankfurt a.M. 1914 bis 1933* (Frankfurt: P. Lang), 69–131.

——— (2000). "'...für die schwierige Aufgabe die rechten Leute, Juden und Christen finden.' Martin Buber: ersters Lehrer für jüdische Theologie an der Frankfurter Universität," *Forschung Frankfurt* (2000): 112–119.

Scott, J. B. (1934). *The Spanish Origin of International Law* (Oxford, UK: Clarendon Press).

Scott, R. (2009). "A Contextual Approach to Women's Rights in the Qur'ān: Readings of 4:34," *The Muslim World* 99/1 (January 2009): 60–85.

Seah, D. (2008). "The ASEAN Charter," *The International and Comparative Law Quarterly* 58 (2008): 197–212.

Searle, J. (1969). *Speech Acts: An Essay in the Philosophy of Language* (Cambridge, UK: Cambridge University Press).

Sedwick, S. (2012). *Hegel's Critique of Kant* (Oxford, UK: Oxford University Press).

Sen, A. (2003). *Human Rights and Asian Values* (New York: Carnegie Council on Ethics and International Affairs).

Sharma, A. (2004). *Hinduism and Human Rights: A Conceptual Approach* (Oxford, UK: Oxford University Press).

Shell, S. (1996). *The Embodiment of Reason. Kant on Spirit, Generation and Community* (Chicago: University of Chicago Press).

Siderits, M. (2007). *Buddhism as Philosophy* (Aldershot: Ashgate).

Smith, R. (2010). *Textbook on International Human Rights* (Oxford, UK: Oxford University Press).

Smith, S. (1987). "Hegel's Idea of a Critical Theory," *Political Theory* 15/1 (February 1987): 99–126.

Still, J. (2010). *Derrida and Hospitality: Theory and Practice* (Edinburgh: Edinburgh University Press).

Stirk, M. R. (2000). *Critical Theory, Politics, and Society: An Introduction* (New York: Continuum).

Stowers, S. (2011). "The Concept of 'Community' and the History of Early Christianity," *Method and Theory in the Study of Religion* 23 (2010): 238–256.

Strawson, P. (1966). *The Bounds of Sense: An Essay on Kant's Critique of Pure Reason* (London: Methuen).

Talbott, W. (2005). *Which Rights Should be Universal?* (Oxford, UK: Oxford University Press).

Tan, K.-Ch. (2004). *Justice without borders: Cosmopolitanism, Nationalism, and Patriotism* (Cambridge, UK: Cambridge University Press).

Tar, Z. (1977). *The Frankfurt School: The Critical Theories of Max Horkheimer and Theodor W. Adorno* (New York: John Wiley & Sons).

Taylor, C. (1958). "Alienation and Community," *Universities and Left Review* 5 (Autumn 1958): 11–18.

——— (1960). "Clericalism," *Downside Review* 78/252 (1960): 167–180.

——— (1975). *Hegel* (Cambridge, UK: Cambridge University Press).

——— (1985a). *Human Agency and Language: Philosophical Papers 1* (Cambridge, UK: Cambridge University Press).

——— (1985b). *Philosophy and the Human Sciences: Philosophical Papers 2* (Cambridge, UK: Cambridge University Press).

——— (1989). *Sources of the Self: The Making of the Modern Identity* (Cambridge, MA: Harvard University Press).

——— (1991). *The Ethics of Authenticity* [US 1992 edition of *The Malaise of Modenrity*] (Cambridge, MA: Harvard University Press).

——— (1995). *Philosophical Arguments* (Cambridge, MA: Harvard University Press).

——— (1999). "Conditions of an Unforced Consensus on Human Rights," in J. Bauer and D. Bell [Eds.], *The East Asian Challenge for Human Rights* (Cambridge, UK: Cambridge University Press), 124–144.

——— (2007). *A Secular Age* (Cambridge, MA: Harvard University Press).

——— (2012). "Multiculturalism or Interculturalism?," *Philosophy and Social Criticism* 38/4–5 (May/June 2012): 413 –423.

Taylor, C., and A. Gutman (1992). *Multiculturalism and the 'Politics of Recognition': An Essay* (Princeton, NJ: Princeton University Press).

Teitel, R. (1997). "Human Rights Genealogy," *Fordham Law Review* 66/2 (1997): 301–317.

Teubner, G. (1996). "Globale Bukowina: Zur Emergenz eines transnationalen Rechtspluralismus," *Rechtshistorisches Journal* 15 (1996): 255–290.

Teubner, G., and A. Fischer-Lescano (2006). *Regime-Kollisionen: Zur Fragmentierung des globalen Rechts* (Frankfurt: Suhrkamp).

Thomas Aquinas (1957). *Summa Theologiae* (Madrid: Biblioteca de Autores Cristianos [BAC]).

Tiedemann, R. (1973). *Studien zur Philosophie Walter Benjamins* (Frankfurt: Suhrkamp).

——— (1983). *Dialektik im Stillstand. Versuche zum Spätwerk Walter Benjamins* (Frankfurt: Surhkamp).

——— (2007). *Niemandsland. Studien mit und über Theodor W. Adorno* (München: Edition Text+Kritik).

Tierney, B. (1997). *The Idea of Natural Rights. Studies on Natural Rights, Natural Law and Church Law* [Emory University Studies in Law and Religion 5] (Atlanta, GA: Scholars Press).

Tully, J. (1980). *A Discourse on Property, John Locke and His Adversaries* (Cambridge, UK: Cambridge University Press).

——— (1993). *An Approach to Political Philosophy: Locke in Contexts* (Cambridge, UK: Cambridge University Press).

Vaihinger, H. (1892). *Commentar zu Kants Kritik der reinen Vernunft* (Stuttgart: Union Deutsche Verlagsgesellschaft).

Van Dijk, P. (1995). "A Common Standard of Achievement: About Universal Validity and Uniform Interpretation of International Human Rights Norms," *Netherlands Quarterly of Human Rights* 13 (1995): 105–121.

Van Hooft, S., and W. Vandekerckhove [Eds.] (2011). *Questioning Cosmopolitanism* (Dordrecht: Springer).

Verene, D. P. (1981). *Vico's Science of Imagination* (Ithaca, NY: Cornell University Press).

VerSteeg, J. R. (2001). "The Machinery of Law in Pharaonic Egypt: Organizations, Courts, and Judges on the Ancient Nile," *Cardozo Journal of International and Comparative Law* (2001): 105–133.

——— (2004). "Law in Ancient Egypt," *American Journal of Legal History* 46/1 (2004): 91–94.

Vertotec, S., and R. Cohen [Eds.] (2002). *Conceiving Cosmopolitanism: Theory, Context, and Practice* (Oxford, UK: Oxford University Press).

Vico, G. (1725). *Scienza Nuova* (Torino: Giulio Einaudi editore, 1959) [English translation *New Science*, ed. L. Pompa] (Cambridge, UK: Cambridge University Press, 2002)]

Vieten, U. (2012). *Gender and Cosmopolitanism in Europe: A Feminist Perspective* (Surrey: Ahsgate).

Vitoria, F. (1934). *Commentarium in II–II* [qu. 57–66], in *Comentarios a la Secunda secundae de Santo Tomás—Vol. III: De justicia* [Hrsg. v. Vicente Beltran de Heredia] (Salamanca: Apartado 17).

——— (1943). *Las relecciones* De Indis y De iure belli [ed. J. Brown Scott] (Washington, DC: Imprenta de la Unión Panamericana).

Vogt, K. (2008). *Law, Reason, and the Cosmic City: Political Philosophy in the Early Stoa* (Oxford, UK: Oxford University Press).

von Friedeburg, L. (1989). *Bildungsreform in Deutschland. Geschichte und gesellschaftlicher Widerspruch* (Frankfurt: Suhrkamp).

von Friedeburg, L., J. Habermas, C. Oehler, and F. Weltz (1961). *Student und Politik. Eine soziologische Untersuchung zum politischen Bewußtsein Frankfurter Studenten* (Neuwied: Luchterhand).

Waldron, J. (1993). *Liberal Rights: Collected Papers, 1981–1991* (Cambridge, UK: Cambridge University Press).

Walzer, M. (1983). *Spheres of Justice. A Defence of Pluralism and Equality* (New York: Basic Books).

——— (1985). *Exodus and Revolution* (New York: Basic Books).

———(1987). *Interpretation and Social Criticism* (Cambridge, MA: Harvard University Press).

Walzer, M., M. Lorberbaum, and N. Zohar [Eds.] (2000). *Jewish Political Tradition* (New Haven, CT: Yale University Press)

Ward, L. (1972). *The Politics of Liberty in England and Revolutionary America* (Cambridge, UK: Cambridge University Press).

Wellmer, A. (1969). *Kritische Gesellschaftstheorie und Positivismus* (Frankfurt: Suhrkamp).

——— (1985). *Zur Dialektik von Moderne und Postmoderne. Vernunftkritik nach Adorno* (Frankfurt: Suhrkamp).

———(1986). *Ethik und Dialog* (Frankfurt: Suhrkamp).

———(1991). *Endspiele: Die unversöhnliche Moderne. Essays und Vorträge* (Frankfurt: Suhrkamp).

Wendell, C. (1972). *The Evolution of the Egyptian National Image: From Its Origins to Ahmad Lutfī al-Sayyid* (Berkeley, CA: University of California Press).

West, C. (1989). *The American Evasion of Philosophy: A Genealogy of Pragmatism* (Madison, WI: University of Wisconsin Press).

Westphal, K. (1998). "On Hegel's Early Critique of Kant's Metaphysical Foundations of Natural Science," in S. Houlgate [Ed.], *Hegel and the Philosophy of Nature* (Albany, NY: State University of New York Press), 137–166.

Wheatland, T. (2009). *The Frankfurt School in America: A Transatlantic Odyssey from Exile to Acclaim* (Minneapolis, MN: University of Minnesota Press).

Wiggershaus, R. (1989). *Die Frankfurter Schule* (Frankfurt: Fischer).

Willaschek, M. (1991). "Die Tat der Vernunft: Zur Bedeutung der Kantischen These vom 'Factum der Vernunft,'" in Gerhard Funke [Ed.], *Akten des Siebenten Internationalen Kant-Kongresses* [Band II.1] (Bonn: Bouvier), 455–466.

Williamson, A. (1996). "Scots, Indians, and Empire: The Scottish Politics of Civilization: 1519–1609," *Past and Present* 150/1 (1996): 46–83.

Winch, P. (1958). *The Idea of a Social Science and Its relation to Philosophy* (London: Routledge).

Wiredu, K. (1996). "An Akan Perspective on Human Rights," in *Cultural Universals and Particulars: An African Perspective* (Bloomington, IN: Indiana University Press).

Witte, J., and J. van der Vyver [Eds.] (1996). *Religious Human Rights in Global Perspective: Religious Perspectives* (Dordrecht: Martinus Nijhoff).

Wittgenstein, L. (1937). *Remarks on the Foundations of Mathematics* (Cambridge, MA: MIT Press).

———— (1953). *Philosophical Investigations* (Oxford, UK: Blackwell).

Wood, A. (1999). *Kant's Ethical Thought* (Cambridge, UK: Cambridge University Press).

Young, I. (1990). *Justice and the Politics of Difference* (Princeton, NJ: Princeton University Press).

———— (2000). *Inclusion and Democracy* (Oxford, UK: Oxford University Press).

———— (2011). *Responsibility for Justice* (Oxford, UK: Oxford University Press).

Yu, K.-P., J. Tao, and P. Ivanhoe [Eds.] (2010). *Taking Confucian Ethics Seriously* (Albany, NY: State University of New York).

Zank, M. [Ed.] (2006). *New Perspectives on Martin Buber* [Religion in Philosophy and Theology, Vol. 22] (Tübingen: Mohr Siebeck).

Zolo, D. (1999). "A Cosmopolitan Philosophy of International Law? A Realistic Approach," *Ratio Juris* 12/4 (December 1999): 429–444.

Zuckert, R. (2007). *Kant on Beauty and Biology: An Interpretation* (Cambridge, UK: Cambdrige University Press).

INDEX

individuality, 3, 13–15, 32, 72,
89–92, 94, 103–104, 107,
109, 113–114, 116–118, 120,
123–128, 130–132, 144, 152,
159–160, 175, 178, 195, 211,
216, 221–224, 226. *See also*
autonomy; freedom
institutions, 3, 5, 9, 11, 28, 32,
37–38, 62, 67, 69–73, 76–78,
82, 84–85, 87–88, 90, 92–94,
107, 118, 121, 124, 128, 131,
134, 138–139, 143, 146–147,
149, 151, 153–154, 158, 160,
168, 171, 175–176, 183, 188,
193, 200, 214, 221
intercultural/interculturalism, 4,
6, 15, 49, 54, 91, 93, 111,
124, 128–129, 131, 133–134,
141, 143, 148, 152–153, 157,
163, 170–172, 194, 197, 204,
210–211, 216, 220–221, 223,
225–226

James, W., 102
Jäsche, G.J., 26
Jaspers, K., 134, 136, 143–144
Joas, H., 49
Jünger, E., 104, 203
justification, 4, 15–16, 18, 46, 57,
63, 65–67, 72, 74–76, 78,
79–82, 84, 85, 91, 94, 116,
119, 122, 132, 135, 144, 146,
153–154, 157, 161–166, 174,
198, 199, 202, 220, 222,
223–225

Kant, I., 4–8, 10, 11, 12, 13, 21–35,
37–39, 41–45, 47, 54, 57,
59–65, 70, 81, 85, 88, 108–109,
114, 117, 119, 120–122,
148–150, 154–155, 163, 166,
167, 179, 186–187, 189–191,
195–203, 209–210, 219
Kautsky, K., 36
Kettner, M., 49
Kirchheimer, O., 38

Kirk, R., 106
Kleingeld, P., 25, 30, 167, 179,
184, 185, 186
Kohlberg, L., 51, 72, 89, 116, 117,
146, 194
Korsch, K., 38
Kracauer, S., 38
Kuhn, T., 58, 134, 154, 155
Kuhlmann, W., 49

Lafont, C., 23, 52, 138, 198
Landauer, G., 37
Las Casas, B., 163
Latin America, 17–18, 51–54,
104–107, 126, 129, 143
law, 6, 12, 14–15, 21, 28–30, 31–33,
35, 40, 46–47, 52, 63., 66, 69,
73–75, 77–78, 81, 86, 88, 92,
101, 117–120, 134–138, 140,
142–143, 145–147, 149, 152,
154, 156–157, 159, 161–168,
170–172, 173, 179–180, 182,
184–187, 191–193, 196,
198–200, 202–204, 208–212,
214–215, 221, 226. *See also*
Discourse Theory
of world citizenship/
cosmopolitan law
[*Weltbürgerrecht*], 4, 5, 13,
167, 187, 196, 209
legitimation/legitimacy, 46, 66, 93,
116, 118, 132, 143, 148–149,
167, 173, 190, 209, 211
Leibniz, G., 10, 26
Lenin, W., 36
lifeworld [*Lebenswelt*], 54, 71,
78–79, 83, 93, 116–118, 120,
128, 146, 157
linguistic turn, 7, 22, 45–47, 49,
58–60, 88, 145, 155
Linklater, A., 50, 176
Locke, J., 9, 23, 101, 164, 165
Löwenthal, L., 38
Luhmann, N., 42, 46, 68, 73, 116,
117
Luther, M., 10

Printed in the United States of America